NATURE WALKS IN SOUTHERN MAINE

An AMC Nature Walks Book

Jan M. Collins and Joseph E. McCarthy

APPALACHIAN MOUNTAIN CLUB BOOKS
BOSTON, MASSACHUSETTS

Cover Photograph: Joseph E. McCarthy
Book Design: Carol Bast Tyler
All photographs by the authors unless otherwise indicated.

Distributed by The Globe Pequot Press, GPP., Inc., Old Saybrook, CT.

Library of Congress Cataloging-in-Publication Data

Collins, Jan M.
Nature walks in southern Maine / Jan M. Collins and Joseph E. McCarthy.
p. cm.
"An AMC nature walks book."
Includes bibliographical references and index.
ISBN 1-878239-46-5 (alk. paper)
1. Walking—Maine—Guidebooks. 2. Hiking—Maine—Guidebooks. 3. Nature study—Maine—Guidebooks. 4. Maine—Guidebooks. I. McCarthy, Joseph E., 1940– . II. Appalachian Mountain Club. III. Title.
GV199.42.M2C65 1996
796.5'1'09741—dc20 95-44595
CIP

The paper used in this publication meets the minimum requirements of the American National Standard for Information Sciences—Permanence of Paper for Printed Library Materials, ANSI Z39.48–1984.∞

Due to changes in conditions, use of the information in this book is at the sole risk of the user.

Printed on recycled paper using soy-based inks.

Printed in the United States of America.

10 9 8 7 6 5 4 3 2 1 96 97 98 99 00

Contents

Portland and Northeast

Northwest

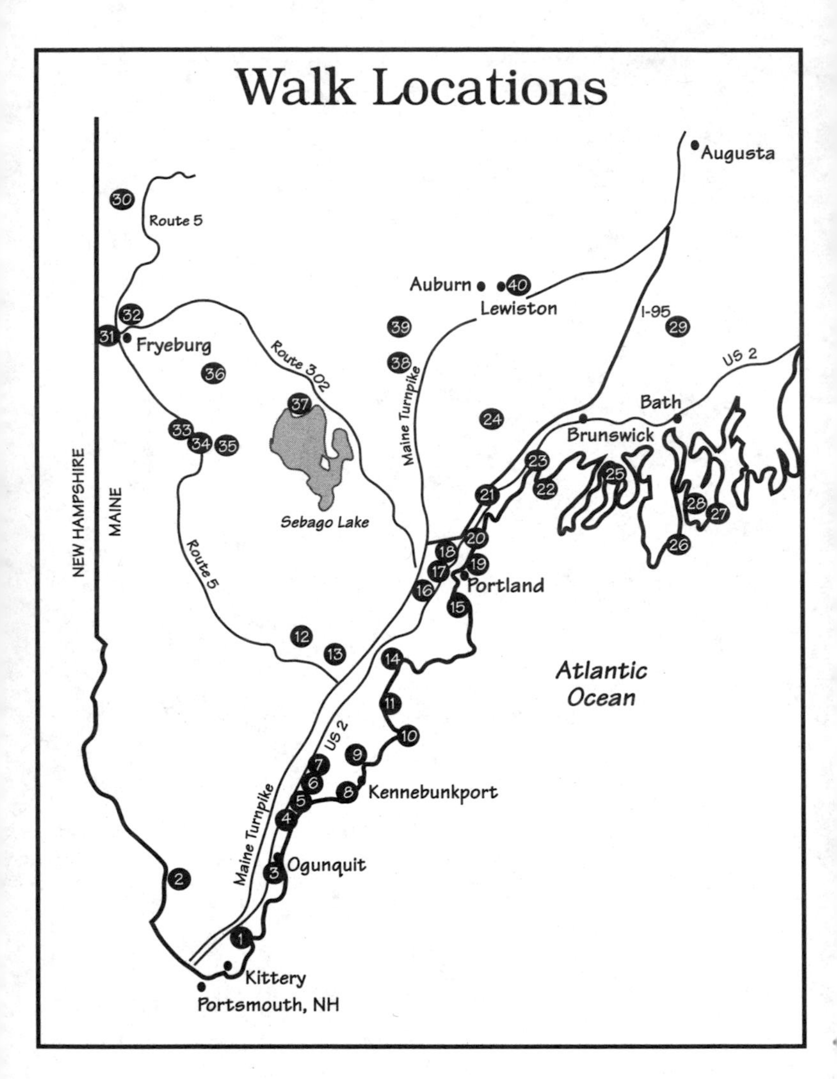
Walk Locations
Augusta
30
Route 5
Auburn
40
Lewiston
32
31
Fryeburg
39
I-95
29
Route 302
38
Maine Turnpike
US 2
36
37
Bath
24
Brunswick
33
34
35
23
25
21
22
28
27
NEW HAMPSHIRE
MAINE
Sebago Lake
20
18
19
26
17
Route 5
16
Portland
15
12
13
14
Atlantic
Ocean
11
10
US 2
9
7
6
8
Kennebunkport
5
Maine Turnpike
4
3
Ogunquit
2
1
Kittery
Portsmouth, NH

Key to Walk Locations

1. Charles R. Steedman Woods
2. Vaughan Woods
3. Marginal Way
4. Laudholm Farm
5. Rachel Carson National Wildlife Refuge
6. Kennebunk Bridle Path
7. Wonderbrook Park
8. Vaughn Island
9. Emmons Preserve
10. East Point Sanctuary
11. Ferry Beach State Park
12. Pleasant Point
13. Saco Heath Preserve
14. Scarborough Marsh
15. Spring Point
16. Fore River Sanctuary
17. Back Cove
18. Gilsland Farm Sanctuary
19. Mackworth Island
20. Falmouth Nature Preserve
21. Royal River Park
22. Wolfe's Neck Woods State Park
23. Mast Landing Sanctuary
24. Bradbury Mountain State Park
25. Austin Cary Lot
26. Popham Beach State Park
27. Reid State Park
28. Josephine Newman Sanctuary
29. Steve Powell Management Area—Swan Island
30. Lord Hill
31. Jockey Cap
32. Mount Tom
33. Mount Cutler
34. Hiram Nature Study Area
35. Douglas Mountain Preserve
36. Pleasant Mountain
37. Sebago Lake State Park
38. Gray Game Farm and Visitors Center
39. Range Ponds State Park
40. Thorncrag Bird Sanctuary

To the many people who taught me
to love all plants & animals.
Particular, special thanks to Santa
and the stars in my universe,
Victoria & Kevin.
J. McCarthy, Ph.D.

To my Mom
who taught me to love.
Jan M. Collins

Acknowledgments

As authors we do not prep and perspire over words and phrases in a vacuum. The finished written material sits at the top of a pyramid of places, hikes, and ideas generated over the last year. The blocks of this work are mixed, mortared, and braced by friends, family, and endless contacts who gave of their time and knowledge. For all their comments, letters, and ideas we thank the following: Mr. Dan Beard, Mr. Thomas Collins, Mr. Rusty Dyke, Mr. Stephen Emmons, Mr. Calvin Fox, Mr. Nate Greene, Ms. Carol Manning, Mr. John Polackwich, Mr. Dennis Pratt, Mrs. Gail Roller, Mr. Eric Richardson, Ms. Kim Round, Mrs. [illegible] Skofield, Mr. David Wiggin, and Mrs. Agnes Innes Wiggin. Also the employees of Maine Audubon; the Maine park system; the Appalachian Mountain Club; Central Maine Power Company; the town offices of Harpswell, Fryeburg, and Kennebunk, who freely answered our queries and energized our quests for background information. In particular, we thank our editor, Gordon Hardy, for the belief we could succeed and his help in the publication of this work.

Introduction

This is a book about secrets. We are bringing you the secrets of southern Maine, our back yard. We are sharing our favorite places—some hidden, some very public—that illustrate the grandeur of the flora, fauna, and topography we know as southern Maine. Like a preferred fishing hole, not all secrets are easily shared. They need to be protected and cherished. When you visit these areas, treat them as you would a friend's back yard: enjoy them and leave them enjoyable for others who follow.

As we worked on this book we discovered a tremendous wealth of locations, more than could fit into a pocket-sized book. Thus, we had to be selective. We have offered you bits and pieces of a larger picture that is the natural landscape of southern Maine. It is by no means complete; your own travels can add to what we have begun. Explore, learn, and absorb the material we present, then carry it further by adding to what we have started. Like a favored family recipe, experience it, treasure it, and share it with friends. Carry some of the regard and love for nature to your own back yard. Let your interest, and that of your family, grow. Join or support such organizations as the local conservation commission, the Appalachian Mountain Club, The Nature Conservancy, or the Audubon Society. Help protect wild areas. In this ever more crowded world, these places and the wildlife they support need to be cared for by each and every one of us.

Hiking Tips

Creature Comforts

Dressing for the weather is always tricky. What you wear and what the weather does don't always match. Play the Scout and "Be Prepared."

Even short hikes can take you from a warm, sunny spot to a cool, breezy area, especially in our coastal region. A day pack with an extra sweater or light jacket can increase your comfort with minimal effort. Add a sandwich, water, binoculars, and camera to stretch a short hike into several hours and increase your enjoyment of the wild world about you.

Other Creatures

What is out there to bother or bite you? The simple answer is not much, though a few precautions are wise. Your best weapons in this area are a modicum of knowledge and a bit of bug repellent.

Poison ivy is prevalent in southern Maine. Learn to identify it. It can be an eight-inch plant or run vinelike up a tree or telephone pole. Occasionally it can be a rather robust bush several feet tall. One thing all these forms have in common is a three-part leaf. "Leaves of three, let it be" is very sound advice. Poison ivy also has a highly waxed gloss on the upper leaf surface, though in some shaded areas this sheen may not be present. In spring it produces small greenish flowers and later white berries. In the fall, it joins the merry maples, turning red and gold. It is an attractive plant but just look, don't touch! If you should blunder into it, wash exposed areas quickly. Be sure to wash your clothing later to remove any remaining irritating oils.

Jewelweed (spotted touch-me-not) provides a poison-ivy remedy from the juice of the crushed plant. It is found in damp areas. The paired leaves are egg-shaped with rounded teeth, and its spotted orange blossom hangs from hollow, succulent stems.

Although we discuss the medicinal and nutritional aspects of many plants, they never should be picked on public lands. Even at home, never taste or eat plants without positive identification.

Another major concern among visitors to southern Maine is Lyme disease. It is carried by the deer tick. A few confirmed cases of Lyme disease have been reported from the area. Again, the best weapons are preparation and knowledge. Dress to eliminate exposed areas of skin. Wear long sleeves and pants. If you do wear shorts, check your ankles and other areas where clothing binds closely for the possibility of a hidden tick. After hiking, check everyone thoroughly for ticks. At the infective stage the tick is a tiny, one-sixteenth-inch-long spot with eight legs. A bite will normally produce a small ring-shaped rash and low-grade fever. It requires medical treatment or serious long-term damage could occur.

Beyond poison ivy and the remote possibility of the deer tick, the only real pests are mosquitoes, black flies (claimed by some as the state bird), and a variety of stinging bees and wasps. The repellent DEET comes in many cream and spray formulas to keep mosquitoes and black flies from biting. Natural alternatives to DEET include citronella-based repellents and large amounts of garlic and vitamin E in your diet. Avoid perfumed soaps and shampoos and the bees will show less interest in you. Stay quiet and calm in the presence of bees. Running, shouting, and wildly swatting about is apt to cause more damage to you than any free-flying insect.

Environmental Care

For several years, the state of Maine and many local communities have removed all trash containers from parks and trail areas. The message is "Carry in, Carry out!" This has worked to a great degree because we are becoming quite conscious about environmental cleanup. If you have not already done so, join the effort. Enjoy the areas you visit, and remember to leave them as clean as, if not cleaner than, you found them. Keep a resealable bag in your pack for orange peels, paper, plastic wraps, and aluminum foil, and we can all have a cleaner world.

Part of environmental care involves watching where you tread. Stay on the trail as much as possible to avoid trampling plants and tiny animals, compacting the soil, and creating excessive runoff and erosion.

Humans are collectors and classifiers. We often want a sample or souvenir of a pleasant place or thing—a rock, flower, or twig. If everyone follows this quest, soon the landscape will look like it's been ravaged by locusts. Bring your camera, take a picture, and leave the blossoms, stones, and shells for all to enjoy.

Accessibility

Society in general is becoming more aware of the needs of disabled persons. Unfortunately, many parks do not yet have easily accessible trails. We have made an effort to point out the wheelchair-accessible trails, but they are few and far between. In this book we use the following numerical system to describe the wheelchair-accessible areas:

Level 1: trails are a flat, prepared surface which may include mowed grass. Inclines change fewer than 5 feet over a 100-foot run.

Level 2: trails may include occasional root or rounded stone. Inclines change between 5 and 8 feet over a 100-foot run.

Level 3: trails change 8 to 10 feet in a 100-foot run. While relatively smooth, such trails require strong-armed help or a power wheelchair for the grades.

The wheelchair-accessible areas are:

Marginal Way

Rachel Carson National Wildlife Refuge

Kennebunk Bridle Path

Ferry Beach State Park

Scarborough Marsh

Spring Point

Back Cove

Royal River Park

Wolfe's Neck Woods State Park

Gray Game Farm and Visitors Center

Range Ponds State Park

There are places in southern Maine where all hikers and explorers, disabled or otherwise, must take careful note of their surroundings or risk injury. Any trail can lead to scrapes, bumps, and twisted ankles. The rocky coast presents special dangers to the unwary. The average nine-foot tides have stranded many inattentive people who hike to offshore islands during low tides. The beautiful ledges host slick spots of algae and are unforgiving, especially with wet footwear. Magnificent storm waves, like wild bears, should be viewed from afar. Curious about the restless sea, hikers have been injured or killed on the coast.

Checklist

To keep comfortable while you hike, take a moment to run through the following checklist.

- insect repellent
- rain gear
- area map/guidebook
- sunglasses
- camera
- water/juice
- lunch/snack
- hat
- tide table
- compass
- sweater/jacket
- sunscreen
- binoculars
- field guides
- proper footwear
- resealable plastic storage bags

Southeast Maine

1. Charles R. Steedman Woods

York

16 Acres

Estuarine Uplands

1 mile

1 hour

In the 1880s, York became a summer colony. Like Kennebunkport and Bar Harbor, it attracted wealthy "cottagers" anxious to leave the stuffy confines of the city.

Many of the summer residents took a concrete interest in the town, organizing social clubs, preserving historical sites, and improving roads and bridges. The Charles R. Steedman Woods reservation is dedicated to the memory of a turn-of-the-century cottager and preserves one of the **most scenic and historic parcels of land in York Village**.

Legend has it that Native Americans favored this spot for summer encampments. Smallpox had already decimated their population, however, when the first European, Edward Godfrey, built his house in York in 1630.

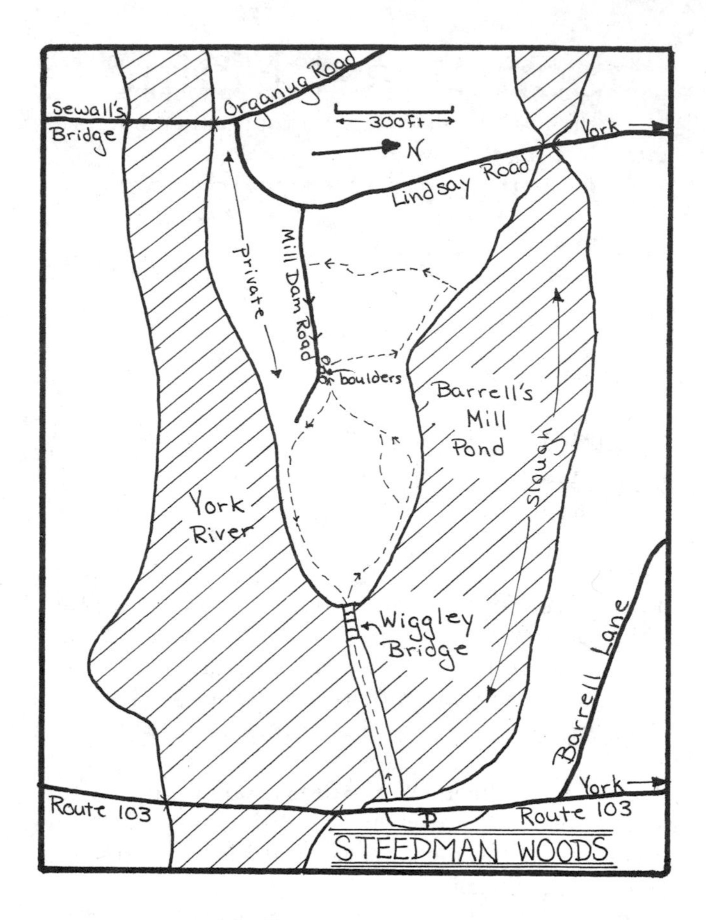

Almost 100 years passed before the slough leading from Meeting House Creek to the York River was dammed, creating Barrell's Mill Pond. In 1727, a **grist-mill and a sawmill were built on the dam.** The mills provided a local source of lumber and flour, the necessary ingredients for the growth of a community.

Paths to the mills were worn on either side of the creek. In 1746, the town voted to make the "road" from the harbor a public right-of-way. In time, the mills fell into disuse, but the path over the dam remained a popular shortcut between York Harbor and Sewall's Bridge.

In 1888, the town refused a request to make the dam a public road and provide a shorter route between York Harbor and Sewall's Bridge (the harbor and the country club). An elaborate plan was drawn in 1890 to develop the land into Villa Sites, a huge hotel, a park, and a wharf. The undertaking failed. Charles R. Steedman bought the parcel for himself a few years later. Private concerns built a bridge in 1896. Charles's son, C. Richard Steedman, from Providence, Rhode Island, donated 16 acres to Old York Historical and Improvement Society in 1978.

Meanwhile, in 1911, the town approved and appropriated $3,940.00 "to construct and maintain a public promenade" over the dam. The result is the picturesque **Wiggley Bridge,** the scenic approach to Steedman Woods.

Reach the reservation by following Route 103 (Lilac Lane) southwest from Route 1A in York Village. As you descend the hill, Wiggley Bridge will immediately catch your eye on the right. Park your car on the left. Watch for traffic as you cross the road.

The causeway is about 12 feet wide. The slough of Meeting House Creek (Barrell's Mill Pond) is on the right and the York River is on the left. In the distance you may see boats anchored in the harbor. At high tide,

Wiggley Bridge, the smallest suspension bridge in Maine, provides access to Steedman Woods.

watch for a multitude of **green crabs** scavenging among the rocks in the water at your feet. As you pass between the cables of the **suspension bridge,** take time to observe the rushing waters below you. The strength of the rising and falling tides was responsible for providing reliable energy to power the grist- and sawmills built on this site more than 250 years ago. At low tide you also may be able to see periwinkles and blue mussels fastened, the former by suction and the latter by threads, to the rocks below. In winter, you may observe buffleheads, red-breasted mergansers, common loons, and mallards dabbling and diving in the water.

After little more than 0.1 mile, you reach the far side of the causeway. The trail forks. It is circular so you will return to this point whether you go right or left.

The trail description follows the path to the right, the one less traveled. *Note:* Many people walk their dogs here so watch your step. In addition, poison ivy grows in profusion along the path.

On the left, honeysuckles nestle amongst the white pines. On the right is an old apple tree and several poplars. The trail borders the slough on the right. When the tide is low, the sandy bottom can be glimpsed through clear blue water. The forest is open here with birch trees and large red oaks. The ground cover includes partridgeberry, blueberry, and juniper bushes. The footpath occasionally branches and rejoins itself. To the left, it climbs to higher, flatter picnicking ground, while the right brings you closer to the water.

At about 0.3 mile the trail descends slightly. There are pleasant views of the marsh, including **crows** hopping about and cawing to one another. These birds are extremely gregarious. Except during courtship, they are found usually in flocks. During breeding season the young of the previous year often attend their parents, assisting in food scavenging and protection of this year's nest.

If you see a large raucous gathering of crows repeatedly diving about a tree or wooded area, on close inspection you may also discover a great horned owl or a barred owl. At night, barred owls are especially fond of attacking and killing sleeping crows, peeling back the cranium to savor the delicate brain tissue within. In retaliation, crows join forces to harass their common enemy during the day.

In Maine, where vultures are scarce, crows perform the vital function of scavenger, cleaning up roadkills and roadside garbage. For this they are often attacked. They do not receive the respect they deserve from humans.

Walk 200 feet from the first marsh view and you will find the returning loop of the trail. You can extend your hike to a second loop by continuing to the right past three boulders that limit the access of motorized vehicles from the dirt road. This secondary loop does not receive as much traffic and is more obscure. It is also wet, especially in spring. Here the trees must lift their roots above the ground to avoid suffocation and drowning. Slippery roots can make for difficult walking. In amidst the white pine and black cherry are red maples, honeysuckle, and huge clinging vines. The different levels of vegetation—ground cover, understory, and canopy—all provide a **diverse habitat for birds.** Rufous-sided towhees, goldfinches, and warblers can be heard weaving their songs among the branches and leaves of the dense vegetation.

The trail reaches the dirt Mill Dam Road at 0.55 mile. The sign above the trail recognizes that this is a "nature preserve given to Old York Historical Society by Charles Richard Steedman to be kept forever wild for the residents of York. No litter, fires or motorized vehicles." As you walk down the road to the left, notice signs of the area's earlier inhabitants. Bayberry and multiflowered rose both bear mute testimony to the presence of early settlers who planted them as borders and made use of their fruit.

When you return to the three boulders mentioned earlier, pass through them and turn right. In 250 feet you will come to a long border of rhododendrons next to a

Partridgeberry covers the ground near the paths of Charles Steedman Woods.

private residence. The trail now follows the banks of the York River. At low tide you may glimpse clammers on the mudflats digging steamers. Unfortunately, many flats are closed now due to pollution and to the scarcity of clams; one southern Maine resident made the news in 1994 by camping in the parking lot of the town office for one month to be sure of getting one of a handful of clamming permits. His family had been clammers for generations, and he was determined to preserve the tradition.

The colorful, bright, green-and-orange buoys in the York River and harbor mark boat moorings. You may also notice platforms used to store lobster traps. A symbol of the Maine coast, the lobsters and the industry they support are also suffering from overharvesting.

Reach the Wiggley Bridge again at 0.9 mile and return across the causeway to your car.

Getting There

From the intersection of Route 1 and Route 1A in York, follow Route 1A 1.4 miles to Route 103 (Lilac Lane) in York Village. Travel southwest 0.2 mile on Route 103. There is parking on the left side of the road for six small cars. The trail begins on the right. There is a crosswalk painted in white on the road.

For more information contact Old York Historical Society, P.O. Box 312, York, ME 03909, or call 207-363-4974.

2. Vaughan Woods

South Berwick
250 Acres

Woodlands
3 miles
4 hours

The **Salmon Falls River** flows south into the Piscataqua River. Together they form the southwestern border between New Hampshire and Maine. The rivers are tidal past Vaughan Woods all the way to Salmon Falls in South Berwick. When the first European settlers arrived, the river teemed with Atlantic salmon, shad, and alewives each spring. Native Americans and Europeans alike depended on the fish as a rich source of protein, especially if the winter had been hard and the hunting difficult. The fishes' annual migration was a sign of spring, a symbol of the cycle of rebirth, and an indication of the bounty of the coming summer season.

Today the Atlantic salmon is a rare sight. Fishing limits are strictly enforced. Habitat destruction and overharvesting have taken their toll on a once-abundant fish. Attempts to reintroduce the salmon have been stymied by the presence of hydroelectric dams. Even when expensive fish ladders are built into the dams, 10 percent of the migrating population is lost at each site.

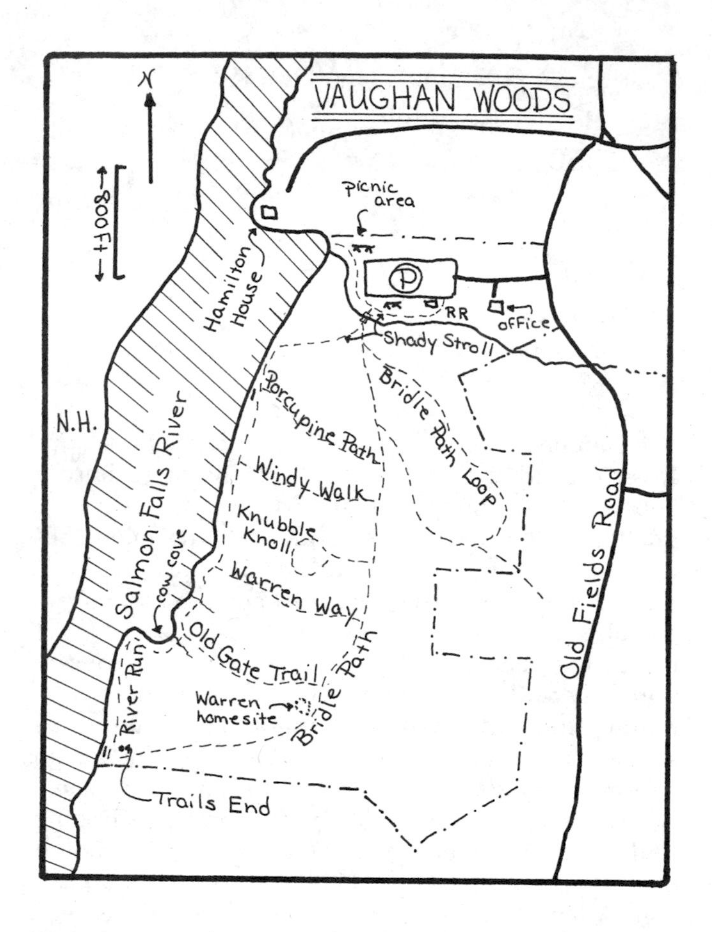

If six or more dams are placed on a river, the impact is large enough to minimize successful breeding. Maintaining a self-sustaining population becomes close to impossible.

Although you are unlikely to see a spring run of Atlantic salmon, much of the abundance experienced by the settlers who arrived here in the early 1600s may still be glimpsed. In the late 1700s and early 1800s, Vaughan Woods and the Hamilton house were part of the same estate. Jonathan Hamilton was a wealthy shipping merchant whose sailing ships did a handsome business until the Civil War. When sailing ships went bust, so did the Hamilton fortunes. The estate was purchased by Henry Vaughan. He married Hamilton's daughter Elizabeth. The two family names are preserved in separate state parks. In the 1940 will of Elizabeth Hamilton Vaughan, she indicated that the 250-acre parcel that now makes up the Vaughan Woods Memorial State Park was to be a **wildlife sanctuary** kept in its natural state. As a result, deer, moose, rabbits, porcupines, hawks, and more make their home here.

Although the park is officially open from Memorial Day to the end of September, visitors are welcome throughout the year. There is a small area available outside the locked gates for approximately 4 or 5 cars in the off-season. The walk or drive to the main parking lot is 700 feet. Here there is space for 40 to 50 cars. There are pit toilets for men and women, a hand pump with cool refreshing water, and seven picnic tables with barbecue grills. The entrance fee is one dollar for adults. Children under 12 are free. A small drive-by box is provided for paying on the honor system.

Begin your hike by taking the path to the left of the bathrooms. This walk is appropriately named Shady Stroll. Huge old hemlocks tower above as they do throughout the park. It is hard to imagine this area was once completely cleared for fields—the trees appear to be as old as time. Watch for poison ivy in this vicinity.

Beside the trail is a wet area blessed with a profusion of **skunk cabbage.** The flowers appear early in spring soon after the snow melts and are gone by the beginning of May. They bloom before they put up leaves. Viewed in July, it would be difficult to believe the leaf and the flower belong to the same plant. The flower is protected by a mottled purple-and-brown fleshy "hood." This gives it the appearance of a cabbage nestled on the wet ground. The leaves, on the other hand, are huge, broad, and tropical in appearance.

The flowers of skunk cabbage appear early in spring and are gone by the beginning of May.

They stand one to three feet tall and are found in many of the washes along the trail as it parallels the Salmon Falls River. True to its name, when the leaves are crushed the plant gives off a distinctly fetid odor. This is to the plant's advantage, especially in spring. Bees have not yet ended their winter hibernation when the skunk cabbage is in bloom. Instead, it must depend on flies as its pollinator. A good stink is as likely to call in a fly as just about anything.

After only 0.1 mile reach an intersection. To the right the trail returns to the parking lot, the Bridle Path enters on the left, and Shady Stroll continues straight ahead. The Bridle Path and Bridle Path Loop are woods trails approximately 1.3 miles in length. Shady Stroll will become River Run in 0.1 mile. Here it will parallel the river for approximately 0.75 mile, then join the Bridle Path, creating a large 2-mile loop.

The Bridle Path receives less use than Shady Stroll but is nonetheless a wide, well-established footpath. Like all the other trails in the park, it's frequented by horseback riders, continuing the tradition established by Elizabeth Vaughan 100 years ago. The Bridle Path Loop is a left-hand turn 80 feet from the junction with Shady Stroll. It rejoins the Bridle Path in approximately 0.5 mile after climbing then descending through **hemlock,** young white pine, and more hemlock.

One of the most interesting sites on this loop is a huge old red oak about 0.15 mile on the right. The tree is probably an ancient remnant of the days when this area was still in field. It is older than the evergreens that surround it and likely provided a shady respite for the livestock that grazed beneath its branches. Today it is experiencing the decline of old age but continues to provide shelter for wildlife. If you approach the tree to investigate the large hole in its trunk, do so quietly and respectfully so as not to disturb the residents that may be sleeping there. Beneath the tree you will find a pile of scat that advertises the identity of the owner. Look closely (and carefully) and you also will discover quills scattered about. This is a **porcupine tree.**

While it is not true that porcupines can throw their quills, it is true that the quills have barbs on them that embed the shaft in would-be attackers. This can be done quickly and effectively with a swish of the tail. The result is quite painful and can easily progress to a serious infection. Quills scattered on the ground can have the same effect. If you handle them, be extremely careful. Porcupines are themselves quiet, peaceful animals. They are vegetarians, spending their nights gnawing on the tender inner bark of trees and their days snoozing in the same trees or in underground burrows. They use their quills only in self-defense.

In 0.1 mile the Bridle Path Loop intersects a private path. Descend to the right and rejoin the Bridle Path in 0.2 mile. If you haven't walked the Bridle Path Loop, continue straight ahead on the Bridle Path. In 0.1 mile you reach the Porcupine Path, coming in on the right. This trail is a little over 0.1 mile in length and connects with River Run.

Proceed 150 feet on the Bridle Path to its intersection with the Bridle Path Loop on the left. Several trees in the area are marked by the excavations of pileated woodpeckers. These giant woodpeckers can be one and a half feet tall. The holes they make in their never-ending quest for wood-boring insects can be four or more inches deep and several feet long, providing excellent habitat for other wildlife.

As you continue along the Bridle Path, you will pass four more trails branching off to the right: Windy Walk, Knubble Knoll, Warren Way, and Old Gate Trail. Each is 0.1 to 0.2 mile in length and parallels Porcupine Path. All except Knubble Knoll connect to River Run. Less than 0.1 mile beyond the Old Gate Trail is the **Warren homesite.** As a plaque at the site explains, James Warren was one of the original settlers. Born in Scotland in 1620, he was taken as a prisoner in the battle of Dunbar. As a Covenanter—one who adhered to the Scottish National Covenant of 1638—he was given a grant in America and settled here with his wife, Margaret, in 1650, probably exchanging his labor for freedom and land. He died in 1702. His grave and the graves of his wife and at least six children can be seen behind the old foundation and at a site on the Old Gate Trail. Unfortunately, the stones have been broken and vandalized, erasing an important part of local history and desecrating sacred ground.

The site itself is open and sunny. At the time of the Warren occupancy, a carriage road would have run in front of the house. The woods leading down to the river would have been cleared for fields, not only for the grazing of livestock but also for the commanding view of the valley. The view allowed the residents to receive immediate notice of anyone approaching by water. This was important both for greeting ships carrying supplies and for defense.

As you continue along the Bridle Path, you will pass through a short section of wet trail. Watch for red-shouldered hawks circling and crying overhead during spring migration. You will also hear the repetitious call of the black-capped chickadee and the red-breasted nuthatch. These two little woodland birds are important to the ecology of the forest. Each of them spends its summer days searching bark and branches for insects. In winter, it must change its feeding strategies to survive the frigid, insectless winters of Maine. It is then that it begins searching for seeds to supplement its diet and often will frequent nearby back yard bird feeders.

From the tip of the tail to the tip of the beak the chickadee is only five inches long. It has a black cap and bib and white cheeks and chest. Its back and wings are gray. The red-breasted nuthatch is about the same size as the chickadee and also has a black cap and gray back, but its bib is white, it has a black eye stripe, and a rusty red breast. The nuthatch's bill is longer and more pointed than the chickadee's. Both birds are acrobatic and may be seen hanging upside down on a branch searching for insects.

The Bridle Path becomes River Run at Trails End, 0.3 mile from the Warren homesite. Take a seat on the bench provided and watch for osprey flying overhead and ducks plying the river. In spring, the annoyed whistle of the **osprey** can be heard as it dives for fish at the same time as rafts of migrating **double-crested cormorants** mix with common goldeneye ducks on their travels north. Bald eagles also have been sighted here on occasion.

Returning to the picnic area via River Run, the trail curves right along a deep inlet called Cow Cove. Some of the **first cows to arrive in the New World** disembarked from the ship the *Pied Cow* in 1634 at this site. It is difficult to imagine the fortitude necessary for both crew and cows on a trans-Atlantic voyage that must have taken weeks to complete and included its share of rough seas. The ship also delivered saw and grist tide mills (which harnessed the movement of tides to grind grain or saw logs) and the artisans to erect them to York Village.

The first side trail branching over a wooden bridge on your right has been discontinued and is blocked by a fallen tree. River Run Trail slabs the steep bank of the Salmon Falls River, zigzagging in and out of small washes that are traversed by wood or stone bridges. To help control bank erosion, the park has moved sections of trail away from the edge of the river. Please assist in land reclamation by staying on the new trail.

The hip-roofed, federal-style Hamilton house stands above the Salmon Falls River at Vaughan Woods.

At intervals of approximately 0.1 mile, you will pass Old Gate Trail, Warren Way, Windy Walk, and Porcupine Path. There are occasional benches provided for the relief of weary wanderers and for the welcome opportunity to drink in the solitude of the quiet woods. At the intersection of River Run and Shady Stroll, a bench provides a picture-postcard view of the Hamilton house, a federal-style mansion with hip roof.

As you sit admiring the house and imagining the view of the river from its parlor windows, you may also hear the rattle of a belted kingfisher's cry. This foot-long, crested, bluish gray bird hovers over the water, then plunges headfirst after small fish that swim too near the surface. These birds make their homes by tunneling into the riverbank.

From the bench, climb gradually 0.1 mile to the intersection with the Bridle Path and another 0.1 mile to the parking lot.

Getting There

From South Berwick travel south 0.5 mile on Route 236. Turn right opposite the junior high school onto Vine Street. Travel 1.0 mile to the intersection of Vine Street and Old Fields Road. Turn right and watch for the entrance to Vaughan Woods on the right.

From the junction of I-95 and Route 236, drive north 9.1 miles to Old South Road. Turn left and travel 1.0 mile to Old Fields Road. Turn left again and watch for the entrance to Vaughan Woods on the right.

For more information call 207-693-6231.

3. Marginal Way
Ogunquit

Rocky Coast

0.8 mile (one way)

1 hour

Wheelchair accessible: level 1–3 (see p. xiv)

The Atlantic Ocean can be quite pacific, though that is not its usual state. Most of the time it rolls onto the rocks in three-to-five-foot swells. During seasonal storms the waves can be violent and dangerous, but at other times the water can also be calm and inviting. Whether a gentle surf or a foaming crest comes to mind when you picture the Atlantic, the Marginal Way is a unique place to view the **rocky coast** of Maine.

The Marginal Way is just that, a 15-foot public strip cutting between landward dwellings and the ledges that line the coast from downtown Ogunquit to Perkins Cove. The trail is blacktop, accessible from several points, and open throughout the year. Parking, limited to a few cars at the northern end and barely available along the route, is most convenient at the southern terminus in Perkins Cove. Here, space for at least 50 cars is readily available, although it can fill up at the height of the tourist season.

Birding and maritime beauty are the main attractions to the Marginal Way. The extensive sweep of the

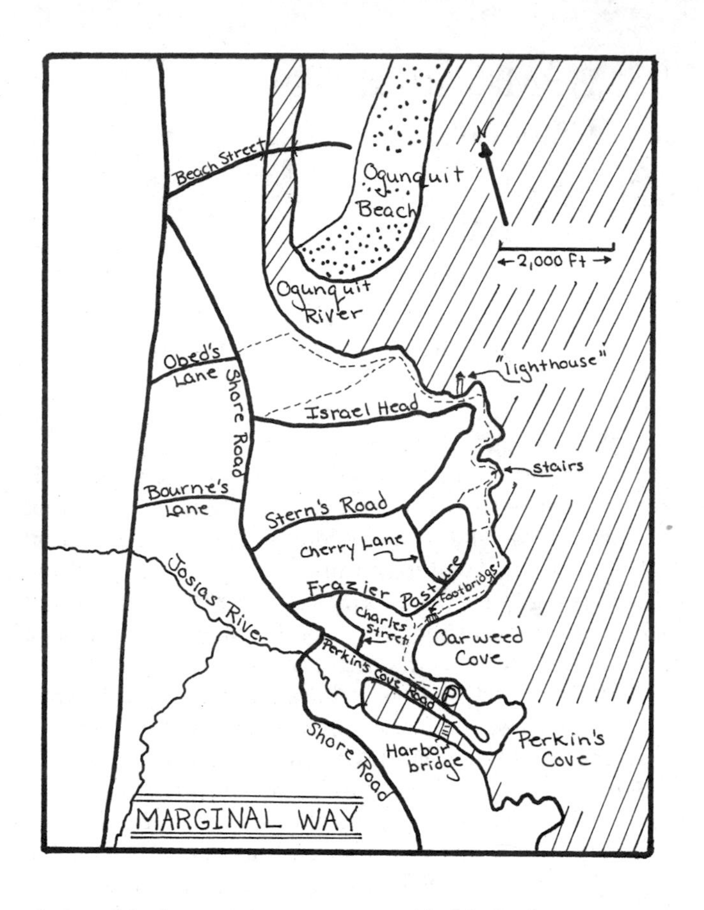

elevated ledges gives a person with binoculars or spotting scope intimate contact with birds diving and dabbling in the white-foamed water and seaweed. Beneath your feet, the fabric of the dry soil gives way to the warp and woof of the supporting metamorphic rocks often seen along the coast. The horizon brings out the rocky splendor of the coast of Maine.

From the parking lot in Perkins Cove the trail is wheelchair accessible up to a set of four stairs midway along the trail (see map). There are some inclines that favor the use of a motorized chair or a strong set of biceps, but the view is certainly worth the trip.

The first 50 feet of trail in Perkins Cove is crushed gravel. This quickly leads to firmer blacktop as one walks around the head of **Oarweed Cove.** Here, you can see the buoys marking lobster pots or boats with divers searching out the lucrative green **sea urchin.** Ten years ago the urchin was an unwanted bait thief in lobster traps. Today, marketed in Japan for its valued roe, it is threatened by overfishing.

On the northern edge of the cove the trail begins to climb though shrubbery dotted with small red cedar. You approach a wooden bridge over a break in the ledges 25 feet above the waterline. On the horizon to the southeast, beyond the buoys marking the channel to Perkins Cove, a thin sentinel stands out on a clear day. This is Boon Island Light, the tallest lighthouse in Maine waters.

From this point on, the hiker approaches a bit of **birding paradise.** Rafting and diving birds move in to feed on the mussels, crabs, and algae growing on the ledges in the surf below. Winter extremes can bring in birds like the northern gannet and the black-and-white dovekie, smallest of the auks. Feeding right at the waterline may be a small goose, the brant, and occasional rare ducks like the colorful harlequin. Birding can be interesting in all seasons as several species of gulls, ducks, and hardy shorebirds are year-round residents.

Most people can identify easily a gull but are unaware that several common species visit the rocks and beaches of southern Maine. The most prevalent is the herring gull. The adult has a white head and tail, a yellow bill with a red dot on the end, a gray back, and gray wings with black tips. Although they fiercely protect their personal space in winter, in early spring you will see lifelong mates standing side by side. By mid- to late-summer, you may see their immature offspring, the same size as adults but mottled dark brown in color. With outstretched necks they plaintively beg for food. For four to five weeks, the parents take turns providing tasty morsels for their demanding young. The chicks then must learn to fend for themselves. It will take three years of gradual change before the **young gulls** will acquire their full complement of adult plumage.

Sharing the same habitat as the herring gull are the greater black-backed gull and the ring-billed gull. The black-backed gull is larger than the herring gull. Its black back contrasts starkly with its white underbelly. Its voice is also deeper and often sounds as though the bird is choking. The ring-billed gull has markings almost identical to the herring gull. It is a few inches smaller and has a circle of black around the bill instead of a red dot under the tip. For all three birds, the marking on the bill is a target for chicks. When the parent returns to the nest, the young peck at the beak marking and the parent regurgitates food into the chick's mouth.

Egg hunting and human **predation** reduced the gull and seabird populations during the early history of our country. However, the gulls have recovered, partly due to their penchant for garbage dumps. With the proliferation of this easily available food source, gull populations have thrived. In some cases, gulls have driven other native species from offshore nesting islands. As a result, their prevalence has contributed to the decline of such birds as puffins, terns, and petrels.

The common eider, a native duck, is often seen in large numbers swimming among and resting upon rock outcrops draped in seaweed. In early spring, the rafts of eiders contain a mix of gently cooing breeding birds. The stunning males—with black bellies and white backs—display, compete, and pursue for the affections of the duller-hued brown females. In late spring and summer, mothers, daughters, aunts, and cousins form roving nurseries, with mature females sharing the care and responsibility of the young birds. The adults circle

Rose hips along Marginal Way in Ogunquit.

around their offspring as each takes a turn diving for tender morsels. The buoyant chicks literally pop to the surface after each foray. The juveniles are very vulnerable to predation. Numbers can drop considerably in the first two weeks if there are lots of hungry, marauding gulls, herons, or large fish. In late afternoon, common eiders will climb out onto seaweed-covered rocks to rest, the chicks cuddled next to mom. A furious round of preening usually ensues, then heads are tucked under wings for an after-dinner nap. The rising tide presents no danger to the resting birds, for even the young have an incredible ability to withstand crashing surf. Their clawed, webbed feet allow them to hold onto slippery rocks in waves that would send a person sprawling.

One of the unique features of the Marginal Way is a clear view of the ocean and the distant shoreline. To aid the visitor, there are many benches along the path. They are the gifts of families and charitable organizations. Here, you can lunch, break out the binoculars, and relax amid the marine scenery.

As you approach the middle of the hike, there is a point overlooking a 100-yard gash into the land. Here you must negotiate four steps that will pose a problem for wheelchairs. In addition, there is a steep incline with a hairpin curve tracing the margin of the fissure carved by the sea. A short distance beyond this sharp curve, the trail meets the road at Israel Head near a decorative **lighthouse** about 15 feet tall. At this point there are 10 parking spaces for those wishing to hike from the north end of the Marginal Way.

From the parking area at Israel Head, the way climbs east past two small cobble beaches reached by concrete stairways. Just past the high point of the head, the trail takes a long turn toward the Ogunquit River. A sweeping sandy view stretches beyond the far shore. From this overlook, you can watch diving **mergansers** year-round and, in winter, the added grace of the loon. The point of land on the distant horizon, about 10 miles away, is Goat Island at Cape Porpoise. This is just beyond the summer home of former President George Bush. The green water tower along this same horizon sits on Crow Hill, also in Cape Porpoise. Very close to the water tower you may distinguish the large white structure of the Colony Hotel in Kennebunkport, 8 miles away.

The last section of the trail is bordered on both sides by a chain-link fence. The traveler walks some 20 feet above the stone-lined embankment of the Ogunquit River. The trail borders the front lawns of several seaside motels. A left-hand turn brings you to the sidewalk on Shore Road. This exit may serve as an easy point of entry for some to explore the north end of the Marginal Way, but as there is no parking nearby, it can be used only as a drop-off and pickup point. If you wish to retrace your steps to Perkins Cove, this will make a 1.5-mile round-trip.

Getting There

Route 1 is Main Street in the village of Ogunquit. Approaching from either north or south, drive through the downtown center. Watch for Beach Street and Shore Road, angling in to join Route 1 from the east. Turn onto Shore Road. Note the blue sign for Marginal Way and follow Shore Road for 0.2 mile. On your right is Obed's Lane and on the left is the first of several smaller access paths to Marginal Way. At 0.4 mile from Route 1, you reach Israel Head Road and a second access path on your left. You can follow Israel Head Road to a small lighthouse and leave your car in the three-hour parking zone. For the best approach to Marginal Way, follow Shore Road 0.9 mile from Route 1 to a left turn onto Perkins Cove Road. Just beyond the junction, pass a private parking lot, the Oarweed Restaurant, a second private parking lot, and finally a two-hour public parking area for more than 50 vehicles, all on the left. On any sunny day during the year, this is a heavy-use area. Visitors should be prepared to search for a parking spot. There are public rest rooms on the loop beyond the public parking lot.

For more information call the Ogunquit Chamber of Commerce Visitor Information at 207-646-5533.

4. Laudholm Farm

Wells
1,600 Acres

Estuarine Uplands
7 miles total
up to 6 hours

Laudholm Farm is part of the Wells National Estuarine Research Reserve, a 1,600-acre parcel made up of **estuaries, marshes, shore front, and upland fields and woods.** Composed of local, state, and federal lands, the reserve was created in 1983 through private initiative and public support. The visitor center is housed in a nineteenth-century farmhouse and offers a gift shop, an auditorium with slide shows and video presentations, educational exhibits, trail maps, and brochures. A variety of walking tours are offered from May through October. The topics include the historic buildings, wildflowers, birds, and estuarine research. If you are visiting with children, inquire about the discovery program. For a small fee, discovery packs and guides for two different age levels are available for each of the reserve's five main trail loops. In July and August there is a parking fee of $5.00, tour fee included. Tours scheduled from May to October, excluding July and August, are $2.50 for individuals or $5.00 for a family and parking is free.

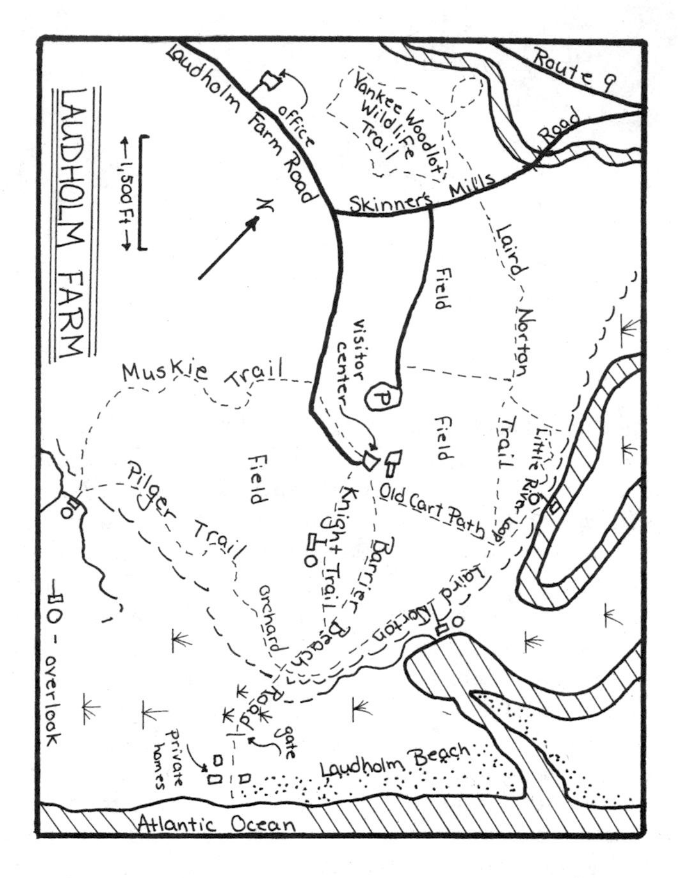

Despite the variety of services available, Laudholm is still a place where solitude can be found. Begin your walk at the visitor center. The farmhouse and outbuildings have been restored to reveal the original Greek Revival architecture. The first European settlers arrived in 1643, and this site has sustained a working farm for the last 300 years.

Prior to 1643 the area was inhabited by the Pentacook. They farmed corn as well as fished, hunted, and gathered plants and shellfish. In the years prior to the arrival of Europeans, large areas were kept in field.

In 1616, a plague—possibly smallpox—wiped out 90 percent of the Native American population in New England. Following the plague large areas were abandoned. Europeans moved in and claimed the area for their own use. Maine was colonized by the French in the north coastal area and the British in the south. Many British considered the Indians to be less than human, without souls, and akin to animals, but the French were more respectful and concentrated their energies on saving souls.

As the general treatment of Maine's native peoples deteriorated, the Indians took action. Attacks were made on Wells in 1675, 1690, and 1692. During one of these forays, the cabin on this farm was burned. The family escaped to a garrison house but a servant was killed. The hostilities ended with the massacre of the Norridgewock Indians and the French priest who had been guiding them.

The present farmhouse was built in the nineteenth century and retains the flavor of a working farm. The lands are now managed to maximize wildlife habitat and to protect the fragile wetlands and their inhabitants. Several endangered species are found on the reserve including **bald eagles, peregrine falcons, least terns, piping plovers, slender blue flag iris,** and **arethusa orchid.** Please observe all posted restrictions and stay on the trails to avoid damaging precious habitat.

The Laudholm Farm visitor center, a restored Greek Revival farmhouse.

The trail most frequently used by first-time visitors is the Barrier Beach Road. The round-trip from the visitor center to the beach and back via the Barrier Beach Road and the Knight Trail is 1.4 miles. Look for the sign in front of the visitor center indicating directions for this and other trails. The Barrier Beach Road descends gradually and is wheelchair accessible except for the last 150 feet to the beach, where a gate limits access across the road and a stepped boardwalk crosses the dunes. The old road begins by passing through open field bordered by viburnum, honeysuckle, and lilacs. In springtime, the sweet smells and vibrant white, yellow, and lavender colors fill the senses. At 0.1 mile, the Old Cart Path intersects on the left. This trail connects the Barrier Beach Road and the Laird Norton Trail by skirting the parking lot and passing through old fields.

Continue 0.2 mile on the Barrier Beach Road to intersect with the Knight Trail on the right. To vary your return from the beach, take the Knight Trail to loop back to the visitor center. The trail edges the top of the glacial moraine on which the farmhouse sits and has wide, bucolic views over open fields. There are benches along the trail for those with a more leisurely schedule.

Past the intersection with the Knight Trail, the Barrier Beach Road passes through a wooded area for a distance of 0.1 mile before intersecting with the Laird Norton Trail on the left and the Pilger Trail on the right. Each of these trails can substantially lengthen your hike if you choose to follow them back to the visitor center. These trails will be discussed more thoroughly below. Continue less than 0.1 mile to a marsh crossing. An educational display discussing **wading birds** is on your left. With luck you may see bittern, willet, heron, or yellowlegs stalking aquatic prey. The bittern and heron will be standing, silently poised, ready to use their daggerlike bills to capture unwary fish. The willet will make itself known by its sharp piercing call of "will-willet," repeated ad nauseam, and by the white band visible on its spread tail feathers as it is landing. The yellowlegs will be seen only in the spring and fall during migration. Its most obvious feature as it probes for food is its long yellow legs.

A few hundred feet ahead is a gate limiting access and marking the boundary with private property. There are beach houses on either side. The right-of-way belongs to the reserve, but respect the privacy of residents. Pass through the gate and cross the boardwalk to the wide sweep of sand that is Laudholm Beach. The raised wooden walkway allows dune grasses to grow beneath the planks and helps limit erosion. During storm surges, the roots of these plants hold sand in place.

Descend the boardwalk. You may see the tangled remains of a large yellow nylon net. Glancing up at the bank, notice a significant cut into its now vertical slope. As sea level rises and development destroys the naturally netted root systems of beach grasses, erosion threatens damage to the homes along the beach. The nylon net is a modern effort to hold the rocks and sand in place.

This beach is a very special sanctuary, as it harbors two federally endangered bird species. Least terns and piping plovers are perched on the edge of extinction. Once plentiful, their numbers continue to decline each year. Both birds nest only on sand beaches. Today, undeveloped stretches of sand are rare. Most of the houses and condominiums within sight were built during the last two decades. Each house may contain a cat or a dog as well as several human inhabitants. The garbage they produce attracts such scavengers as raccoons. Any one of these factors may further threaten the survival of these species.

Human shoreline development limits the space available for nesting. People are often unaware of the birds and their nests and may approach too closely, frightening the birds from their nests or even inadvertently trampling the camouflaged eggs. Oblivious to the repeated warning cries of the birds, bathers may park themselves and their towels too close to nests. Cats, dogs, fox, and raccoons also take their toll eating parents, fledglings, and eggs. That is one of the most important reasons why no pets are allowed on the reserve—they pose a threat to nesting birds.

Along with human impact, nests are often lost to unusually high tides or storm surges. In the past, populations were large enough to absorb these natural stresses but not so today. Walk north along this half-mile stretch of beach to enjoy the crashing waves and glimpse the plovers and terns, but please remember to give the birds a wide berth and observe all posted warnings. Fences have been raised to protect nesting areas. Please do not approach the fences or try to peer around them. There are plenty of opportunities to see the terns flying overhead on fishing expeditions and the plovers scurrying along the beach probing the sand for invertebrates.

If you would like to extend your hike to include a quiet wooded walk and views of the marsh, return via the Laird Norton Trail and the Old Cart Path. Excluding any walk along the beach, this loop is 1.3 miles. Backtrack 0.2 mile along the Barrier Beach Road to the intersection with the Laird Norton Trail on the right.

The Laird Norton Trail leads along the edge of the woods and the border of the salt marsh. Several benches are provided along the way for rest or quiet contemplation. There is an extensive boardwalk. Two-tenths of a mile from the intersection is a large raised platform on the right, providing sweeping vistas of the marsh, Little River, and the barrier beach. This view alone is worth the hike. An educational display discusses the ecology of the barrier beach.

From here the trail moves away from the marsh into the woods. Walk 0.2 mile to the junction with the Old Cart Path on your left and the Little River Loop on your right. The Old Cart Path connects with the Barrier Beach Road in less than 0.2 mile and reaches the visitor center in an additional 0.1 mile.

The 1.8-mile Little River Loop is also a wooded walk. Cross a **freshwater swamp** and travel 0.1 mile along the winding trail to the Little River overlook on your right. In winter and spring this is an especially good place to see **waterfowl.** Mallards, black ducks, buffleheads, and red-breasted mergansers find food and shelter in the quiet backwaters of the Little River estuary. In the spring and fall Canada geese migrate through the area. Occasionally, osprey call overhead or a bald eagle glides past.

From the overlook it is 0.1 mile to an intersection. The right turn is an unmaintained trail. To the left, about 100 feet, the Little River Loop crosses the Laird Norton Trail. Follow the trail 50 feet to the right, then take a left to return to the parking lot and visitor center in 0.2 mile. This trail is mostly wooded with occasional views of open fields.

If you prefer to go on, the Laird Norton Trail continues 0.6 mile along the field edge to Skinner's Mills Road. Cross the road here and continue to enter the Yankee Woodlot Wildlife Trail. This is an ecologically managed woodlot with 0.75 mile of trails. Inquire at the Laudholm Trust Office on Laudholm Farm Road for more information.

The final loop of trail also can be accessed via the Barrier Beach Road. The Pilger Trail connects with the Muskie Trail to make a 2.0-mile round-trip. As you leave the Barrier Beach Road, 0.4 mile from the visitor center on the right you will enter an old apple orchard. The area under the trees was once mowed regularly to keep it open. Now, speckled alder, sweet fern, honeysuckle, and thistle have moved into the once grassy area. This transitional vegetation provides a rich and varied habitat for many species of wildlife, including **woodcock, snow-**

shoe hare, and **white-tailed deer.** Local people often take the opportunity on a warm summer evening to stop at Big Daddy's on Route 1 for ice cream, then take a leisurely drive along Laudholm Farm Road to watch the deer grazing in the south field at sunset.

The Pilger Trail skirts the field, then enters a wet woodland. If you have not used fly repellent up to this point, you will probably need it now. In addition, be aware that the sanctuary does have ticks, including the carrier of Lyme disease. To reach the Salt Hay overlook, turn left at the intersection with the Muskie Trail. Dabbling ducks, muskrat, and river otter may be seen here. Continuing along the Muskie Trail, cross over wood plank bridges provided in wet areas. The trail skirts the edge of the field, popping in and out of the woods until it reaches the Laudholm Farm Road. Cross the road and walk along the edge of the field back to the visitor center.

Getting There

From the south, take the Maine Turnpike to Wells (Exit 2). Turn left onto Routes 9 and 109 and proceed to the traffic lights. Turn left on Route 1, continue 1.5 miles, and turn right at the second blinking light onto Laudholm Farm Road. Travel 0.1 mile, turn left at the fork, and then right into the reserve entrance.

Coming from Kennebunk, at the junctions of Routes 9 and 1 (just over the Wells line), travel 0.5 mile to Laudholm Farm Road. Turn left and travel 0.1 mile, turn left at the fork, and right at the reserve entrance.

For information call 207-646-1555.

5. Rachel Carson National Wildlife Refuge

Wells
4,000 Acres in Several Parcels

Salt Marshes
1-mile loop
up to 1 hour
Wheelchair accessible: level 1 (see p. xiv)

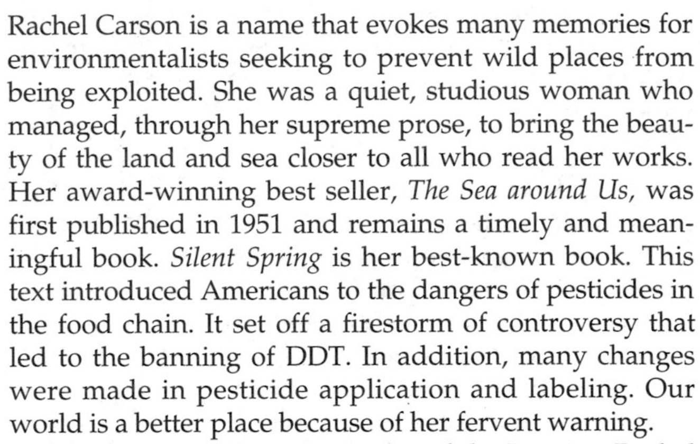

Rachel Carson is a name that evokes many memories for environmentalists seeking to prevent wild places from being exploited. She was a quiet, studious woman who managed, through her supreme prose, to bring the beauty of the land and sea closer to all who read her works. Her award-winning best seller, *The Sea around Us,* was first published in 1951 and remains a timely and meaningful book. *Silent Spring* is her best-known book. This text introduced Americans to the dangers of pesticides in the food chain. It set off a firestorm of controversy that led to the banning of DDT. In addition, many changes were made in pesticide application and labeling. Our world is a better place because of her fervent warning.

Operated by the Department of the Interior, Rachel Carson National Wildlife Refuge is dedicated to her work and her memory. It seeks to preserve the mistreated marshes that border the edge of the sea, a world she dearly loved. Actually, the refuge is not a single marsh

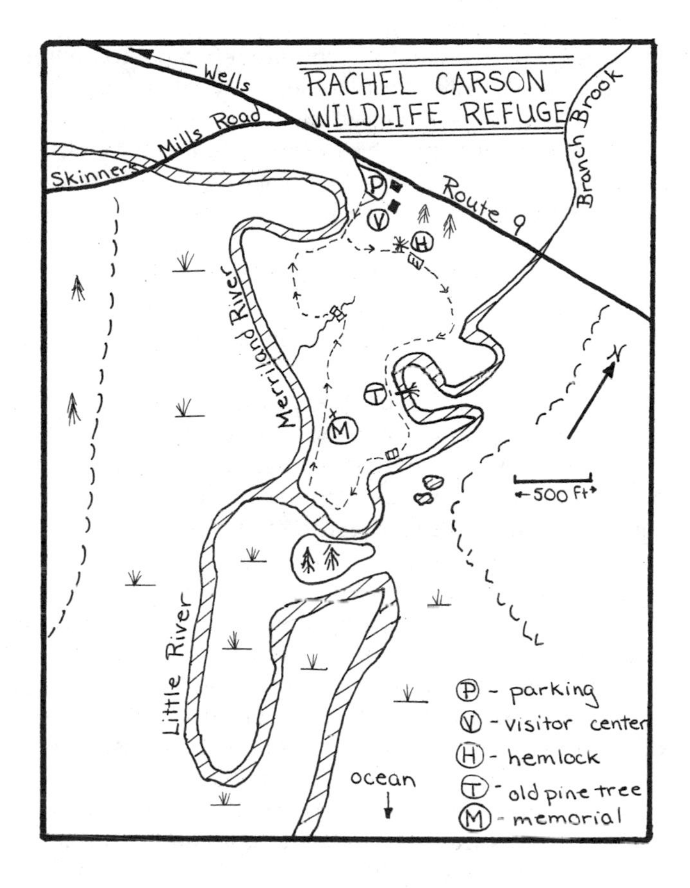

but a series of wetlands extending from the York/Kittery area to Scarborough and Cape Elizabeth, Maine. The land in Wells is one of the few places you can get a close and instructive look at the **salt marsh ecosystem** while staying dry and doing the tender marsh no harm.

The visitor's area of the wildlife refuge is deceiving. From Route 9, enter on a crushed gravel drive in the midst of a young stand of white pine. There is no marsh in sight. Step out into the hushed silence of the trees surrounding the visitor center. There is a parking area for a couple dozen cars, including a designated handicapped zone. Nearby, a display area with trail guide brochures shows the refuge map with its one-mile-loop hike and lists the flora and fauna common to the marsh. Also available is a checklist of the 250 species of birds sighted on the refuge.

The trailhead from the parking lot is clearly marked. It leads into the forest on a finely packed, even surface, suitable for feet or wheelchairs. There are benches located at various points around the one-mile course to rest oneself or just to sit and enjoy. The first 200 feet of trail lead through the white pine grove with ground cover of bunchberry and wild lily of the valley. Beware of poison ivy along the left side of the trail. There is no need to worry if you remain on the path.

The trail opens onto the first overlook on the edge of the **Merriland River,** a small tidal stream that meanders through the southern margin of the marsh. Here, the wetland area of the refuge becomes visible. The river has four-to-five-foot tides twice a day that flush plant **nutrients** from the marsh grasses and carry algae out to sea. Because of this food supply, such marsh areas are nurseries to many young fish that later become part of our offshore harvest. Early settlers and Native Americans realized the value of this property. Only recently have marshlands become dumping grounds and seaside developments.

Follow the white arrow left, away from the marsh into the darker area beneath the canopy of white pine and red oak. Along this section of the walkway look for Indian cucumber-root. The two-foot stem has two separate whorls of leaves with a yellow blossom at the tip in spring and deep blue berries by midsummer. Also there is the red trillium, with its solitary blossom surrounded by three large leaves on a single stem. The large pink blossom of the lady's slipper usually fades by late June. There is also a scattering of low-bush blueberries.

Two hundred feet from the first overlook, the trail widens under the boughs of a beautiful **hemlock** that is probably close to 200 years old and one of the largest trees in the refuge. Stand here in the spring and look out over a sea of green cinnamon ferns. In the spring, these ferns produce a three-foot-high spray of greenery with a brown spike carrying the cinnamon brown spores. In the fall, they will take on a beautiful golden hue. Among these ferns is a small shiny plant similar in shape to the wild strawberry. This is goldthread, a plant whose roots are still sought as a treatment for mouth cankers and sore throats. Beside the large hemlock is the rotting trunk of a fallen red oak. It serves as a reminder of the slow origin of nutrient-rich topsoil.

The next overlook faces part of the marsh and **Branch Brook.** The large gooseneck turns of the brook indicate the old age of the stream: marshes in New England date back to the last Ice Age, and time has created this nearly level waterway cutting wide swinging curves on its way to the sea. The expansive marsh grasses and shallow wet spots are perfect feeding areas for the local and migratory bird populations.

Stately pines grace the walkway at Rachel Carson National Wildlife Refuge.

The trail continues abreast of Branch Brook in a long arc, remaining about 20 feet above the surface of the marsh. Looking down the sandy banking you can see where large trees cling to the soil's edge in the eroding waters. At the third overlook a large white pine has lost the battle to stay erect. It now lies across Branch Brook, a decaying captive of the marsh. The path dips back into the woods, where red spruce, wintergreen, and clintonia line the walkway leading to the next overlook. The clintonia have large basal leaves like the lady's slipper, but the flowers are a pale yellow green that will form deep blue berries by summer. In the distance you can glimpse the open ocean. In the foreground, there are bird houses posted to help draw insectivorous birds as a **biological control** on the local bugs.

Handrails mark the next section of the path as it descends gently to a wide boardwalk and bench. On a sunny day you may note a distinct temperature change between the tree-covered trail and the open marsh. The wooden bridge brings you to the very edge of Branch Brook and presents a wide vista of the marsh. The trestle not only keeps your feet dry, it also keeps them from destroying the fragile marsh grasses and forming an eroded walkway in the rich vegetation and organic matter that are the foundation of the marsh.

Great blue herons and snowy egrets are common throughout the refuge, spring through fall. Deer frequently graze the borders of the marsh. Tall trees in the distance usually support a native band of heckling black crows. More than 250 species of birds, some rather rare, have been recorded in the refuge. Remember though, this is primarily an area for transient species. At times, birds and other wildlife are scarce. You just have to come more frequently to view them!

Continue from the bridge through the woods to a sharp turn in the trail with a bench nearby. The Merriland River and Branch Brook join at this point and flow on to the ocean as the **Little River.** On the beach horizon you can make out low sand dunes where the river breaks through the beach to the open sea. These isolated dunes provide nesting areas for the least tern and the piping plover. Populations of both birds have been decimated by the careless invasion of current nesting sites by humans and household pets. Locally, this isolated sand spit may be the last refuge for their reproduction.

From the corner bench, move alongside the Merriland River to an open area heavily bedded with pine needles. Squirrels frequent this area, leaving many piles of pine-cone scales in their search for seeds. Another bench overlooks the **plaque** dedicating the area to the memory of Rachel Carson. This is the most scenic vantage point on the whole walk, overlooking the immediate marsh, woods, and the distant sea. It is a perfect spot for quiet reflection.

Proceed along the trail to the small bridge over a seasonal stream. Beneath is an intermittent dribble of water that supports rather large cinnamon ferns and a springtime array of wild blue flag. Beyond the bridge, a rest stop lets you take a last look over the length of the refuge and out to sea. Continue toward the beginning of the loop trail. There are gray birches here. In early summer the white flowers of the hobblebush bloom nearby, and pale, ghostly Indian pipes push up through the leaf litter in July and August.

Close the loop by reaching the junction with the outbound trail and return the 200 feet to the parking area. If you do not need your trail guides, return them to the box to be used by other visitors.

Getting There

From the junction of Routes 1 and 9 in Wells, travel about 0.6 mile east on Route 9. On your right will be a large brown-and-yellow sign marking the entrance to the Rachel Carson Wildlife Refuge. Follow the short gravel drive to the parking area. There are public rest rooms.

You may also leave Route 1 in Kennebunk and travel down Route 35 to its junction with Route 9. Turn right and drive 3.6 miles on Route 9 west to the entrance of the refuge. For information call 207-646-9226.

6. Kennebunk Bridle Path
Kennebunk

Estuarine Uplands

3.1 miles

2 hours

Wheelchair accessible: level 1 (see p. xiv)

In 1873, the land developers of the Boston and Kennebunkport Seashore Company saw the Kennebunks as a prime development site for a destination resort equal to that of Mt. Desert Island. A core of well-to-do families from Boston already had built summer cottages overlooking the crashing waves of the rocky coastline. The Kennebunkport community also had built a reputation for its active harbor and thriving shipping industry.

By the turn of the century, a new electric train (trolley) was being built to connect Cape Porpoise and the Kennebunks to Sanford, Wells, and Biddeford; a steamship carried passengers from Boston and Portsmouth, New Hampshire; and a spur of the Boston and Maine Railroad built in 1883 connected Kennebunk's Upper Village to Parson's Beach, Kennebunk Beach, and Kennebunkport.

The Boston and Maine ran nine trains a day each way between Boston and Kennebunkport, Monday through Saturday. Some of the wealthier summer residents owned their own railroad cars and transferred entire households from their estates in Boston to their

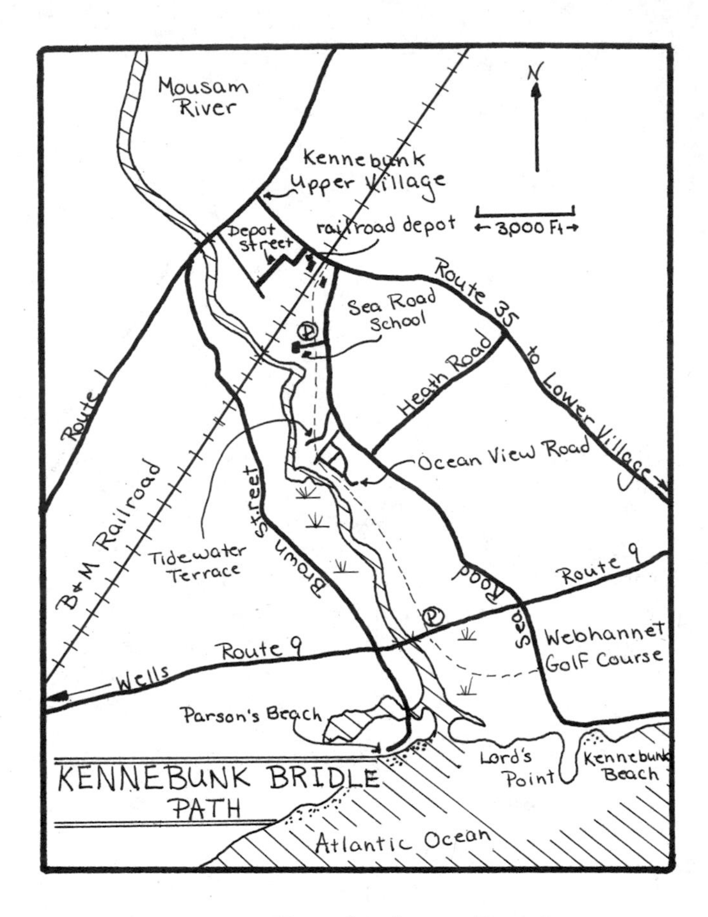

summer cottages in Kennebunkport. Favorite servants, trunks full of clothes, and carriages were all delivered in a timely three-and-a-half-hour ride. In those days, rail service was essential to the sustenance of the thriving summer community. As automobiles grew in popularity, railroad passenger service declined. Finally, in 1926, the rails from Kennebunk to Kennebunkport were abandoned and the tracks were removed to be used elsewhere. Today, little remains to mark the era of passenger rail transport in the Kennebunks.

Following the line's demise, the **railroad bed** from the Kennebunk depot to the Webhannet Golf Course was renamed the Bridle Path. Whether it was ever used regularly for horseback riding is unclear. It is certain, however, that its popularity as a means of getting from one place to another remains. On a Saturday morning you will meet runners, walkers, bicyclists, birders, and, in winter, skiers.

Railroad beds are ideal for walking. Indeed, the section of this path from Sea Road to Route 9 is wheelchair accessible for those with wide-tread tires. Here the footpath is level, wide, and dry.

The path begins on Depot Street in Kennebunk's Upper Village at the site of the old railroad station. However, the easiest access point, with plentiful parking in summer, is at the middle school (Sea Road School) on Sea Road. The trail crosses the school driveway before the first parking lot. The path on the right goes north 0.4 mile through a forest of white pine and red oak, crossing a telephone line right-of-way and a very small wetland of sweet gale and sheep sorrel before reaching Depot Street.

To the left is the more scenic walk, approximately 2.0 miles to Route 9 and an additional 0.7 mile to Sea Road and the greens of the Webhannet Golf Course.

The 2 miles to Route 9 is due south and runs parallel to the Mousam River. The river is not apparent in the first 0.8 mile, as a forest of oak and pine blocks a view of the water. Immediately after passing the small development of Tidewater Terrace and crossing Ocean View Road, the trail opens onto an expansive view of the Mousam and its attendant marshes.

Trees, shrubs, and tall grasses have been removed by a landowner to provide this vista. The few trees remaining, all oaks, have reaped the benefits of full exposure to the sun. They are large, symmetrical, and robust. As a result, they often produce an abundance of

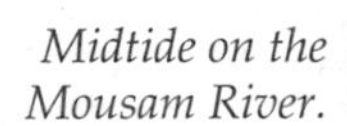

Midtide on the Mousam River.

fruit, in this case, acorns. Trees with prolific fruit production are called mast trees. They attract a variety of wildlife that feast on the bounty: squirrels and blue jays are ever present; deer, grouse, and the recently reintroduced wild turkey are a rarer find. In the fall, the densely packed acorns create a carpet of rolling pointy fruit that may be difficult to walk on for several yards.

From this point, **views of the marsh** become more frequent as do the opportunities to view the large migratory wading birds that inhabit the tidal wetlands from spring to fall. **Great blue heron** may be seen well into November. You may also spot the **green heron,** the **black-crowned night heron,** and the **snowy egret.** Although these birds are long legged and large bodied, they may be difficult to see. The heron and egrets stand perfectly still in ankle-deep pools waiting for small fish to seek refuge in their shadow. At just the right moment, the bird strikes with lightning speed, its large pointed bill as lethal as a dagger.

The **ducks** you see floating on the river are likely to be mallards or black ducks, with buffleheads and red-breasted mergansers accompanying them in spring, fall, and winter. The buffleheads are the smallest of the four species with a characteristic well-rounded puffy head, the males with a large patch of white on the crest and the females with a smaller white patch behind the eye. The red-breasted merganser has a crest that looks like a cowlick after a restless night sticking straight out in back. The male has a green head while the female's is rusty red. In fact, of the four types only the male and female black ducks look alike. Bufflehead, merganser, and mallard males are more colorful than the females, who are camouflaged in brown to sit safely unnoticed on their nests.

At 1.4 miles from Sea Road School, a side trail leads through large white pines to the river and a rope swing. Standing here at low tide, it is difficult to imagine that the swing ever reaches out over the water. But at high tide on very warm summer days, there are those who dare to take the shocking plunge into the brisk Atlantic estuarine waters. Apply the term hardy or foolish according to your own inclinations. Walkers should not use the swing without scouting the water and checking the condition of the rope first.

In the last 0.5 mile to Route 9, the visible acreage of marsh expands. Even on a hot day you may want to

A salt marsh estuary leads to the sea along the Kennebunk Bridle Path.

bring an extra sweater to ward off the chill of an ocean breeze as it sweeps across the large open expanse of grass and water. This is true especially on afternoons in May and June, when land temperatures are considerably warmer than the ocean's.

Where the railroad bed crosses small tributaries of the larger Mousam River, note the huge culverts made of massive granite blocks. Rock is the perfect building material for the harsh conditions of the marsh. Salt water would corrode steel girders and rot wooden supports, but the granite likely will outlast each of us as it has already outlasted the railroad.

At Route 9, there is a small parking area that may accommodate three or four cars. If two families decide to walk the trail on the same afternoon but only wish to walk one way on the trail, park a car on each end of the trail and exchange keys when you meet along the trail.

Carefully cross Route 9. There is no crosswalk and traffic is heavy in summer. The Bridle Path continues an additional 0.7 mile to Sea Road and Webhannet Golf Course. This section feels wilder. The shrubbery has grown into the trail, so it is no longer passable by wheelchair and the path is rutted. At 0.1 mile, winter storms have breached the railroad bed to create a low, wet area. At high tide, especially during new and full moons, this crossing may be difficult without rubber boots. On a warm summer afternoon, bare feet and shorts would be the order of the day.

At 0.25 mile past Route 9, the trail enters a forest of red oak and pitch pine. These trees dominate the marsh area because of their tolerance for salt. During severe winter storms, at spring tides, or as the result of sea spray, they are exposed to concentrations of salt that would kill more-sensitive plants.

Scanning the ground beside the trail you may discover two small plants sporting red berries in late summer and fall. The checkerberry, or **wintergreen,** is known locally as teaberry. The flavor of its berries and leaves mimics the chewing gum of the same name. The leaves are thick, dark green pointed ovals, waxy on top, and form clusters of three. The **bunchberry,** the smallest member of the dogwood family, is identified by its parallel veined leaves set in whorled clusters of four or six. The bunchberry is bland and tasteless, though very nutritious. Both plants prefer the cool shade of thick woods and thrive in sandy soils, especially near evergreens.

As you approach the end of the Bridle Path, you will glimpse cultivated shrubs sprinkled throughout the near woods marking the site of an old farmstead. Among them you will find barberry, which makes a delightful tart jam; honeysuckle's fragrant flower; wild rose, which also makes a great jam; and an old apple tree, which provides fruit for pies and sauce. (For a description of these plants see the chapter on East Point, p. 72.) As with the railroad, the people who planted these trees and shrubs may be lost to memory, but their handiwork continues to give pleasure to hikers passing this way.

Getting There

From the junction of Routes 1 and 9 in Wells, turn right onto Route 9 east. The Bridle Path will be 2.4 miles on the left. There is limited parking in front of a small blue clapboard pump house surrounded by a chain-link fence. To reach the Sea Road School and better parking, continue 0.6 mile to the first traffic light. Turn left onto Sea Road. The driveway for Sea Road School is 2.2 miles on the left (parking is available for individuals but not large groups).

From the junction of Routes 9 and 35 in Lower Village, Kennebunk, continue west on Route 9 1.8 miles to the blue clapboard pump house, or turn right at 1.2 miles onto Sea Road and continue 2.2 miles to the driveway for Sea Road School on the left.

Approaching from the junction of Routes 1, 9A, and 35 in Upper Village, Kennebunk, drive south on Route 35 0.6 mile. Turn right on Sea Road and continue 0.4 mile to the Sea Road School on your right.

7. Wonderbrook Park

Kennebunk
37 Acres

Estuarine Uplands
1.2 miles
1 hour

A plaque embedded in a rock at the beginning of the trail proclaims, "This land was procured in 1975 through the efforts of the Kennebunk Conservation Commission." The park was not a gift but a parcel of land significant to the town and its inhabitants because of its intrinsic value. At the time of its purchase it was about to be sold to developers for a huge subdivision. It contains a small tributary of the Kennebunk River, and the trail leads across the brook to the banks of the river. Protecting watersheds has become an essential environmental concern to many communities. Preserving lands in their natural state protects the quality of water for both humans and wildlife. Development on land next to a water source often blocks access or destroys habitat necessary for the survival of many species. Wonderbrook Park is dedicated to such crucial protection.

Parking for up to six cars is available at the end of Plummer Street, on the right. The trail begins amidst meadowsweet, alternate-leaf dogwood, alder, honeysuckle, and cherry. It immediately enters a stand of

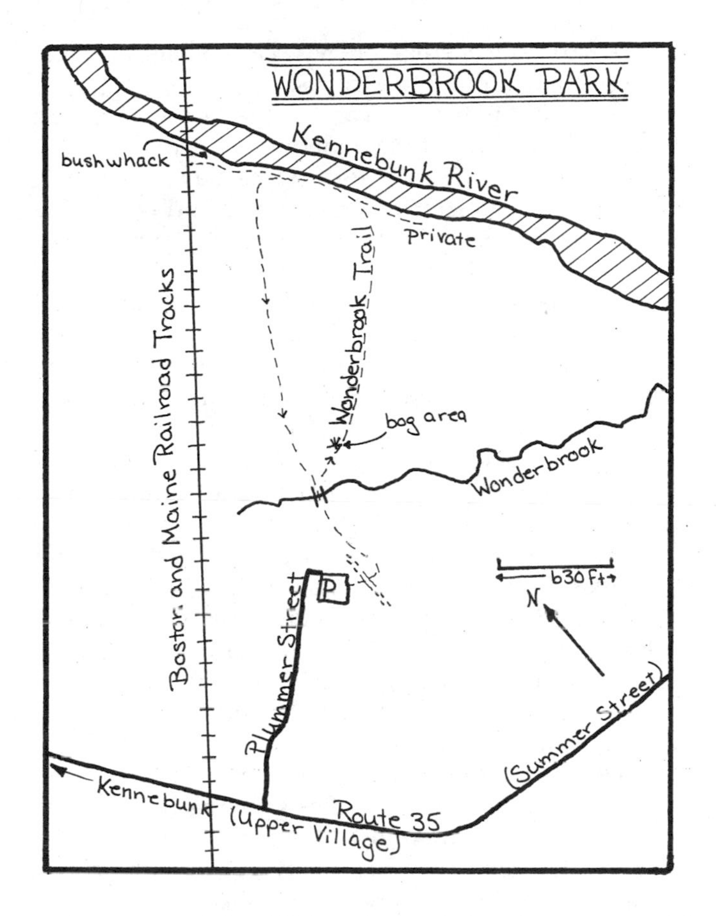

white pine. Within 30 feet, the path is crossed by an old woods road. Continue straight ahead following faded white over fluorescent orange blazes. Gray squirrels greet you as they busily gather the fruit of surrounding trees—especially acorns—or chase each other mercilessly around and around tree trunks.

The trail swings sharply to the left at 175 feet. Because there is very little undergrowth here to act as a barrier, you may miss this turn. Soon you begin a short descent to a small stream. Cross on a log bridge, noting the precarious perch of the sugar maple immediately downstream to the right. The leaves of the red and sugar maple are very similar—both sport the characteristic three lobes of the maple family and are not heavily toothed; however, the dip between the lobes of the sugar maple is wide and curved like a sugaring bucket, while the red maple is sharply pointed like an arrow.

Water striders searching for prey skim the surface of this still, slow-moving stream. Their feet are covered with dense hairs that act like snowshoes, spreading their tiny weight over a relatively large area and enabling them literally to walk, or run, on water. They are attracted to any small disturbance of the surface tension and will race toward it in hopes of discovering an adequate meal. Like some spiders, they sink their fangs into the hapless victim, then suck out its body fluids.

The trail climbs again on the stream's far side, passing between tall old maples on the left and white pine on the right. The younger trees growing beneath are balsam fir, one of the most pleasantly aromatic trees found in the Maine woods. Seventy-five feet after crossing the bridge, the trail forks with white blazes in either direction. This marks the beginning of a loop. The trail description follows the right-hand lead.

In a short while the trail crosses a wet spot on two logs. Note the **sphagnum moss** to the left. This plant

Wonderbrook Park protects a portion of the Kennebunk River watershed.

thrives on wet acidic soils. The woods beyond harbor a rich variety of ground cover including partridgeberry, teaberry (winterberry), false lily of the valley, and goldthread. Each of these can provide sustenance for wildlife, or humans, in the form of fruit or berries. The root of goldthread is also used medicinally by holistic healers for toothaches.

At 0.3 mile from the trail's beginning, another log bridge has been placed over an intermittent stream. Upstream, to the left, Mother Nature was equally accommodating, dropping a large maple that now provides a natural bridge. From here the trail swings right and crosses a low spot before climbing through a large sweep of **hay-scented ferns.** Their aroma is particularly strong in autumn after the first frost, when they are also the color of straw.

In any of these wet areas, listen carefully for the trill of an American toad or the pip of a spring peeper. You are more apt to hear both in late April, but they are most pleasant, perhaps because they are so unexpected, in October.

At 0.4 mile from the trailhead, reach a T intersection. The path joining from the right crosses private property while the Wonderbrook Trail veers left. Follow the white blazes past a large carpet of partridgeberry, its evergreen leaves set off by bright red fruit in September and October.

As you walk, notice the height, diameter, and species of the trees around you. Stands that are all the same size are likely to be about the same age, indicating that the land was once cleared. In York County, that may affirm the passing of a more agrarian lifestyle as old fields grow into forest. It may also bear testament to the huge fire that swept the southern coast in the 1940s. Occasionally, it attests to clear-cut logging practices. Do you find evidence for any one of these three possibilities? The fire burned accumulated organic matter—dead leaves, dead weeds, fallen branches—and left barren ground and exposed bedrock. Occasionally, charcoal is found captured in the roots of overturned trees.

Stone walls and barbed wire embedded in a tree trunk attest to the past presence of a field. Piles of rotting logs and rusty oilcans indicate logging operations.

At 0.6 mile there is an intersection on the left. Turn here to close the loop back to the small stream with the overhanging sugar maple. If you continue straight ahead, in 200 feet the path meets the Boston and Maine Railroad tracks.

This is also the best point to bushwhack down to the **Kennebunk River.** The bank is steep and the area next to the stream is wet, slippery clay. Be careful. Although the stream is tidal, it is quite shallow. If you do decide to scamper below to the water's edge, it is a great place to find footprints and **identify tracks,** especially those of the raccoon. Red squirrels will scold you from the branches of the overhanging hemlocks. In autumn the red, gold, and brown of the maple and oak trees reflect in the quiet, slow-moving waters of the creek.

Backtrack 200 feet to the intersection, now on your right. The returning trail is bordered by oak, maple, and

The mud on the river shore is a good place to find raccoon footprints.

an occasional white pine. Some blueberries mix with the usual ground cover of partridgeberry and teaberry.

At 0.9 mile cross a wet area on two small logs. Notice the shelf fungi growing on the log. The multicolored horizontal stripes give it the common name turkey's tail. One hundred and fifty feet beyond the featherless fan-tailed fungi is a double-branched oak splitting down the middle. The tree is literally tearing itself apart as the weight of the huge limbs pulls each half to the ground.

Close the loop at 1.1 miles among the balsam fir. Keep right to return to the parking area.

Getting There

Travel south on Routes 35 and 9A out of Kennebunk Upper Village. In less than 0.1 mile, cross railroad tracks and make an immediate left onto Plummer Street. At the end of Plummer (0.2 mile), turn right onto a gravel drive and park.

For more information contact the Kennebunk Conservation Commission, Kennebunk, ME 04043.

8. Vaughn Island
Kennebunkport
40 Acres

Rocky Coast
1.0 mile round-trip
1 hour

Nooks and crannies make the Maine coastline. They create the major and minor indentations outlining the craggy seacoast. Tucked away between Turbats Creek and Cape Porpoise Harbor, Vaughn Island is part of this irregular network. The island introduces itself from the tiny parking area on a dead-end road abutting the creek dividing Vaughn Island from the mainland.

Ledges form a **buttress** beneath gnarled red oaks where the island faces the small mainland beach. At high tide, several hundred feet of water keep the island protected from all but the most dedicated visitor. Low tide drains the creek and surrounding marsh almost to the point where dry feet can make the crossing, but usually the muddy sand and remaining inches of water ensure wet feet, so carry your shoes. The window of opportunity to explore the island is one hour on each side of low tide. Time **miscalculations** create the risk of a cold-water swim or need of a boat to return to the parking area. Between the time limitation and the very small parking area, the island is somewhat protected. It

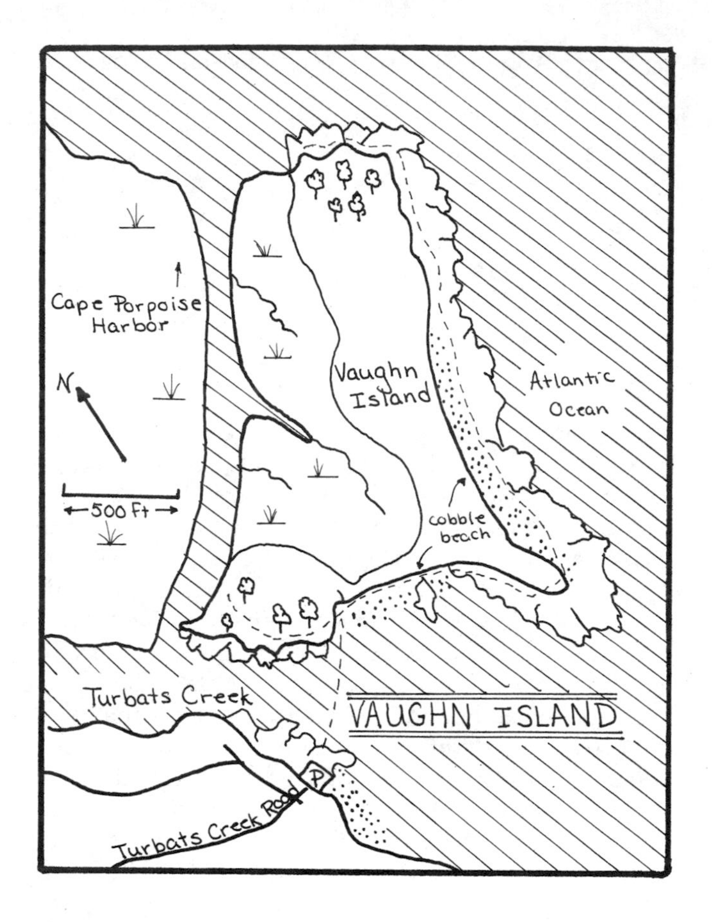

was much more accessible in the early 1900s, when a bridge carried picnickers across the creek to the island. The upright timbers on the left end of the beach are all that remains of the bridge. Today the island is part of a program training youngsters about coastal ecology and no-trace camping.

Across the intervening flats, the next obstacle for the hiker is the **rocky cobble** leading up to a grassy knoll. On the higher ground, under the oaks, are signs of heavy use: pummeled paths, trees nicked by axes, and bark stripped from birches show the thoughtless side of earlier visitors. Sadly, limited access to the island has not protected it from those who do not respect nature.

Turning from this more heavily utilized area, walk the cobble berm that leads seaward from the oak grove. The intertidal sands might be more appealing to bare feet. The berm is really a natural, narrow barrier of broken rocks protecting the marshy back side of the island from the direct force of storm seas breaking in from the southeast. Beach rose, poison ivy, and some honeysuckle top the berm, making it tough for people to penetrate. The beach rose, in spite of its inviting pink flowers, has a heavy coat of large thorns. These plants are a haven for birds and other small wildlife who find food and shelter in the dense shrubbery.

The rocky beach on this side of the island continues for several hundred feet over and around metamorphic and granite ledges to a point that makes a sharp left to the east. Here, at low tide, an extensive series of ledges stretches seaward. This is excellent lobster habitat, but boaters must be wary. Local fishermen, raised with a working knowledge of all the unmarked **reefs**, operate when high tide covers the rocks that threaten planked and fiberglass hulls alike.

Turning eastward along the beach, still cobbled and broken by ledges, the best view from Vaughn Island lies before you. Here the island effect settles over the adventurer. Imagine being alone and civilization slips away. Rock and sea sweep across the visual field, and the cries of seabirds greet the ears.

Almost due north, in the distance, is **Goat Island Light**—one of the last in Maine to be automated—guarding both Cape Porpoise Harbor, on the near side, and Stage Island Harbor beyond. In summer and fall the working drone of lobster boats may also be noticed.

Many large **tidal pools** invite exploration. Rocky spots support a few oysters, a mollusk no longer common on Maine shores. Occasionally after a storm, small pteropods (pelagic sea snails lacking shells) wash into the tide pools. Their expanded bodies and delicate swimming movements justify the nickname sea butterfly. There is much to explore on this rock garden of the sea, but remember to watch the **time** and tide to prevent being stranded on the island.

Moving along the beach toward Goat Island, you will find a series of smaller islands that fill in the southwestern margin of Cape Porpoise Harbor. In between them, and behind Vaughn Island itself, a series of mudflats are home to the soft-shell clam, or steamer. Harvesting clams has been limited by **pollution.** As the beach arcs back to the north, there is a pastoral view of the wharf and homes along the harbor. Another large clump of aged red oaks dominates the high land on this end of the island. The shards of rock thrown up into the trees attest to the force of storm waves along this shore.

It is not wise to circumnavigate the island. This would mean tramping and damaging the delicate marsh grasses and crossing some of the mudflats that line the

High tide limits access to Vaughn Island, where oak trees line the ledges facing the mainland.

north side of the island. Instead, return along the scenic beach area, capturing the view from another direction, noticing the colorful geology, plants, or birds you missed on the first pass. Between walking, viewing, a few photographs, and a quick sketch, you will return to the beach just in time to beat the incoming tide. Oops! Not in time? Better start waving at someone on the dry side.

Getting There

Route 9 is the coastal road of southern Maine. From Biddeford or Saco, follow it west through Cape Porpoise

1.8 miles to a stop sign at Main Street, Kennebunkport. Turn left onto Main Street; go 0.4 mile and bear left onto Wildes District Road. At 0.3 mile bear right at the Wildwood Fire Company onto Shore Road (it also has a Turbats Creek sign). At the next junction (0.6 mile), Shore Road will bear right while Turbats Creek Road bears left. Turn left onto Turbats Creek Road (a dead end), and follow it 0.2 mile to a very small parking area right on the beach.

From Wells or Kennebunk, follow Route 9 east into Dock Square in Kennebunkport. On the right, in the square, is a white pylon marking Shore Drive. Turn here and follow the very scenic route 3.2 miles down the river, out around the beach, and past the home of former President George Bush (2.1 miles). As the road curves away from the beaches, Turbats Creek Road comes up as a hairpin turn to the right, at a sign for the Shawmut Inn. Parking will accommodate only three cars at any one time.

9. Emmons Preserve

Kennebunkport
150 Acres

Woodlands
0.4-mile loop
0.5 hour

Henry David Thoreau said we need **wilderness.** There is certainly proof of Thoreau's idea in our advertising and consumerism campaigns. How many of our cars, foods, clothes, and creations are sold with mountains, trees, or bubbling streams in the background or on the printed label? How many homes for sale promise a special view at an enhanced price? As urban areas expand, wilderness becomes more and more precious to animals and humans alike.

The days of large-scale **conservationist** work by such people as John Muir, Teddy Roosevelt, and Aldo Leopold are gone. Huge wilderness areas have been exploited to suit the pressures and needs of a growing population. If we are to continue to save habitat for other species and fulfill our own need for "wilderness," it will most likely involve smaller plots created by informal groups and private organizations.

A prime example of this grassroots effort is the creation of the Emmons Preserve through the work of the Kennebunkport Conservation Trust. This local group,

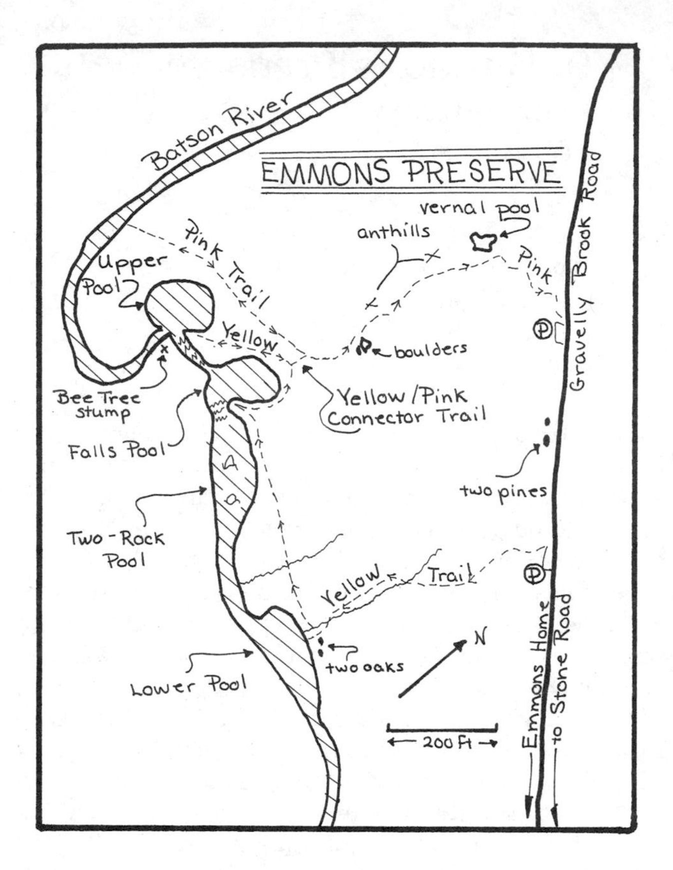

with about 700 members, has helped to purchase and set aside more than two dozen different properties for flora, fauna, and people. The newest addition is a 110-acre parcel of farmland donated by Mr. and Mrs. Stephen Emmons. With an additional purchased tract, the preserve now totals 150 acres.

Painted blazes delineate a trail system established in 1994. The preserve entrance, purposely **inconspicuous**, is off Gravelly Brook Road 0.2 mile past the Emmons's home (the only house on the left side of the road). Look for a 20-foot clearing on the left between a large red oak and a white pine. Park on the shoulder of the gravel road and step out into rural Maine air. About 200 feet before two large white pines, there is an opening into the woods, also on the left. About 20 feet into the trees is a handmade informational sign. Beyond this, the Yellow Trail leads you through a grove of young white pine, evidence of **succession** from the harvested fields of years past and an intense fire in 1947. Birches, small-toothed aspen, alder, and old apple trees add to the mix of leaves and detritus along the path. Needles, ferns, and mosses carpet the heavy clay soil that angles down toward the Batson River (Gravelly Brook on some maps). Granite ledges break the surface, swathed in common juniper. The trail snakes for several hundred feet, crosses a seasonal stream, and jogs left to the margin of the Batson River.

The far bank is lined with red oak and drops steeply to the water. The trail rests beneath the canopy of two enormous red oaks, the larger of which has stood watch for more than 200 years. Here the river expands to create the elongated Lower Pool. Summer and fall create colorful reflections on the surface, and winter produces a snowy cover sprinkled with the tracks of the gray squirrel. These attractive rodents are one of the agents of change in an area such as the preserve. Many of the seeds they bury are never retrieved and sprout into young trees that reclaim the old fields.

Returning 40 feet from the bank, the path cuts left and parallels the Batson River upstream. In addition to the young white pines and older red oaks along the river's edge, small eastern hemlock and balsam fir are just beginning to settle into the gentle slope of the transient **clay soil.** About 150 feet from the large oaks, the trail crosses another seasonal streamlet and the distant gurgling of **falling water** grows stronger. The trail rises gently to a sharp curve. Step onto the pointed ledge where water drops from Falls Pool into Two-Rock Pool on the left. Caution—the rocks are not far above the water and

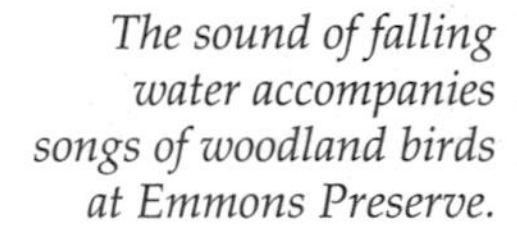

The sound of falling water accompanies songs of woodland birds at Emmons Preserve.

they may be slippery. On hot summer days when the surrounding fields were worked, these pools provided a cool respite to field hands, the "old swimming hole."

The path arcs right, around the border of Falls Pool, and joins the Yellow/Pink Connector Trail. Stay left and follow the Yellow Trail along granite ledges that create a 100-foot-long cascade splashing from the Upper Pool into Falls Pool. On the near side are the fallen remains of a large white pine, once a honey tree, home to an enormous contingent of native bees pollinating domestic and wildflowers alike. The stump of the bygone "**bee tree**" remains upright on the large granite outcrop guarding the top of the falls across the river.

Linger in the surrounding sound of the river. When you are ready, retrace your steps to the junction and bear left onto the Yellow/Pink Connector Trail. Sixty feet farther, take a sharp left onto the Pink Trail. It moves gently upward through more young, closely packed white pine and opens onto a wide terrace populated with red maple and red oak in an almost parklike area. Royal fern, lycopodium, some teaberry, and a leafy ground cover create a soft cushion underfoot. The moist ground and nearby forest, combined with the pastures on the far side of the Batson River, produce a unique area for **wildlife,** especially birds. The American woodcock can find food in the damp ground and run its buzzy breeding ritual in the nearby open spaces. The harsh croak of the ring-necked pheasant is heard in the fields, and the ever-increasing number of wild turkey can add to a birder's life list. In spring, ruffed grouse patrol the grounds with their chicks in attentive array or startle hikers with their explosive launch technique.

Again, retrace your steps and, bearing left at the junction, follow the Pink Trail. This initiates your return trip to Gravelly Brook Road. For 50 feet the trail climbs, then levels out, again snaking through a dense growth of white pine. About 150 feet from the junction, the path moves between granite boulders. On the left is an unusual sight. Several mounds, 5 or 6 feet across at the base and almost 3 feet high, rise out of a low area beneath the pines. Do not disturb or step on these hills—they are the industrious work of **ants.** Like earthworms, these insects turn over and aerate the soil, resulting in a user-friendly mulch for plant roots. These are unusually large hillocks, likely due to the shallow soils over the granite ledge that force the ants to build high-rise **condominiums.**

One hundred and seventy feet farther along on the right, a white pine straddles the ledges and hovers over a collection of common polypody fern. This hardy little fern is a pioneer plant, invading and clinging to the rock face even before soil begins to collect. Beyond and to the left is another set of anthills, somewhat smaller than those in the initial group. Continuing along, the trail quickly reaches a mossy green area on the left. Keep an eye out for water underfoot. In winter the area is iced over. In spring and summer it holds the **Vernal Pool,** temporary home and breeding area to the spring peeper. This tiny tree frog creates one of the more welcome sounds of spring, a sure cure for cabin fever. In late summer, this same pool dries out beneath the gray birches, and the remaining cool bed of moss is a rest area for the local red fox.

It is only a couple of hundred feet from the Vernal Pool to the roadway. Parked by the Yellow Trail, vehicles are 350 feet away down the road, making an easy return loop. Step into your car refreshed from a pleasant walk and this small patch of "wilderness." Consider looking into the organizations in your town, city, or state that sponsor conservancy and preservation. A patchwork quilt of wilderness habitat is beneficial to all, including our economy. Take another step—join and **support your local group**, and you, too, will make a difference.

Getting There

Route 9, the local coastal road, provides the most direct access to the vicinity of the Emmons Preserve. Follow it 5.4 miles east from its junction with Route 35 in Kennebunk, through Cape Porpoise, to the intersection with Goose Rocks Road. Turn left here, by a striking white farmhouse and adjacent barn topped with a large clock (Clock Farm Corner). Follow Goose Rocks Road 1.4 miles to a left turn onto Stone Road. Turn right 0.6 mile farther onto the unpaved Gravelly Brook Road. Pass a small home on the left (the Emmons residence dated 1815), and the trail entrance is 0.2 mile beyond on the left. It is set back from the road in some red oaks. There are two large white pines 150 feet past the entrance on the road. Watch for these if you have trouble finding the trailhead. Parking is along the edge of the roadway.

Coming from Biddeford on Route 9 west, travel 3.7 miles beyond its junction with Route 208, turning right at Clock Farm Corner. Continue on Goose Rocks Road as noted above.

10. East Point Sanctuary

Biddeford Pool

30 Acres

Rocky Coast

1.6 miles

1 hour

You can visit East Point in the early morning darkness, hoping for just enough heavy weather for the rising sun to color the sky in shades of red, orange, and purple. You can almost shut out the world in a shroud of heavy fog, or gaze for miles out to sea on a clear summer day, or stand at the point and marvel at the energy and fury of the crashing waves following a winter storm. In winter, cross-country skiers on perimeter trails may glimpse the snow-covered peaks of Mt. Washington and the Presidential Range 75 miles away. Each encounter with East Point offers some new gift or unlocks one more secret.

Year-round residents and visitors alike can travel to East Point to experience the Maine coast as it looked a century ago. Though bordered today by residential homes and a private golf course, at East Point it is surprisingly easy to leave the modern world behind once you glimpse the open ocean, hear the ringing of a channel buoy, and taste the salty air.

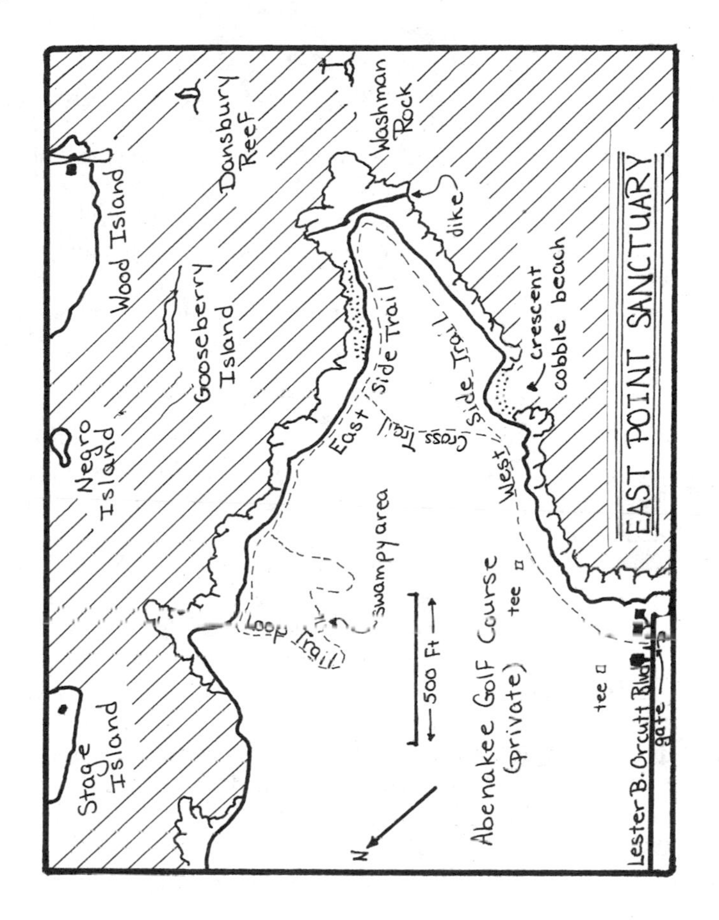

South-coastal Maine hosted some of the earliest European settlements in North America. Prior to their arrival the native peoples had occupied the area for at least 5,000 years, enjoying the bounty the sea offered up and making little lasting impact on the local ecology. The Europeans came hoping to transform the wilderness into the land they had left behind. Many of the **plants** they transported on their ocean voyage from the old country found the New England climate hospitable. They thrived, escaped into the surrounding countryside, and have become so well established that most of us assume they are native plants.

At East Point, aliens—among them locusts, beach rose, and beach pea—are sprinkled about, intermingling with the hardy native flora.

Climate also affects plant and animal life here. The steady, sometimes severe sea wind has selected for varieties of low-growing herbs and shrubs. Fog and surf have chosen those with a tolerance for salt. Plants in the open field or on exposed rocks must also contend with scorching sun in summer and the potential for severe desiccation. Denizens of the **intertidal zone** must struggle with the force of the powerful, twice-daily, crashing surf.

As you walk the preserve, look for five distinct ecological zones: the open field of the headland; the dense shrubbery behind the headland; gnarled low-growing trees in the lee of the shrubs; the rocky intertidal zone; and a small wetland ecosystem midway through the Loop Trail. Each area contains life adapted to the rigors and competition found in that specific environment.

Whether you are ready for a crisp 45-minute hike or a leisurely four-hour stroll, you begin your jaunt at a 15-foot section of chain-link fence adjacent to the on-street parking. The barrier has an opening wide enough for people but does not admit bikes or motorized vehicles. Visitors are welcome from sunup to sundown.

One of the first trees encountered on either side of the path is an exotic, the black locust. Usually planted along the edges of fields, the black locust has beautiful, edible clusters of flowers (in fritters) but is otherwise inedible. It is also protected by paired thorns at the base of its leafstalk. The tree is easily identifiable not only by its thorns but by the compound leaves that are divided into 6 to 20 leaflets.

As you continue along the well-worn dirt and grass road, the greens of the golf course will be on your left and the remnants of a windbreak on your right. Here you will find a variety of apple trees that bear fruit to the delight of the local population of squirrels, chipmunks, skunks, raccoons, and porcupines.

Growing among the locust and apple trees are two of the most common shrubs found on East Point, honeysuckle and bayberry. The bayberry, or wax myrtle, is most easily identifiable in late summer and fall by its clusters of hard blue berries covered by white wax. The fruit is inedible by humans (though it appears to be palatable to some birds). The berries were boiled by early European settlers to remove the richly scented wax for the production of candles. The thin green leaves give off a sweet herbal aroma when crushed, as do two of its close relatives also found growing at East Point, sweet fern and sweet gale. Bayberry's leaves are arranged alternately along the stem and have margins that are smooth or have only one or two teeth. From a distance the shrub can be identified by the densely packed growth of its branches. It's an ideal place for birds to build nests as some thickets are virtually impenetrable to humans and larger animals.

Past the golf course, about 100 yards from the gate, the trail opens out onto a grassy field. Here you will receive a **sweeping view** of ledges, the open ocean, channel buoys, and rafts of ducks. This is a perfect place to survey the effects of the near-shore climate on the growth of vegetation. The plants closest to the open water (mostly grasses) are low growing and must be salt tolerant. In amongst the grasses are wild strawberries, yellow rattle, and cinquefoil. Although deer and sometimes even moose visit this field, the most common inhabitants are meadow voles and field mice. They tunnel through the thick grass and feed on seeds and fruit that fall to the ground. In turn they become food for fox, hawks, and even the beautiful snowy owls that occasionally migrate here in the dead of winter when the Arctic tundra has become inhospitable and their food is scarce or hidden beneath the snow.

As you stand at the head of the field, the Cross Trail joins from the east and is bordered on the north side by a very large stand of **staghorn sumac.** In winter the staghorn's large compound leaves, which are divided into 11 to 31 leaflets, drop to the ground, exposing the stout hairy branches of the sumac. At this time they resemble the velvet-covered antlers of a very large stag. The clusters of fuzzy red berries serve as food for winter wildlife (in summer when the berries are first ripe, you can prepare a strained mixture of the berries, honey, and water to make a wild pink "lemonade").

From the head of the field, proceed to the right down the West Side Trail. Stay close to the shore, watching for the crescent-shaped **bank** that drops 25 feet to a rocky beach. This steep slope has been cut back some 20 feet in the last decade, demonstrating the pressing power of the ocean waves. The exposed area is a bank of cobbles and soil from glacial outwash formed more than 8,000 years ago. The lower portion of the exposed material is an ancient sand beach. At the bottom of the cut, the beach is made up of cleaned cobbles that rattle in the surf with each breaking wave. Many of the rocks found here are not part of the local bedrock. They were carried here by the mantle of ice abrading the land from the north during the last great Ice Age.

At the base of the eroded cut, the most recently revealed ledges show evidence of the glacier. The smooth unweathered outcrop of rock bears scratches running north-south, where tons of ice in a sheet 10,000 feet high pressed boulders along the ledge, leaving

Horizontal glacial striations indicate the glacier's direction of travel across metamorphic rock at East Point.

marks of its passage. Such scratches are found throughout Maine. The ice locked up so much of Earth's water that the sea level was approximately 300 feet lower, and dry land extended miles out into what you now see as open ocean.

As you walk farther out the trail to the literal point of the land, you can see the nature of the **bedrock** clearly. Stretching out into the surf are the sandwiched sedimentary rocks of an ancient seafloor. These layers have been heated, compressed, twisted, and turned on end by the continental forces that built the Atlantic Ocean and the Appalachian Mountains. Now the onetime sediments are considered metamorphic rocks made up of quartzites and slates. Within 10 feet of the embankment is a large northeast-southwest "dike" of dark brown **basalt** that cuts directly across the layers of older stone. This rock was formed deep in the earth when a crack in the metamorphic material filled with molten lava. It is younger, going back less than 100 million years, than the surrounding metamorphic rocks (which date back several hundred million years). The basalt also weathers more easily than the surrounding rocks, leaving narrow channels in some areas.

The horizon reveals open ocean, distant points of land, nearby green-mantled islands, and a lighthouse. The **Wood Island** lighthouse is the fourth oldest in Maine, constructed in 1808 under the administration of Thomas Jefferson. The light stands 71 feet above the sea and flashes green and white at six-second intervals. Wood Island was partly cleared of timber to accommodate the sweep of the beacon. (This island is, along with East Point, part of the Maine Audubon Society's chain

A frequent sight on Maine's rocky coast: a basalt dike that intruded into metamorphic rock millions of years ago.

of protected lands for the breeding and maintenance of our declining bird population.)

Between the mainland and Wood Island is Gooseberry Island, an exposed ledge often covered with seabirds and their guano, but no gooseberries. Instead, you might see double-crested cormorants and a smaller number of great cormorants. Herring gulls, great black-backed gulls, and the smaller ring-billed gulls mix their mews and cries with those of the cormorants on the ledges. Storms at sea will occasionally bring in seldom-seen visitors like the northern gannet, Wilson's storm petrel, the black guillemot, and the little dovekie. For the newcomer who might wonder, the favored Atlantic puffin does not come this far south.

To the left of Wood Island is a small, rounded green knob, Negro Island. This very small, island was the last stop for slaves escaping to Canada on the Underground Railroad.

Moving away from the point to your left and toward Negro Island, the path, now called the East Side Trail, parallels the rocky shore, where there is a semblance of a beach with some soil and a lot of cobbles. If you choose to walk the beach, you will find many shells unbroken by the churn of water and rock. Common periwinkles, blue mussels, and horse mussels abound with many of the larger seaweeds like rockweed, horsetail, southern kelp, and Irish moss. This last supplies carrageenan, a common ingredient in ice cream and pudding desserts.

To resist the pounding wave action of the **intertidal zone,** the periwinkles and limpets use excellent suction cup feet to lock themselves to the rock surface. Limpets, in particular, are almost impossible to remove from a rock face once they have attached themselves. Barnacles cement their shells to the rocks and as adults must remain forever in one place. Blue mussels make a series of cables called byssus threads to attach to the rock's surface. As we humans do not have suction cups, cement, or cables, we must move with care around the slick rocks and extreme surf. Please use caution near the waterline and keep a protective eye on children. The ledges are covered with seaweed and other forms of algae, making them predictably slippery. Children enjoy exploring the intertidal zone and can while away hours looking under seaweed for green crabs or gazing into tide pools at periwinkles, tortoiseshell limpets, and barnacles.

Just above the high-tide mark, you will discover beach peas, wild mustard, and sea rocket. The beach pea is an alien from Japan, where it was believed to be an aphrodisiac. Like the common garden pea, it is quite edible and has tendrils for climbing other plants. Nearly all the mustards are spicy and are used as mustard plasters for healing fevers, rheumatism, and blood congestion. You will recognize wild mustard by its yellow flowers composed of four petals arranged in a cross. Sea rocket is also a mustard, with rather thick edible leaves and purple flowers. Best when used in salads, it has a strong peppery taste that tells one to use it sparingly.

From the area of the rocky shore, approach the juncture with the short Cross Trail, and another larger island comes into view. This is **Stage Island.** The name dates back to the seventeenth century when stages, or benches, were used to dry the split bodies of cod before they were shipped to Europe. During the War of 1812, Stage Island was the platform from which the men of the British ship HMS *Bulldog* attacked and burned four local ships and the Cutts store on Biddeford Pool. The island's conical stone tower was erected in 1825 to mark the mouth of the Saco River and Wood Island Harbor. Stage Island is now home to breeding colonies of white egrets, common terns, eider ducks, and many local gulls.

At this point, the East Side Trail begins to narrow to a single-file footpath, and the beach again gives way to ledge. Strewn about the path and underbrush are rocks thrown up from the beach by storms. It takes quite a strong surf to throw 30- and 40-pound rocks this far.

Imagine what it takes for animals and plants to exist under such fierce conditions.

Beware of the occasional sprig of poison ivy along this path, but also notice more bayberry and beach rose blooming in pink or white. There is also a strange parasitic plant known as dodder along this portion of the walk. It is a thin yellow wire with sparse flowers and no leaves. Lacking chlorophyll to make its food, dodder wraps about other plants, stealing nourishment with little suckers.

The dense thickets that are a large part of the East Point Sanctuary make it a great birding location. But the shrubs can also make sighting birds extremely frustrating if you are trying to determine where that L.B.J. (Little Brown Job) is among the tangle of branches. Some of the birds you may hear, if not see, at various times of the year include goldfinches, yellow warblers, common yellow-throated warblers, yellow-rumped warblers, black-and-white warblers, white-throated sparrows, song sparrows, rufous-sided towhees, northern mockingbirds, and gray catbirds.

The underbrush provides **shelter** and protection for lots of medium-sized wildlife. In among the poison ivy and roses go groundhogs, fox, snowshoe hare, ring-necked pheasant, porcupines, and possibly otter. You may also run into a skunk or a raccoon.

At the end of the East Point Trail is the aptly named Loop Trail. It provides the hiker with a little more challenging foot fare, turning and twisting sharply with a few small ledges thrown in for good measure. Most hikers can handle this easily. You might have to use your hands in addition to your feet on a couple of the steeper rocks. There is also a **swampy spot** that, depending on the season, may be either bone-dry or ankle deep with mud. Strategically placed rocks and logs can help you get across. Some of the plants you will notice here include marsh Saint-John's-wort, sweet gale, and jack-in-the-pulpit. There is also an abundance of jewelweed, whose crushed leaves can be rubbed on skin exposed to poison ivy to remove the irritating oils.

Past the swampy area, the Loop Trail provides the fourth ecological habitat of East Point. The moment you move in from the beach, the sea breeze diminishes and the air seems warmer. Behind the protection of the shrubs grow pitch pine, scrub and red oak, and sugar and red maple. As you enter this miniature forest, notice how some of the trees have been sculpted by severe wind, rain, and ice in winter. The elements render them short and stout in appearance, with close-cropped, gnarled branches. If a tree loses its tip in a storm, lower limbs will form a double top, adding to the apparent bulk. Lower branches, protected from the full force of nature, spread out, giving the tree a wider stance than one might normally expect. This mix of trees and dense shrubbery, and the relative isolation of the Loop Trail, provide protection for more birds and mammals.

The Loop Trail rejoins the East Side Trail. You can backtrack to the Cross Trail, providing a second opportunity to savor the sweeping vista of open ocean, the fragrance of honeysuckle, and the raucous cry of gulls as you make your way back to your vehicle.

Getting There

From Route 9 between Kennebunkport and Biddeford, turn east onto Route 208 toward Biddeford Pool. Pass over a small bridge and come to a stop sign. Turn left onto Mile Stretch. Pass Hattie's Deli on your left and continue up the hill past Yates Street, also on the left. At the top of the second rise, bear right on Lester B. Orcutt Boulevard. Maintain this route past a series of rather large "summer cottages" sometimes referred to as soap row (for the homes associated with names like Gillette, Proctor & Gamble, and Colgate). When you are in sight of the ocean, you will see a 15-foot length of chain-link fence on the left in the shrubbery just before the last two driveways. There is limited parking on either side of the roadway. Leave your vehicle and begin your walk through the fence. You might also take a moment to walk over to the corner at Ocean Drive, where you can roam out onto the attractive rock beach and ledges.

11. Ferry Beach State Park

Saco

100 Acres

Sandy Beach

1 mile

1 hour

Wheelchair accessible: level 1 (see p. xiv)

Much of our present shoreline is devastated. It is reshaped to suit the needs and desires of modern development. The end result is usually an unstable, receding beach or shore that is very expensive to stabilize and support. We have yet to recognize that seashores represent a continuum of change over many human lifetimes. In most cases where the beach **stabilization** process has been studied in depth, we find that nature and her sand dune grasses are better than most modern engineering at solving shore erosion problems.

Ferry Beach State Park represents a small section of native sand dunes and the **ecological conditions** these dunes create. Here you can see the natural balance of elements existing before humans began to landscape the shoreline. Along the sandy berm, the dominant plant is the dune grass *Ammophila breviligulata* (ammophila means sand lover). This is the main pioneer plant that takes hold in the hostile, hot, and salty soil. Once established, the dune grass holds the sand in place with its

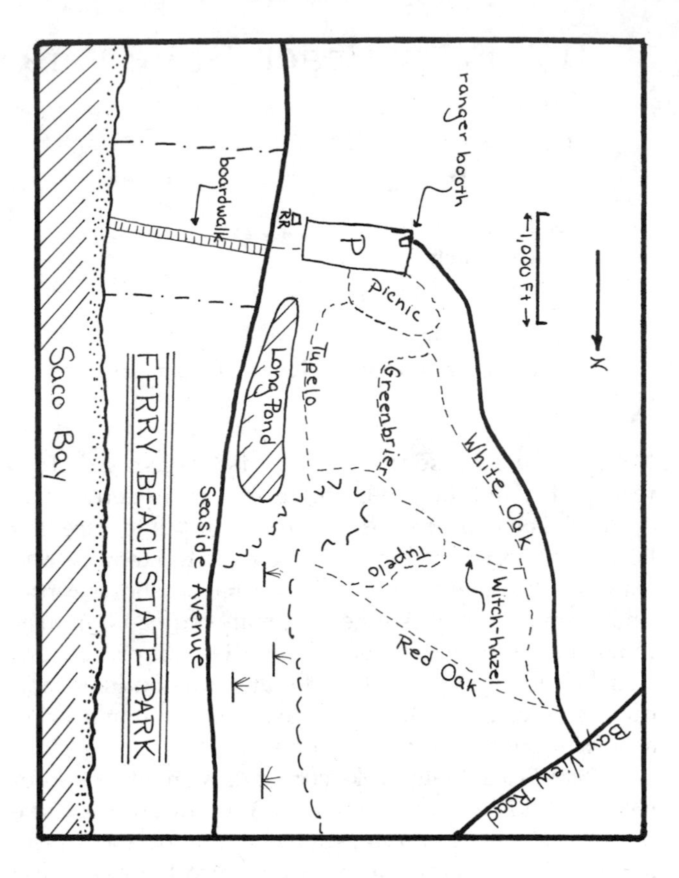

roots, and its highly flexible stalk resists the forces of wind and water. The stalks also weaken the power of the wind and catch blowing grains of sand, building dunes higher. Underground **runners** send up new shoots along the seaward face of sand dunes. The habits of this tough plant allow protective dune systems to actually migrate forward over a period of years or retreat in the face of overwhelming storms. This flexible system usually proves superior to fixed granite groins and jetties.

Once the dune grass has established itself, other **plants** readily take hold in the freshly stabilized soil. Beach pea, beach rose, seaside heather, and wormwood join the floral show that spreads across the dunes. Mixed in the dune grass, beach pea produces a deep purple blossom through the summer and delicate pea pods in August. It closely resembles its commercial garden cousin. The beach rose has five pink (occasionally white) petals that precede a one-to-two-inch red rose hip used in jams and tea. Wormwood, or artemisia, has deeply cut, finely divided leaves covered in silvery green hairs, a protection against the sun and blowing sand. If these plants in the system remain stable for a long period, larger shrubs and the hardy pitch pine add their own root systems to the holding pattern. Delicate lichens and earthstar puffballs grow among the needles strewn beneath the pines. The unusual puffball opens in a star-shaped pattern, spreading its spores into the sea breezes. The **endangered** least tern and piping plover use such areas for nesting. The diverse life of a dune area can be damaged by uncommonly large storms or simple foot traffic compacting the soil and the plants. Please follow the signs and remain on the trails to protect this **fragile** ecosystem.

The open sand beach gives an expansive view of Saco Bay. Biddeford Pool and Wood Island Light are to the southeast past the jetty guarding the mouth of the Saco River. To the northeast, the beach extends to Old Orchard,

Prouts Neck, and Cape Elizabeth. About one mile offshore is Eagle Island. This and the many other islands of the bay are protected breeding areas for blue herons, white egrets, terns, and gulls that frequent the Maine coast.

A hundred yards behind the dune and beach zone sits a chain of ponds and swamps that represent an **ancient shoreline.** Glacial outwash and the long-shore current carried sand from the Saco River along the beach, building dunes and enclosing shallows. With the ocean cut off, freshwater filled the area creating a totally new environment. Water lilies, pickerelweed with its purple flower spikes, sphagnum moss, and painted turtles soak in the plentiful supply of freshwater a short distance from the desertlike environment of the dunes.

As you enter the parking area, a short trail in the far left corner leads to a sign giving a quick summary of trails. The longest possible loop, one mile, combines the Red and White Oak Trails with the Tupelo Trail. The latter carries you out past Long Pond and the ancient beach shoreline.

Toward the northern end of the pond, the trail takes a sharp left. A raised walkway carries you above a **sphagnum swamp** full of highbush blueberry, maleberry, sweet gale, and winterberry holly. The green oval leaves of maleberry and the holly are similar. The fruits are quite distinctive. The holly produces individual bright red orange berries while the maleberry forms a cluster of five-parted fruits. The trail brings you almost immediately to a stand of black tupelo (sour gum) on the right. This tree is usually associated with southern swamps. It has a deeply cut bark, and the limbs tend to come off the tree at right angles to the trunk. The Red and the White Oak Trails carry you into an upland, drier forest shortly beyond the tupelo swamp. Eastern hemlock is mixed in heavily with the trees that name the trails. The chatter of both the red squirrel and the eastern gray squirrel accompany the hiker through this area. There is a rich soil built up by deep leaf litter. This heavy layer of decaying vegetation creates a habitat that favors larger poisonous fungi like the fly mushroom, *Amanita muscaria,* and the destroying angel, *A. virosa.* Both can be six to eight inches tall and quite poisonous. The fly mushroom has a warty yellow cap, and the destroying angel is usually a stark white outline against the dark pine forest floor.

A boardwalk along the shady inland trails of the tupelo swamp provides a cool retreat.

The obvious pleasures of the sand beach and quiet ponds and the variety of vegetation in the protected confines of Ferry Beach State Park create a special area. In addition to the uncommon black tupelo, sassafras, prevalent to the south, is represented in the park. The durable wood from the tupelo has been used in barrels, buckets, and dugout canoes. The root and most parts of sassafras have been made into a popular tea used as a **cure-all.** This plant was a major export item in the seventeenth century. It gained an undeserved reputation for treating syphilis. This single fact discouraged the common use of the tea for some folks. Other unusual plants within this 100-acre wood include the earthstar puffball, now locally rare due to habitat destruction. The dwarf ginseng, rare for the same reason, is also cautiously watched over by park rangers.

Visiting this enclave of healthy **coastal habitat** tucked away along a highly developed shoreline is a rare pleasure for young and old. If we are to have an equally healthy world for humans, we must have such spaces that are viable for all forms of life.

Getting There

From Route 1 in Saco, follow Route 9 east (Beach Street) 2.9 miles to a left turn onto Bay View Road. Follow Bay View for 0.3 mile to the large brown sign on the right for Ferry Beach State Park. It is 0.5 mile to the spacious parking lot just beyond the ranger's tollbooth. There is a minimal entry fee and a senior citizen discount (free to date).

For information call 207-283-0067.

12. Pleasant Point

Buxton

60 Acres

Woodlands

1.5 miles

1 hour

Pleasant Point is a place of big trees and, especially in the fall, big quiet. The trees, in some cases more than 10 feet in circumference, rustle gently in the breeze, whispering the secrets gathered during decades of standing sentinel over carriage paths and open pastures.

It is a wonderful place to picnic beneath **tall pines,** walk wooded paths, launch a canoe into the now placid waters of the impounded Saco River, or sit with eyes closed, leaning against a 200-year-old oak envisioning an earlier time. There are centuries of history in this place. It is easy to imagine the shadows of early inhabitants enjoying a carriage ride under the shady, bowed oaks or a picnic on the sun-washed sand beach at the point.

In 1740, the first Europeans arrived at Pleasant Point. They were attracted to the huge trees they could market for lumber. There were waterfalls they could harness for power; the wide river on which they could transport raw timber in log drives; and the hill that rose

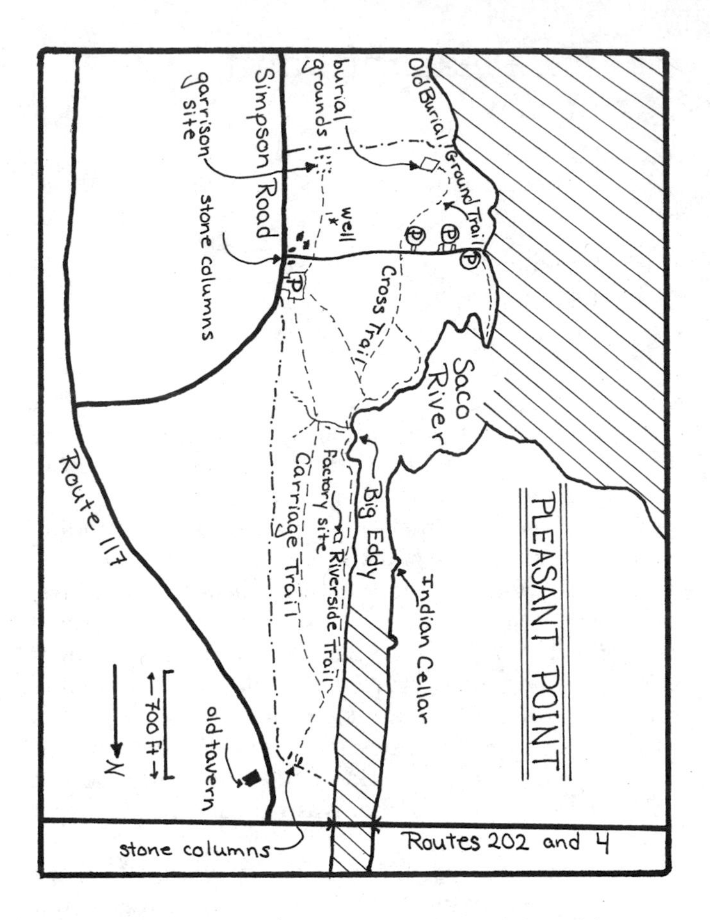

from the riverbank that, when cleared, would give a wide view of the river valley, making it easily defensible.

It was at Pleasant Point that the roiling Saco River tumbled over Salmon Falls and through the rock-strewn

gorge, slowed, dropping the sands it carried, and created a gently sloping sandbar. Fresh, cool water bubbled from a nearby spring. It was as inviting a site as one can imagine.

The settlers worked at clearing land for fields, and by 1754 a small fort was built on the top of the hill and a plot was laid out for the **burying ground.** In 1906, after 150 years of service as pastureland, the property was given to the Appalachian Mountain Club as a recreation site for public use and as a memorial to one of the first settlers, Cyrus Woodman. It is now owned and maintained by the town of Buxton. The trees have grown back in all their grandeur. Today, Pleasant Point looks much like it might have when European settlers first arrived.

It is Pleasant Point's majestic white pine, white ash, and red oak that distinguish it from other parks. You may crane your neck to find the tops of pines that would have been masts carrying ships of the colonial days across the realm of the British navy. These are the kinds of trees that helped the USS *Constitution*—"Old Ironsides"—set records in the defense of our country. They allowed shipping to carry the people and goods of a growing nation.

Pleasant Point offers a glimpse into the **ecology** of a mature northern mixed forest of conifers and hardwoods. Though some of the areas beneath the trees have been cleared by human intervention, much of the park area close to the river, beneath the mature growth, is quite clear and park-like due to nature. The heavy canopy of leaf and needle growth absorbs or reflects 95 percent of the sunlight. Little of this energy

Tall white pines dwarf hikers at Pleasant Point.

reaches the forest floor to support a heavy undergrowth. The result is an area rich in leaf litter and relatively few shrubs.

Movies and adventure books often show wild areas as impenetrable jungles, yet our early colonial forests were often clear of such thick growth. Passage on foot or on horseback was easy under the protective cover of the climax forest. The Native Americans did not spend their time chopping their way through junglelike growth. They made blaze marks on trunks of trees to mark a trail through an accessible forest.

As one drives down Simpson Road, the main entrance to Pleasant point is announced by 8-foot **stone columns** posted on each side of the gravel road leading to the river. On the west side of the entrance, the unpaved parking lot will handle about 20 vehicles. You can use this lot or drive about 1,000 feet down the gravel road to the point. There is limited parking near the picnic table along the road and at the end of the road for a half-dozen cars. The absence of trash barrels reminds you to carry out all your garbage.

Where the road terminates, walk to the right 200 feet and you will arrive at the actual point, a corner along the original Saco River bed. You are standing on a clay and gravel bank. The roots of very tall white pines, accompanied by much smaller northern red oak and beech, hold the soil against the **erosive forces** of the river and the water impounded by Union Falls (also called Skelton) Dam. Stumps and fallen trees along the river's edge show that the water has won a few rounds in the battle against the clay bank. There are two picnic tables, an attractive view, and access to a small sandy beach.

There are many trails in the park that you may enjoy. Choose between the Old Burial Ground Trail, a 0.25-mile round-trip, or connect the Carriage and Riverside Trails for a loop about 1 mile in length that covers a major portion of the park. Consult the map for additional trails not described in this text and be on the lookout for occasional clumps of poison ivy.

Halfway down the entrance road, near a picnic table, a sign designates the main trail to the east leading to the burying ground. The cemetery holds the remains of many of the early settlers from the pre-Revolutionary era. Initially the pathway is wide enough for four abreast as it drops 15 feet into a deep cut lined with giant white pines some 7 to 9 feet in circumference. Through these trees one can make out bits of the shoreline and the sparkling surface of the river.

The burying ground itself is a rectangle on the forest floor outlined by rough rocks. The uncut grave markers are made of the same fieldstone. A modern bronze **plaque** lists the names of the early settlers interred in what is a rather idyllic place surrounded by the silent trees, some of which were probably seedlings when the graves were freshly dug.

Some of the pines in the area of the burying ground show the handiwork of pileated woodpeckers. The large oblong holes on trunks and branches indicate the pileated has been hard at work finding food and ridding trees of harmful pests. These holes are important **shelters** for such cavity-nesting birds as chickadees, nuthatches, wood ducks, tree swallows, tufted titmice, and others. If you investigate nearby trees, you may find some excavations two or more feet in length and 6 to 10 inches wide. If you are lucky, you may hear the pileated pair as they make their way through the forest canopy. They are very large birds, the size and color of a crow, with a shocking red crest and large white patches under the wings. Their call resembles a very loud and boisterous chicken cackling in the treetops like Woody Woodpecker.

Retrace your steps to the parking lot along Simpson Road, where you'll find there is a high mound of dirt on the right corner nearest the road. Behind this gravel barrier is the beginning of the Carriage Trail.

Here you tread where horses and oxen once served the community's transportation needs, where settlers and natives walked along the river, and romantics strolled arm in arm. Like the trail to the burying ground, large white pines dominate the area, leaving little underbrush. Ash, red oak, and a few birches are mixed into the surrounding growth. Once there were huge American chestnuts, but they have disappeared since the introduction of the chestnut blight from China in 1906.

The Carriage Road is approximately 0.4 mile long. At 0.3 mile, the road narrows to a path, descends gradually, then passes through a thick carpet of partridgeberry. The plant has dark green, waxy leaves, often sporting variegated white lines. In the spring it displays twin white or light pink flowers at its tip. In the fall, the twin flower produces a single eye-catching, deep red berry. Though it is a potential food source for birds and humans, it is rather tasteless. Native Americans dried and steeped the leaves for medicinal purposes.

The trail continues, exiting the park between two stone columns that are twins to those near the parking lot. Set close to these towers is a plaque embedded in stone explaining that the area was once part of the Maine state park system. The home across Route 117 from this entrance served the area as a tavern well into the twentieth century.

Returning some 300 feet along the Carriage Trail you come to a junction that bears to the right along the Riverside Trail. This scenic route has some sections that run **40 feet** above the river, very close to the edge. If heights are a problem or you have small children in tow, you might want to go back along the Carriage

Trail. Some parts of the Riverside Trail have steel cable along the river's edge, installed to prevent accidents. The cable predates the damming of the river in 1947, when the drop to the ledges and rapids was as much as 70 feet. Now the trail snakes back and forth, rises and drops with the bank, and looks out on a quiet river where canoeists, bass fishermen, and occasional swimmers pass below.

About 0.2 mile from the beginning of the **Riverside Trail,** the path opens onto an area bordered by the river on one side and a rough, broken ledge on the other. If you look closely among the trees, there are a series of cut granite blocks. This is what remains of a building site dating back to 1827. The ledges were blasted out with black powder, and quarried stones were hauled for the foundation of one of New England's first textile mills. Some 90 feet long and about 50 feet wide, the construction halted soon after it began and the project was never completed. The years since construction stopped can be measured by the size of the trees, some 3 feet in diameter, that have buckled the granite blocks along the old foundation line.

Just south of the foundation, the trail opens out into a small clearing where the rocky edge drops 20 feet to the river. Here you get a clear view of a cleft in the rocks on the far side of the river called **Indian Cellar.** The title stems from the belief that the local tribe stored material here. More likely, the rapids that once tore along the base of Indian Cellar were an ideal spot for netting migratory salmon. The more gradual slope at the rear of Indian Cellar might have provided a ready overlook and access down to the riverbank.

Farther along the trail at another small clearing, the river's edge forms a large semicircular area called the Big (or Great) Eddy. If you watch carefully, you can still see the slight river current. It swings into the **eddy** copying the path of the circular current that once formed at the foot of the rapids. The water in this area is about 30 feet deep and is a popular spot for both swimming and fishing.

From the Big Eddy area the trail forks. A short trail to the left through the trees along the rocky bed of an intermittent stream leads back toward the Carriage Trail. The other trail continues along the river in the direction of Pleasant Point. This section of the Riverside Trail drops to the water's edge. Even at this point there are pieces of the old cable protecting wanderers from the once long drop to the river's surface. The far end of this trail circles back to connect with the Cross Trail (see map) and allows you to return to the parking lot via the access road.

Getting There

Traveling from the intersection of Routes 1 and 112 in Saco, drive northwest on Route 112 (North Street) approximately 4.9 miles. Turn left onto the Simpson Road. Continue 4.2 miles. You will notice stone and mortar pillars announcing the Cyrus Woodman Reservation (the 1906 designation for the park) on the left. Fifty feet beyond, on the same side, is a dirt parking lot accommodating up to 20 cars.

Approaching the park from the west, look for the intersection of Route 117 and Routes 202/4 in Hollis. To reach the main parking lot and trailhead, continue along Route 117 for 0.35 mile to Simpson Road. Turn right and travel 0.4 mile to the reservation's main gate on your right.

13. Saco Heath Preserve

Saco

800 Acres

Bog

1 mile round-trip

1 hour

"Let's go to the swamp!" is not the normal suggestion you would expect for a hike. Most people think of slime, muck, and ooze when the word swamp comes up. Visiting places like the Saco Heath reminds us such words paint only part of the picture. Wetlands are productive, necessary, attractive areas. Many species of reptiles, amphibians, **unique plants,** and numerous birds make their homes here. Large tracts of natural and man-made bogs in Massachusetts and Wisconsin are dedicated to growing commercial cranberries. Gardeners prize the peat moss harvested from bogs. Almost anyone who has ever done lawn work has utilized this peat. People are beginning to recognize the beneficial nature of bogs, and attempts are being made to ensure the survival of wetlands.

Land donations by the Joseph Deering family and the work of The Nature Conservancy have preserved some 800 acres of the Saco Heath. Local volunteer groups worked hard to lay a mile-long trail and **boardwalk** through the heath for the enjoyment and educa-

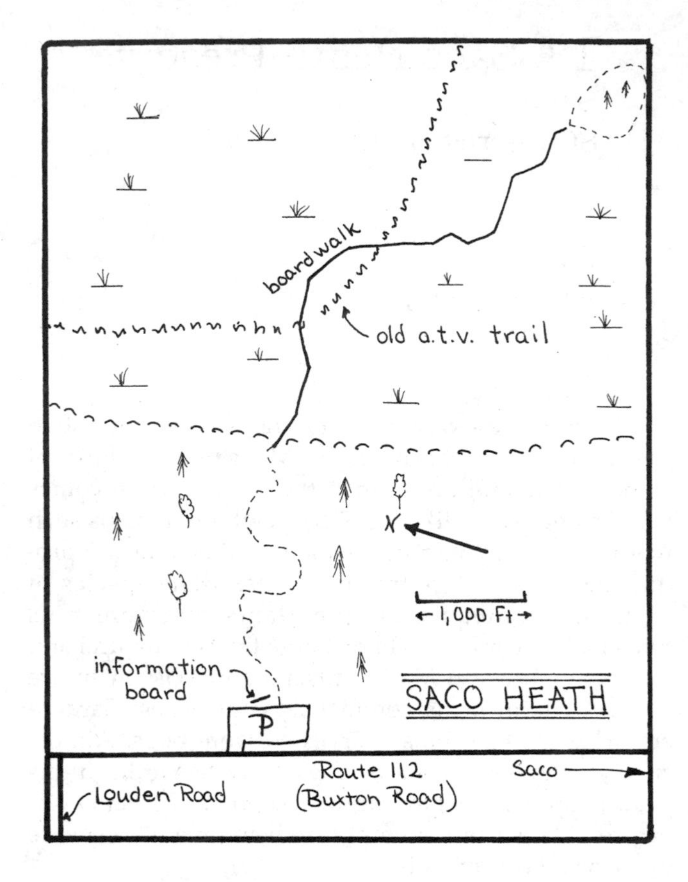

tion of the public. Trail maps are available at the parking lot explaining and delineating the five-foot-wide trail through the woods to the heath.

The Saco Heath, like many features in Maine, is a child of the last Ice Age. Some 12,000 years ago **glacial**

retreat left clear, deep ponds. Vegetation grew and animals moved in along the borders of these ponds. Lack of an outlet encouraged the deposition of sediments. Acidic conditions in the water discouraged the decay of materials, and layers of organic matter built up over time. Ultimately the ponds became shallow marshes, or bogs. Shrubs and trees developed near the drier margins. In Saco Heath, sphagnum moss has continued to grow above the original water level to create a "raised coalesced bog" like those normally found nearer the Arctic tundra.

The hike into the Saco Heath begins at the parking lot parallel to Route 112. Step past the information board into the cool darkness of a canopy composed primarily of eastern hemlock. The gravel- and wood-chip trail turns and twists through damp, wet areas covered by cinnamon ferns, royal ferns, and goldthread. In spring, 12-inch stalks with triple leaves support the deep purple flower of the red trillium. A smaller, more colorful cousin with white petals and a crimson blaze, the painted trillium, dots the forest floor.

During the summer, mud will show deer prints and scratch holes left by the gray squirrel and striped skunk. In wintertime, snow records the tracks and travels of many small mammals and birds. In early summer, the forest rings with the songs of the common yellowthroat, the black-capped chickadee, and the hermit thrush. In particularly wet areas, a boardwalk protects both the hiker and the vegetation. This path continues for about 1,500 feet until it breaks out of the forest into a grassy area dotted sparsely with trees. This is the true heath, protected from traffic by more than 2,000 feet of raised walkway with seating for walkers and watchers.

The heath is an ancient pond now filled with thousands of layers of accumulated **organic matter.** In a sense, the surface of the heath is the most recent page of life in a book that goes back 12,000 years. The special conditions of the heath—the low-nutrient, high-acid environment with abundant organic buildup—create a habitat where unique plants are more notable than animals. The animals here are migrant, moving through many areas to fulfill their life requirements, and are not usually specialized. Plants do not have this option. They must adapt to the **conditions** or die.

About 1,000 feet onto the boardwalk is a green stripe of sedges across the landscape. This abandoned trail was created by motorized all-terrain vehicles. Much of the original vegetation here was destroyed and is slowly making a return. Scanning from the walkway, note the variety of surrounding plants. Mixed with the sphagnum base are various grasslike sedges with their triangular leaves and decorative seed heads. There are endless clusters of leatherleaf, looking much like blueberries but for the leaves folded up against the stem. In late summer and fall, small fluffy tufts of white sprinkled across the marsh announce the sites of a rare sedge, cotton grass. Purple blooms that open in April, before the leaves unfold, mark rhodora—a relative of the household rhododendron. The cautious eye—or nose—will find sweet gale and Labrador tea. More familiar plants like highbush blueberries and huckleberries are also present.

A boardwalk in Saco Heath protects the fragile habitat.

Moving along the boardwalk, note the larger plants. The tamarack (larch) is a tree that does well in the bog. The **tamarack** is unusual: a coniferous, needle-bearing tree, it is not an evergreen, for the needles drop off in winter. The timber of the tamarack, naturally resistant to rot, was sought for posts and was used in the ship's knees (deck braces cut from a single piece of wood) on such vessels as the USS *Constitution*.

One tree attempting to invade the heath area is the white pine. You can see it is just barely holding on. The trees are sparse with poor needle growth. As the heath continues to fill and dry out over centuries, the white pine might grow well here, but now is not the right time in the succession of the heath's life. Even the pitch pine struggles here, taking more than 50 years to grow only three inches in diameter.

The concentrated organic matter, the **acid environment,** and abundant water in a bog create a setting that only specialized plants can tolerate. For example, there is very little nitrogen available. Nitrogen is essential for growth, so plants must develop unique ways to acquire it. Some **bog plants** obtain nitrogen and other nutrients by predation—trapping insects and ingesting them. The pitcher plant is a prime example. Right at the border of the walk, red-veined leaves form water-filled tubes staring up at the hiker. The interior of the leaves have downward-pointing hairs that prevent entrapped insects from escaping. The bugs ultimately drown and are digested in the fluid of the leaf cup, and the pitcher plant soaks up the **nutrients.**

The sundew achieves the same result in another science-fiction way. The leaves on the plant produce sticky solutions on glandular hairs. Insects, attracted to these secretions, become entrapped, dissolve, and are absorbed by the plant. Among the taller vegetation of the bog, the three-quarter-inch leaves of the sundew are hard to spot. Perhaps it is best for us that insectivorous plants have not evolved into specimens large enough to challenge humans. Imagine predatory plants capturing and consuming animals!

Bogs abound with **beauty.** At least 18 of 30 species of eastern orchids grow in swamps, bogs, or wetlands.

The Saco Heath supports a healthy population of the delicate rose pogonia. This attractive flower is similar to the design of the lady's slipper. It is a bright pink, five-lobed blossom at the top of a solitary 10-inch green stem. The lowest petal of the flower has a distinctive fringed border. If we lose these habitats we will lose many orchids—a floral family noted for its graceful, delicate displays.

Boggy areas like the Saco Heath are important to animals as well as plants. This is a prime feeding ground for larger creatures like the eastern white-tailed deer and the occasional **stray moose.** Insects are also an important part of the food chain for many birds in and about the heath.

The acid nature of the heath limits the presence of amphibians. The surrounding wetlands and the trail from the parking lot create habitat for the spotted salamander, found under logs, and the tree frog, often heard on spring evenings and hardly ever seen. These animals rely on standing water when laying eggs, during larval stages, and often as adults. The heath donates generously to the **diversity** of living things. It helps keep wonder alive and makes our own existence fuller.

On the far side of the open heath, the boardwalk leads into a loop trail to another bog-loving tree. The Atlantic white cedar, similar to arborvitae, is a valuable and rare tree. The wood from this cedar found its way into organ pipes, sailing ships, canoes, and the carbon for gunpowder of the American Revolution. It is probably the only tree that was ever mined: When the supply of Atlantic white cedar was exhausted from the bogs of

New Jersey, industrious harvesters dug up the rot-resistant fallen trees buried in the bogs.

When you have completed the loop through the white cedar upland, return as you came. Be sure to take a break on the benches provided. The longer you sit in one spot and contemplate the area, the more you will see among the variety of greens swamping your senses. We can learn much about our surroundings from such unique areas as the Saco Heath.

Getting There

The Saco Heath Preserve is on Route 112, 3.4 miles from the junction of Routes 1 and 112 in Saco. Driving northwest from Saco, watch for Fire Lane 14 on the right. This is about 0.1 mile before reaching the right turn into the gravel parking lot.

If approaching from the west on Route 112, the preserve is 3.3 miles from the junction of Routes 117 and 112. As you approach the preserve, watch for Louden Road on your right. The Saco Heath is an additional 0.3 mile on your left.

Coming from the Maine Turnpike, use Exit 5. Take the first right from the tollbooth and then a left turn onto Industrial Park Road. Turn right at the lights onto Buxton Road (Route 112). In 2.0 miles reach the preserve entrance on the right.

For information call 207-729-5181.

14. Scarborough Marsh

Scarborough
3,000 Acres

Salt Marshes

0.5 mile

1 hour

Wheelchair-accessible platform: level 1 (see p. xiv)

If shorebird identification or photography seems appealing, Scarborough Marsh is the spot to visit. Shorter than most hikes included in this guide, it provides opportunities for great close-up bird **photography** and learning about the delicate salt marsh **ecosystem**. The locality also supplies an alternative to hiking. If you have the time, fully equipped canoes can be rented to cover much of the sea of green that makes up the Scarborough Marsh. The 3,000 acres of marine land belong to the state of Maine. The information center and trail areas are provided by the Maine Audubon Society.

Begin your trek at the visitor center located on Route 9. It is surrounded by grass and water. This combination gift shop, museum, and information center is dedicated to the salt marsh. Wander about on your own or join walks and workshops led by staff and volunteers of the Maine Audubon Society.

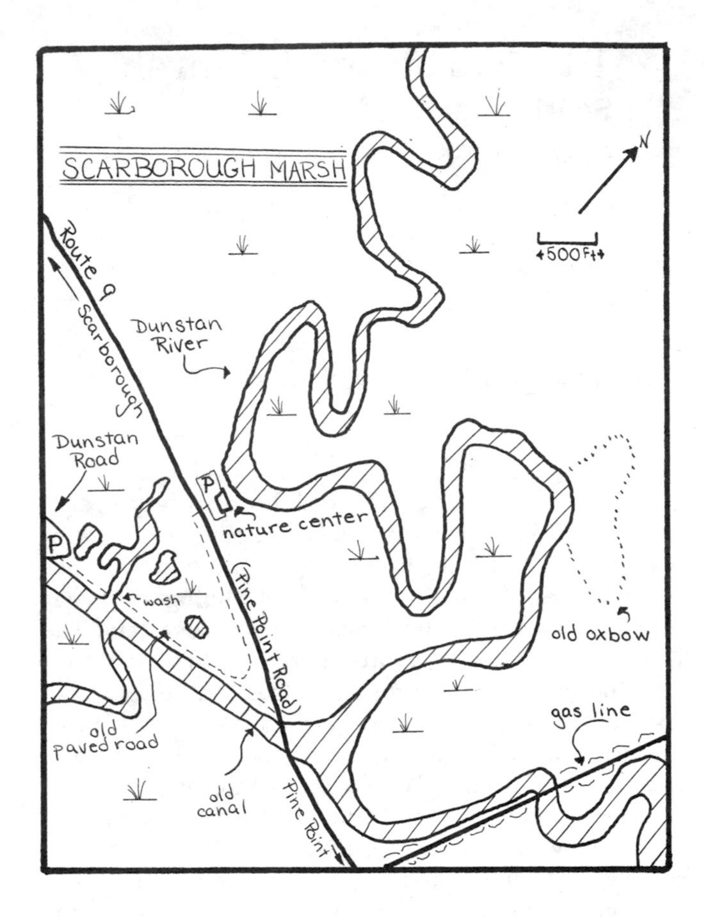

To follow the short trail or to photograph the myriad shorebirds and waders that pass through the marsh, cross the two-lane highway with caution. The path leads 20 feet into the border of the marsh and opens onto a large pool, often coated with **algae.** Egrets frequently hunt here, and some of the smaller sandpipers actually walk on the algal mat in search of tiny crustaceans. The trail turns left and runs parallel to the road through grasses, spirea, and several species of young trees. The rapid motion of finely serrated leaves mark the quaking aspens in their light gray green bark. The locust trees have 10-inch leaves divided into smaller, paired leaflets. Mixed amid these are young chokecherry trees with drooping flower heads in spring and red to black clusters of small cherries in late summer and fall. Among the trees, tidal wet spots are planked to help keep the hiker's feet dry.

After several hundred feet, the path takes a sharp right into a grove of staghorn sumac and more quaking aspen. You may also see shorter smooth sumac mixed in with goldenrod. Distinguish between the two sumacs by looking closely at the terminal twigs. A downy fuzz marks the staghorn sumac, while the smooth sumac's twigs are bald. The path emerges onto an old blacktop road that once extended through the wetlands from Dunstan's Landing. This abandoned route now provides the walking access to the marsh. Shrubs and grasses have overgrown much of the road. Two plants common here are slender glasswort and sea lavender. Glasswort forms shiny leafless stems among the grasses; its thick branches have been used as a celery-like nibble. Sea lavender, sporting tiny purple flowers in late summer and fall, unfortunately is endangered by overharvesting for holiday wreaths.

Follow the macadam through the marsh. Walk quietly on the approach to the open grasses and be rewarded with the sight of willet or lesser yellowlegs a few feet away. Pools on the right and the old canal on the left often have many smaller birds feeding quietly. High tide will also force more birds to the shallow pools.

The marsh is a stopover for **migrating birds,** so spring and late summer see greater numbers and varieties of birds. Summer brings lush grasses with fewer numbers and species of birds. However, a close look at an apparently empty marsh usually reveals several of the shorter shorebirds. More-isolated pools feed members of the heron family. The great blue heron, snowy egret, common egret, and the cattle egret all have been found here.

Farther along on the right margin of the road is a **ditch.** In summer it teems with the mummichog, a

Shorebirds enjoy the shallow feeding areas of Scarborough Marsh.

small fish that inhabits most coastal marshes. This fish is a prized food for many of the larger wading birds. The surface of the shallow pools ripples with the swimming movements of the fish. When the heron or egret crouches, dips, and strikes, this little fish is the most frequent target.

At high tide the walk will end at a washout cutting through the road. At low tide you can cross to a parking area at Dunstan's Landing, birthplace of Maine's first governor, William King.

The old road and the shrubs offer a chance to photograph the wide variety of birds that visit this refuge. The road provides a firm surface for a tripod with a long lens, or a pause among the shrubs with a shorter handheld lens can bring the birds in range. Regardless of the equipment, patience is the most necessary ingredient for the great shot.

In addition to this trail, the marsh can also be crossed in a peace broken only by birdcalls, wind, and the subtle dip of a paddle. **Canoe** along the serpentine river from Route 1 to the gas line and beyond. Removed from the rush of Route 9 traffic, you melt into the tall cordgrass (settlers used it to thatch roofs) that lines the channel. It is best to paddle downstream against the incoming tide. Return with the current lifting you above the steep mud walls. The canoes are available at an hourly or full-day rate. Always have everyone in your group wear a life vest when on the water.

Viewing the marsh from the roadway or the handicapped-accessible **platform** gives an impression similar to the expansive wheat fields of Washington or corn-

Rental canoes from the nature center offer a close-up view of the marsh.

fields of Iowa. There seems to be one type of plant over thousands of acres. In reality, this marsh is a tightly interwoven ecosystem of numerous plants and animals. Many of the plants are microscopic, and the larger forms are the various salt-resistant grasses. The animals also range from microscopic to the dominant fish and birds, both of which are often transient creatures. What we might view as a rather barren area literally ripples with life. Salt marshes need our understanding and protection for the diversity of life they maintain and the often hidden benefits they provide to humans. Acre for acre, salt marshes can outproduce most farms. The resulting food generated is carried to sea where it becomes part of the food web leading from haddock and cod to humans.

Getting There

From Route 1 in Scarborough take Pine Point Road (Route 9) at Dunstan's Corner. Follow Route 9 one mile west across the marsh. The Audubon Nature Center and parking lot will be the sole disturbance in the acres of marshland. During the summer season there are racks of canoes alongside the center that may be rented hourly or for full-day rates.

For more information call 207-781-2330.

Portland and Northeast

15. Spring Point
South Portland

Rocky Coast
1 mile

1 hour
Wheelchair accessible: level 1 (see p. xiv)

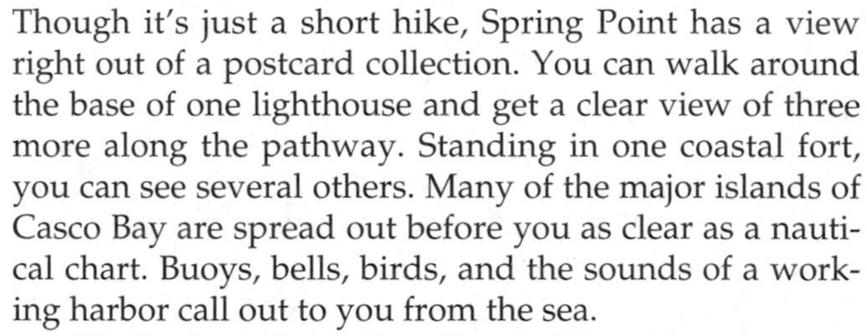

Though it's just a short hike, Spring Point has a view right out of a postcard collection. You can walk around the base of one lighthouse and get a clear view of three more along the pathway. Standing in one coastal fort, you can see several others. Many of the major islands of Casco Bay are spread out before you as clear as a nautical chart. Buoys, bells, birds, and the sounds of a working harbor call out to you from the sea.

The harborside walk at Spring Point is on the campus of Southern Maine Technical College (SMTC). Evenings and weekends are the best times to visit, reducing competition for parking. Except for the sandy beach and the breakwater that leads to the lighthouse, the area has smoothly paved walkways going the length

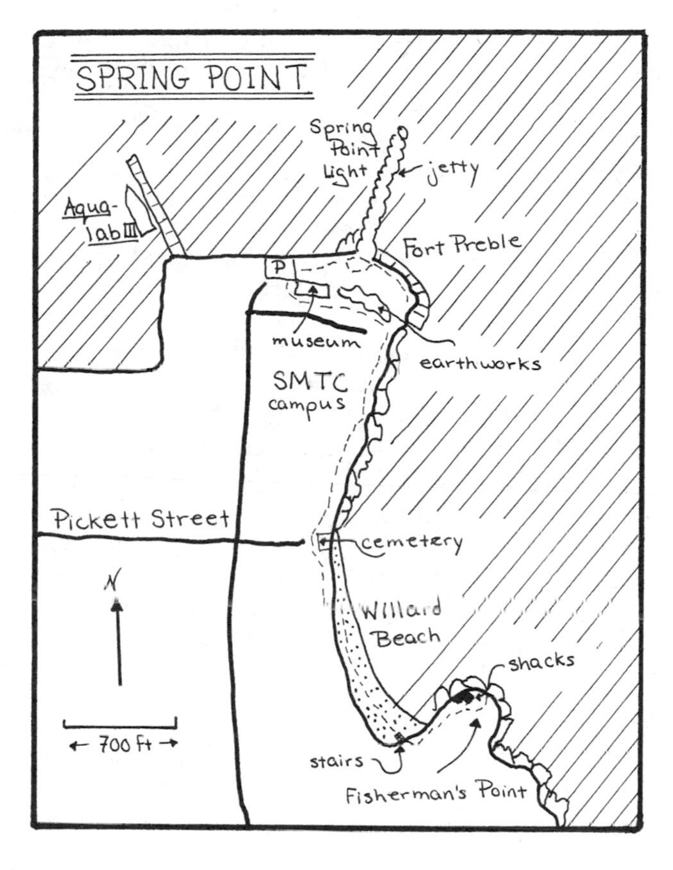

of the shorefront. The shrubbery along the path, mostly varieties of ground cedar and juniper, is an arboretum demonstrating both native and introduced species of salt-tolerant shore plants. There is also the seasonal Spring Point Museum with a ramp and admission fee.

The favored lookout is the 1,000-foot-long **breakwater** to Spring Point Light. The light was constructed in 1897 to protect shipping from a ledge at the point. The breakwater's 50,000 tons of granite were added in 1951. The blocks at the low-tide mark support a heavy concentration of dark brown kelp that houses and feeds a variety of crustaceans and fish. Bright green sheets of sea lettuce wave in the currents. Delicate reddish shades of laver (*porphyra*), a palatable alga the Japanese export under the name *nori,* is also visible scattered along the base of the breakwater. At low tide, it hangs in tissue-thin sheets with ruffled edges. Laver is eaten raw, dried for soups, or rolled around rice to produce a colorful and tasty treat.

To the immediate left of the breakwater is the dock for SMTC's **research vessel,** the *Aqualab III.* This converted minesweeper is part of the marine technology program on the campus. To the far side of this complex is a much longer dock with a variety of large hoses. This is the southern terminus of a pipeline carrying crude oil to Montreal.

Beyond the pipeline, on a point, is the smallest lighthouse constructed on the Maine coast, Bug Light. No longer functional, the tower is an attraction for visitors and is the centerpiece of South Portland's city seal. In its heyday, the light sat at the end of a half-mile jetty, guiding ships into the Fore River. The shallow harbor behind the light has been extensively filled and it now rests on dry land. It is just a few minutes away if you wish to visit.

The large granite structure sitting by itself in the middle of the harbor is Fort Gorges. Completed around the Civil War, it was never fully used. The stone sentinel stands its solitary watch, a curiosity for kayakers and hikers.

Straight out (north) from the Spring Point Light are three islands, Little Diamond, Peaks, and House. From this angle they look almost like a single landmass. The **batteries** of Fort Scammel can be seen facing the point from House Island. These bulwarks, combined with the 20 or so guns at Fort Preble, at the breakwater, created a dangerous field of cross fire that protected the main entrance to Portland Harbor. Though they have guarded the harbor since revolutionary days, these forts have seen little memorable action. During the Civil War a Confederate crew stole into the harbor, boarded the *Caleb Cushing,* and subdued the men on watch. They ultimately burned the vessel and were later captured. This action fueled scuttlebutt and war fever in the local communities. The following week, a small Northern vessel entered the harbor without giving the proper recognition signals. Fort Preble fired a shot across her bow that ricocheted on the water and destroyed the outhouse at Fort Scammel.

Immediately behind the breakwater and the guns of Fort Preble are tall **earthworks** with concrete bunkers and steel doors. These protective measures are among the many remnants of World War II. Nearby is a semicircle of old granite blocks from the wall of Fort Preble. Now they are part of a children's play area—a delightful conversion from wartime to peace.

Along the eastern front of SMTC, a paved walk extends for 2,000 feet. It begins by the earthworks, overlooks the outer entrance to the harbor, and extends to **Willard Beach.** The view from this end of the trail extends from House Island through Whitehead Passage to the light on the horizon, Halfway Rock, eight miles to seaward. Cushing Island, to the right of the passage,

Spring Point Light protects ships passing close to shore.

was one of the first islands settled in Casco Bay. It is now completely private.

The vista continues right, across the harbor entrance, to the majestic outline of the nation's second oldest lighthouse, Portland Head (1791), rising boldly on the cliffs at Fort Williams. In the foreground is a sandy tidal area, home to gulls, ducks, and an occasional loon. At low tide, many peeps and yellowlegs probe the grit for tiny burrowing creatures. In winter, this cove is a protective area harboring several species of **waterfowl.** Loons, in their dark gray-and-white winter coats, may be accompanied by scoter, eider, goldeneye, and bufflehead. On warm days, the area is also frequented by families poking and probing the sand and tide pools, much like their feathered friends.

There are several decked viewpoints and informational signs explaining the wildlife and historical background of the immediate cove. The walk continues south around fuel tanks until it passes by the burying ground of 1658. Here, graves date from the two episodes when settlers were driven from the area during conflicts with Native Americans. It was not until 1716 that peace resumed and the area was permanently settled by Europeans.

From the cemetery, the path begins a 400-foot gentle slope to Willard Beach. Walk the sand an additional 1,200 feet past a bathhouse to a set of stairs mounting to a walkway. This leads to Fisherman's Point, a viewing area above three old fishing shacks. Here is one of the most photogenic spots on the immediate coast. There is a panoramic view from the light at Spring Point all the way around to Portland Head. Rest on this grassy knoll and contemplate the world-class vessels plying their trade in Portland Harbor.

Getting There

Exit 6A from the turnpike brings you to I-295. Exit 1 on 295 will bring you to Route 1, the main thoroughfare into South Portland. Turn left onto Route 1 and follow it for 1.1 miles. Passing the rail yards on the right, come to two sets of lights. At the second one (Cash Corner), bear right onto Broadway. Continue 3.6 miles through the heart of South Portland until you intersect Pickett Street and turn right. At the next stop sign, turn left onto the campus of SMTC. Follow the campus drive straight to the water's edge, and swing right into the parking lot by Spring Point Light, at the end of the marine museum. There are also several parking lots along the waterfront edge of the campus.

16. Fore River Sanctuary
Portland
76 Acres

Salt Marshes
2.5 miles
2 hours

The Portland of 100 years ago was a city of green. There were open spaces and a series of parks created by the sons of Frederick Law Olmsted, noted designer of Central Park in New York City. Portland has grown dramatically since those days. Today it is larger and more crowded, but such beautiful green areas as Deering Oaks, Baxter Woods, and Evergreen Cemetery are still present.

The foresight and ideals that made the original parks possible continue today. The city of Portland has some unused open space and it has people to plan for the future. Dedicated members of the Maine Audubon Society and a private citizens group, Portland Trails, are attempting to create more green, open space for the people of Portland. The Fore River Sanctuary is proof they have made a difference.

The Fore River Sanctuary is part of a system proposed by these organizations that may ultimately provide more than 30 miles of trails in and around the city. Today the Fore River Sanctuary is relatively isolated and

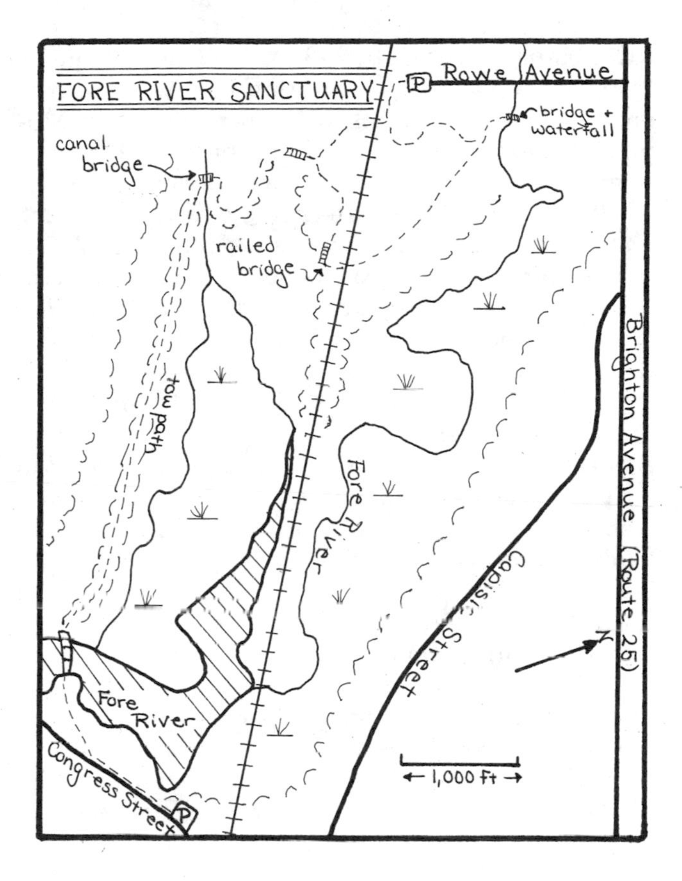

quiet. It was not so more than 150 years ago. In 1828 this was a busy construction site. Here the Cumberland and Oxford Canal was completed in 1830—2 years before Portland was chartered as a new city of 13,000 inhabitants. The canal linked Portland Harbor and the Fore

River estuary with Sebago Lake and the villages of Bridgton and Harrison on Long Lake. This was an important waterway until 1872, when railroads took its place. What remains now is a bit of towpath, rubble from the locks, and the silt-filled memory of a canal.

If you step back in history to the early seventeenth century, the Fore River area was a center of the British colonial **masting trade.** The huge white pines so necessary to the maintenance of the British navy were brought to the masting agent at the mouth of the Fore River for preparation and shipment to England.

The hike begins at the dead end of Rowe Avenue. The trail starts left, parallel to the railroad tracks for about 500 feet until reaching a fork. Follow the left path as it drops steeply through the grass and enters the woods. This blue-blazed trail brings you through a **hardwood forest,** almost shutting out the city surrounding you. Red maple, white pine, beech, and red oak abound. Some 1,500 feet along this path, another trail comes in sharply from the right. Continue to your left. As the number of hemlocks increases, the trailside drops off more steeply to your right and a swampy area can be seen through the trees. As the trail angles down to the level of the bog, there is the sound of falling water. You have arrived at the base of the only waterfall within the boundaries of Portland, Jewell Falls. It is a tree-shaded, 25-foot cascade. The area has been preserved by Portland Trails. This small stream angling down over the rock face becomes the Fore River. At the bottom of the falls the stream quickly disappears into the vegetation of the swamp. The trail climbs stairlike up the left side of the falls to a newly constructed arch bridge at the top. Take a moment to sit and savor the cool air and the soft sounds of falling water. Soak in the birdsongs and watch the water striders dance across the pools in search of prey.

When you are refreshed, retrace your steps to the earlier junction and bear left (you could follow the trail right to return to the parking area). This section of trail is wide and flat, easier to follow than the first segment. The trail breaks out under the power lines and approaches the **railroad tracks** 0.3 mile from the waterfall. Yellow posts mark the rail crossing. Look both ways; this is an active train site.

The path reenters a dark hemlock wood on the far side and begins to drop toward a marsh. The trail emerges into the open and takes an immediate right across a railed **footbridge** about 300 feet from the track. At first glance this looks like a typical salt marsh, but the vegetation is different. The wide blades of the common cattail mix in with tall sedges and rushes. Travel 150 feet across the bridge, reenter a darkened evergreen forest, and begin a slight climb. You quickly arrive at another path dropping to the left. Turn left here, descend gently for a couple of hundred feet, and then step out onto a bridge (no rails) crossing another section of the sedge-rush marsh. As you step off the bridge, the blue-blazed trail turns sharply left and follows the boggy shoreline through a white pine canopy. Several species of fern are at your feet. A white flower head at the tip of an arching 20-inch spray of large leaves marks false Solomon's seal among the ferns. In the fall these flowers are replaced with bright red berries. The trail turns sharply to the right around the tip of land jutting

The bridge provides a scenic, close-up view of the marsh habitat.

into the marsh and comes out on a grassy slope beneath a second power line. Ahead is a 40-foot bridge that spans the former site of the Cumberland and Oxford Canal. Note that the far end of the bridge rests on a ridge extending in a very straight line eastward through the marsh. This is the old **towpath**, where men and horses toiled to ferry boats through the canal.

The bridge stands close to the location of the first of the 27 locks that raised boats and barges more than 250 feet to the level of Sebago and Long Lakes, 50 miles inland. This was the modern highway in 1830. The new bridge carries you to the towpath. As you cross over, imagine what it must have been like in the days horses and oxen tramped the path hauling barges up the canal.

Continue along the raised towpath. Small washes are nicely bridged to keep hikers dry. Salt marsh spartina (or thatch) grows on both sides as you approach the **estuary** of the Fore River. Young white pine, small-toothed aspen, and chokecherry have taken a foothold on the path. About a half-mile from the bridge that spans the old canal, a second bridge spans 90 feet of the Fore River. This overpass returns the hiker to the world of traffic on Congress Street. It is the most recent addition to the trail, providing a second access point to the sanctuary. As of this writing, up the hill to the left, at the large building housing the Maine Orthopedic offices, are five parking spaces designated for hikers.

Getting There

Quickest access to the Fore River Sanctuary is from Exit 8 on the turnpike (I-95). Turn left from the exit and go 0.1 mile to the junction with Route 25 (Brighton Avenue). Turn left onto Route 25 and then take a right onto Rowe Avenue at the third set of lights. Follow Rowe Avenue to its gravel end by the railroad track.

A second access is provided at Exit 5 from I-295 onto Routes 9 and 22 west (Congress Street). About 1.3 miles along this road, just beyond Frost Street on the right, turn into the parking lot of Maine Orthopedic Center, also on the right. Please use only the designated spaces. From here, walk the 100 yards downhill to the Fore River and turn right to reach the new footbridge.

For more information call 207-781-2330.

17. Back Cove
Portland

Salt Marshes
3.5-mile loop
1.5 hours
Wheelchair accessible: level 1–2 (see p. xiv)

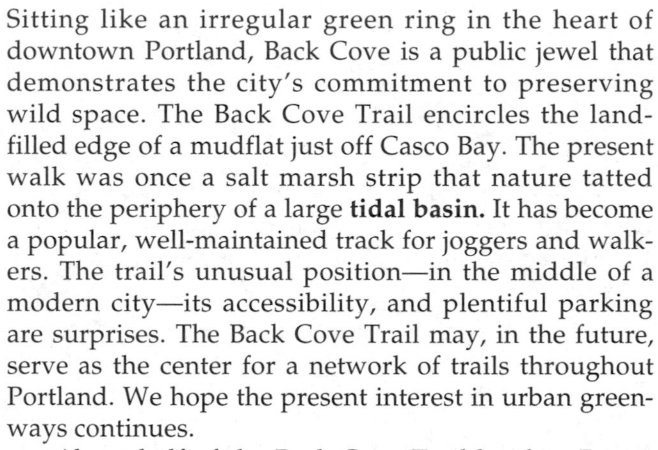

Sitting like an irregular green ring in the heart of downtown Portland, Back Cove is a public jewel that demonstrates the city's commitment to preserving wild space. The Back Cove Trail encircles the landfilled edge of a mudflat just off Casco Bay. The present walk was once a salt marsh strip that nature tatted onto the periphery of a large **tidal basin.** It has become a popular, well-maintained track for joggers and walkers. The trail's unusual position—in the middle of a modern city—its accessibility, and plentiful parking are surprises. The Back Cove Trail may, in the future, serve as the center for a network of trails throughout Portland. We hope the present interest in urban greenways continues.

About half of the Back Cove Trail borders Baxter Boulevard. The wide flat **path** has a fine blue gravel surface. It is a civilized trail with a trimmed grass border and a line of manicured basswood (linden) trees shading the length of the boulevard. In spring, these trees

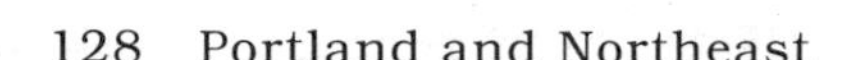

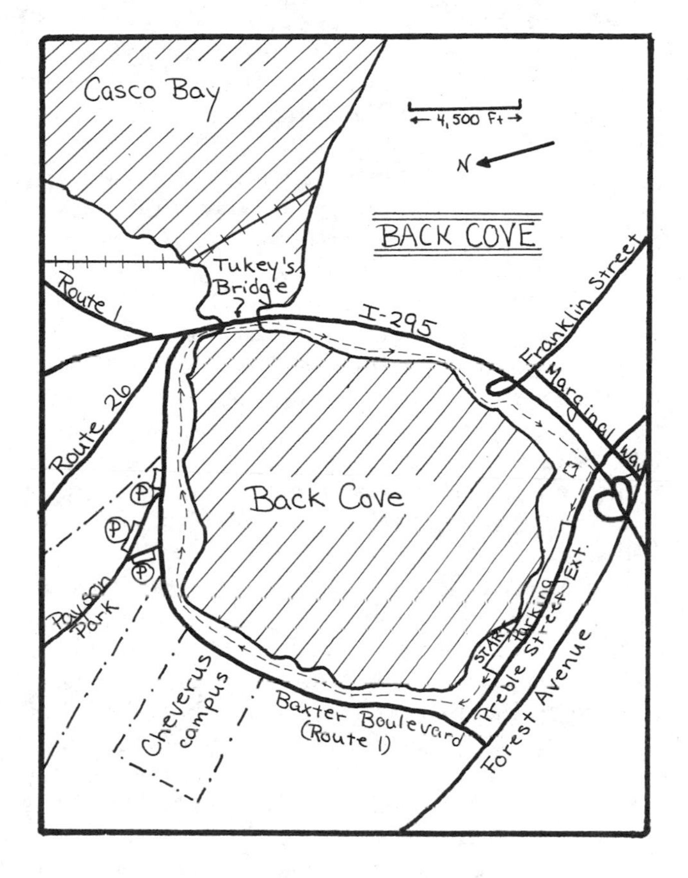

produce plentiful blooms once used as a tea for cramps and indigestion. The walk is more attractive on the flood tide, where you can see a collection of feeding ducks, gulls, herons, and cormorants. Low tide almost completely drains the basin. The exposed acres of **mud-flats** entice a gathering of such wading marine birds as yellowlegs, sandpipers, plovers, and willets. Casual stares from an occasional scavenging crow may follow the hiker along the perimeter path.

Beginning at the parking lot on the southwest corner of the ring, you can see a planned exercise and jogging route. The numbered **activity** posts and assorted gear are for the health-oriented enthusiast wishing to follow a press, pull, or stretch routine. The walk itself is quite level for the length of Baxter Boulevard. The initial 1.5 miles of trail are sandwiched between Back Cove and the boulevard, lined with attractive homes and their manicured lawns. There are two open green areas along the left side of the street. The first is the campus of Cheverus High School and the second, a triangular bit of land, is Payson Park.

As you move along Baxter Boulevard, look east across Back Cove to a sweeping view of the Portland skyline. Note where Interstate 295 rises and passes over Tukey's Bridge. Immediately to the left of the bridge is a large factory and **obvious stack,** the Burnham and Morrill plant, famous for its B&M brand of New England baked beans. To the right of the bridge, the high point of land is Eastern Promenade. Among the jagged clutter of rooftops coming down from the Eastern Promenade, notice a gold dome on a tapering tower that resembles a **lighthouse.** This is the Portland Observatory, built in 1812 to sight incoming ships and alert local merchants to prepare for pending trade. During these early years, the observatory was the only structure on this end of the peninsula. The rest of the land was pasturage broken only by stone walls. The present conglomeration of buildings is the result of almost 200 years of development. Farther to the right of the observatory is another outstanding mark on the skyline, the sharply angled steeple on the Cathedral of the Immaculate Conception. To the right of the cathedral is the small green dome on a large granite building, Portland City Hall.

Approaching the two-mile mark, the trail begins to rise to the level of Tukey's Bridge, spanning the mouth of Back Cove. Starting across the bridge, approach the Burnham and Morrill factory, which is now immediately between the **bridge** and the islands of Casco Bay. The unused rail trestle behind this plant may become part of another Portland waterfront trail.

The bridge, with its eight lanes of traffic, is a noisy stretch mixed with the cool breeze off Casco Bay. On a sunny day, the 50-foot drop to clear water may permit you to watch **cormorants** as they dive to ply their underwater fishing trade. These birds have lower oil levels in their feathers compared to other waterfowl, which allows them to swim underwater in direct pursuit of fish. The ability to submerge can be hazardous, and they must take time to drain and dry their feathers to maintain sufficient buoyancy. You can spot waterlogged birds standing with wings outspread to dry their soggy feathers.

Cross the bridge at the 2.25-mile mark and bear right. Follow the chain-link fence and angle down to the level of Back Cove. This portion of the trail brings you right to the water's edge with riprap banking. Even at low tide, the bordering portion of Back Cove retains

Back Cove is a haven in the midst of a bustling city.

some water and a bevy of **seabirds.** The gray of the herring gull and the large body of the black-backed gull stand out easily. A smaller black-headed species, the laughing gull, has a distinct low chuckle that gives the bird its name. Initially, the trail remains close to the highway as the road moves toward the Franklin Street exit from Interstate 295. It gradually angles away from traffic, traces the edge of a small ball field, and joins the sidewalk just east of the parking lot to complete the Back Cove loop.

Back Cove is not a typical quiet, rural setting for a hike but does provide the metropolitan visitor with a welcome taste of the wild world that lies beyond the city limits. It is a sign of hope for the future of urban trails.

Getting There

The main artery through Portland is I-295. This is also the most direct route to Back Cove. From either north or south, you must take Exit 6B to Forest Avenue (following Routes 1 and 100). Proceed along Forest Avenue to the first light and turn right onto Route 1 (Baxter Boulevard). Take the next right onto Preble Street Extension, and a large parking lot will be on your left. From this lot you can follow the Back Cove Trail in either direction. Our described walk takes the western side along the boulevard. As noted on the map, there is alternative parking along Baxter Boulevard and Payson Park. Presently there is no fee for the use of this area. The Back Cove area is also accessible via a public transit system.

18. Gilsland Farm Sanctuary

Falmouth
60 Acres

Estuarine Uplands
2.5 miles total
up to 3 hours

Gilsland Farm Sanctuary, headquarters for the Maine Audubon Society, is a wonderful place to go if you enjoy the sounds of the changing seasons. Its 2.5 miles of trail wander along a **pond, fields, forest, river,** and **marsh,** all of which provide a symphony of sound ranging from the gentle lapping of waves at high tide to the musical medley of bobolinks; from a chorus of spring peepers to the whistling of the winter wind.

The old visitor center includes a nature store, reading library, and conference center. On exhibit are mounted mammals and birds native to Maine. Literature is available concerning guided tours of the facilities and other natural areas around Maine, school programs, video and slide shows, the Teacher's Resource Center, and International Eco-tours. A free brochure with a map and history of the sanctuary is available. Begin or end your hike by acquainting yourself with the facilities or by picnicking under the apple tree next to the huge whalebones behind the center.

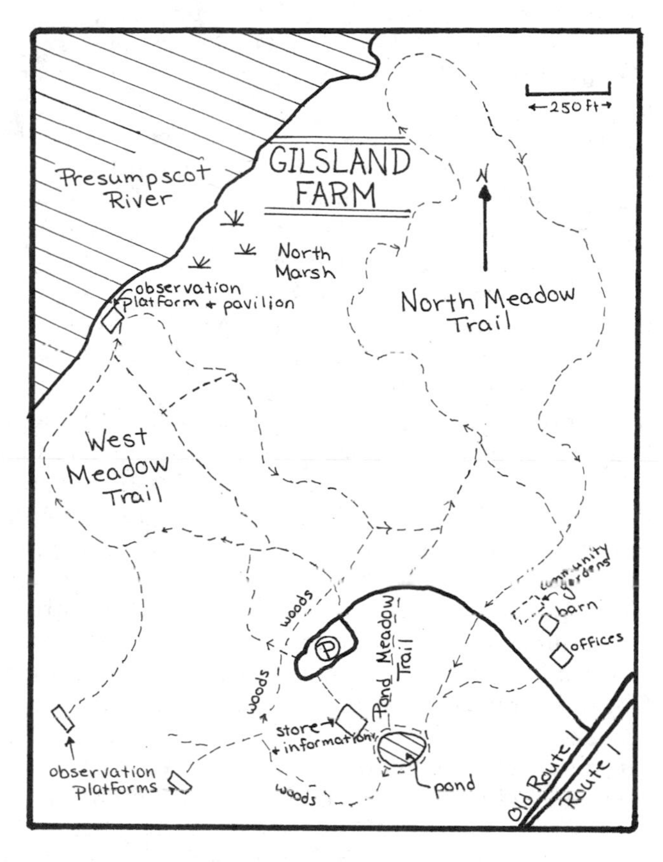

Beginning at the old visitor center (a new one is under construction), you will see tiny black-capped chickadees flitting back and forth to the feeders in front of the building along with blue jays and finches. In February, the black-capped chickadee's song changes from a name saying "chick-a-dee-dee-dee" to courtship's plaintive "fee-bee" (sometimes translated by the romantic as "marry").

Walk through or around the center to the back side and descend to the pond's edge. By the third week of March, regardless of whether all the snow has melted, spring will have officially begun; with it come the male red-winged blackbirds. Perching on the brown stalks of last year's cattails, they will compete for prime breeding territory in the marsh at the edge of the river and next to the pond. Their call is an emphatic "konk-a-ree."

A great place to do **pond studies,** this shallow body of water comes alive in April with a chorus of **frogs.** Wood frogs, the earliest to breed and the most tolerant of cold (some appear in ponds before all the ice has melted), and spring peepers, the smallest frog in Maine, join forces. The cacophony can easily be heard a half-mile away. Because wood frogs prefer vernal ponds surrounded by forest right up to the water, you may not hear many at the Gilsland pond. Where wood frogs are found in large numbers, their voices are sometimes mistaken for a flock of ducks. The mystery concerning the identity of the singers prevails when the frogs fall instantly silent at the approach of humans.

Spring peepers, although they are tree frogs with suction-cup toes, readily throng to ponds in open fields. Their voices are sometimes mistaken for small insects. Crickets and cicadas, however, do not sing in April. That peep, peep, peeping can only be a frog.

By July, the remaining frog calls will be the single note of the green frog, described as much like the plucking of a loose banjo string and the booming call of the bullfrog, a deep-throated "jug-o-rum." Bullfrogs are the latest to breed in Maine. They are the last to emerge from hibernation in the spring, and their tadpoles take the longest time to develop into adults. Three summers and two winters pass before the bullfrog trades in its fishlike tail for legs. During this time the tadpoles will suffer a high mortality, even at the hands of their own parents. Bullfrogs have voracious appetites and consume insects, snakes, fish, crayfish, small turtles, mice, other frogs, and even the young of their own species.

The bird houses around the sanctuary and here at the pond are for **bluebirds,** a species that almost disappeared from Maine a few decades ago as abandoned farms grew to forest and old trees and fence posts that had provided cavities for nests were cut for firewood. Bird watchers prize bluebirds for their stunning color, their beautiful song, and for their voracious insect appetite. If a bluebird does not come to claim a house, the second most preferred bird is the tree swallow, because, like the bluebird, the swallow loves to consume insects. Any home owner bordered by marshes or wetlands has a true appreciation for this bird's ability to ingest hundreds of flying bugs a day. The tree swallow is a deep iridescent blue with a white chest. Its wings are narrow and pointed. At rest the wing tips cross over the tail and are almost as long. Barn swallows, a close relative with a rusty chin and buff-colored belly, build nests of mud and straw inside the barn. They join the tree swallows in swooping and diving over the field and pond, all the while keeping up a constant scolding chatter.

May is the loudest month of all at the pond and elsewhere at the sanctuary and provides the most variety in birdcalls. Visit the sanctuary between five and six o'clock in the morning and be completely enveloped in sound. The migrants, some just passing through on their way north, now combine their voices with those of year-round residents. The warblers arrive from their winter homes in Central and South America, filling this forest with color and song. As you leave the pond take the trail to the right, southeast. The path curves north, passing through an oak forest.

Although the songs continue in June, they do not seem as impetuous. Most birds have found partners and are sitting on nests. As you leave the forest and turn left into the West Meadow, you will hear two additional songsters perched in the tall grasses of the field; the **song sparrow** sings "Maids, maids, maids bring your kettle-ettle-ettle," and the meadowlark pines "Spring of the year."

"In Maine we have two seasons: winter and the Fourth of July," goes the old Down East joke. This may be a bit of an exaggeration, but July is likely to be the only month with consistent warm-to-hot temperatures. For birds, that means an early morning round of singing during the cool hours and conservation of the voice during the heat of the day. At night, lightning bugs may still be flashing their silent messages of love over the field.

During August, **bobolinks** continue to call in the fields. They are solid black below, with white patches on the wings and rump and mustard yellow on the back of

A statue of the great blue heron at Gilsland Farm recognizes the contributions of Lispenard S. Crocker to the Maine Audubon Society.

the neck. Joining them are goldfinches, often mistakenly called wild canaries because of their lemon-yellow livery accented with black cap and wings. The goldfinch waits until August to build its nest and raise its young, while the bobolink may be on its second brood by then. Goldfinches are seed eaters, and in August plenty of food is available to raise their young, as well as thistledown to pad and insulate their nest. Both bobolinks and goldfinches can be seen perched on shrubbery or flying low over the weeds. The **goldfinch** repeats "potato chip, potato chip, potato chip" in flight, while the bobolink call starts with low reedy notes and tumbles upwards joyously.

About 0.25 mile along the West Meadow Trail, a path leads off to the left to an observation deck over the marsh. Continue an additional 0.3 mile to the Presumpscot River and a second platform and small pavilion. The river is tidal here. **Wading shorebirds** collect on the mudflats to catch a meal or two on their journey north to Arctic breeding grounds. Some stay the summer, adding their peeps to the more melodic discourses of the warblers and songbirds. During winter, mallards, black ducks, and goldeneyes find shelter here.

From the platform and pavilion you can return directly to the parking lot by following a swath mowed through the center of the field, or you can skirt the perimeter of the field for a meandering journey back. At the southeast corner of the field reenter the woods briefly, climbing a graded slope to your car, or turn left (northeast) to connect with the North Meadow Trail.

In spring, the arrival of migrating birds is easy to mark. They cheerily announce their presence with singing. Not so their departure in fall. After fledging their brood, they often fall silent. The warblers molt, exchanging their bright yellows, blues, and reds for mottled green. More troublesome to spot and identify, they also become quiet and secretive. In September the black-capped chickadees may join nuthatches, golden-crowned kinglets, and some warblers in feeding flocks moving from tree to tree in the wooded area south and west of the visitor center. They call anxiously back and forth as they scour the limbs and trunks for insects. Birds flying south, and those staying for the winter, must fill up on much-needed fat and protein. Migrating warblers choose to join local chickadee flocks as they can lead them to the best feeding sites. Listen for the soft "tseet" call as the chickadees keep in constant contact.

As the maple turns crimson, the poplar turns gold, and the oak brown, sounds become subdued. By the end of October, the woods are filled with the whisper of rustling leaves. As visitors shuffle down the path, the browns and golds of fallen leaves part, then fall back, like a boat cutting through waves. The gray squirrels and chipmunks are busy gathering and storing acorns for winter. The hardier migrants—robins, woodcocks, and song sparrows—those that travel only short distances south to Cape Cod or Long Island, stay on till Thanksgiving. Most have stopped calling, although somewhere in the field, the song sparrow may occasionally forget itself and begin a solo. The silence that follows is haunting.

November is gray. The ground begs for an insulating layer of new-fallen snow. The sound of the wind through the trees has changed. No longer muted by the paper softness of leaves, it whistles through the empty branches. Gray squirrels haul twigs and leaves up tree trunks. Weaving these materials into vacated nests, they create a warm and cozy winter cottage. Unlike the chipmunk, they do not hibernate but remain active throughout the winter.

If no snow falls in December, the frost will move low into the ground, pushing those animals that seek refuge in the soil deeper and deeper or freezing them alive. Although the wood frog and spotted salamander can survive the Popsicle stage, most animals cannot. The sweetest sound in December is the gentle drifting of big fat snowflakes, clinging to the evergreens and piling up on the roofs of the bird feeders.

January combines plummeting temperatures, bitter winds, and driven snow with still, sunny days. The blue jays, black-capped chickadees, and red-breasted and white-breasted nuthatches make daily pilgrimages to the feeders. All but the nuthatches revel in repeating their names loudly and frequently. Cross-country skiers returning from a spin around the farm are cheerily greeted by these feathered residents.

The trails at Gilsland Farm are well marked, groomed, and easy to follow. Because of the open nature of the sanctuary, it is impossible to get lost. Even without a map, it is easy to pinpoint identifiable landmarks from across the field—the visitor center, original farmhouse, or big red barn—and follow the nearest trail to them or the access road.

The three major trails include West Meadow Trail (0.7 mile), North Meadow Trail (1.2 miles), and Pond Meadow Trail (0.6 mile). Numerous short connector and spur trails add variety and views. Benches are provided at strategic points for listening to and viewing wildlife or just plain relaxing.

Groundhogs (be careful not to turn your ankle in a hole), meadow voles, and chipmunks grace the North Meadow. Red-tailed hawks occasionally circle overhead, and red fox lie in wait for an unwary rodent. Signs of their successful kills may be as graphic as a half-eaten carcass or as subtle as hair-laden scat. Bobolinks, goldfinches, and meadowlarks all know the silhouette of a hawk and find shelter on their passing.

Meadows and marsh overlook the Presumpscot River.

The Pond Meadow Trail joins the North Meadow Trail across the road from the community gardens and the red barn. The trail drops to the pond, circles the edge of the visitor center and energy building, then enters the woods before intersecting with the West Meadow Trail or returning to the parking lot. Hours could be spent just observing the activity at the pond. From aquatic insects and frogs to herons, blackbirds, bats, and muskrats, something is happening, day or night, throughout the spring and summer. The woods provide habitat for warblers, thrushes, chickadees, and squirrels.

The sanctuary is open from dawn to dusk. For security reasons, the gate is closed from 5:00 P.M. to 7:30 A.M. Visitors coming before or after these hours may park outside the gate. Admission is free, but no pets, fires, or collecting samples are allowed. The visitor center is open 9:00 A.M. to 5:00 P.M. Monday through Saturday and 12:00 noon to 5:00 P.M. on Sundays (except during January and February).

Getting There

From Portland travel north on I-295 to Exit 9 (Route 1, Falmouth). After 1.8 miles, turn left at a sign indicating Maine Audubon Society. Travel 0.1 mile to the next sign and turn left again. Continue along the dirt road till it ends at the visitor center parking lot and a sign outlining the trail system.

For more information call the Maine Audubon Society at 207-781-2330.

19. Mackworth Island

Falmouth
100 Acres

Rocky Coast
1.5 miles
2 hours

Percival P. Baxter died in 1969 at the age of 90. He is best known for his gift of Baxter State Park, a wilderness tract totaling 178 square miles and comprising almost five townships. Few, however, know of his other philanthropic interests. He was born into a well-to-do Portland family, entered the state legislature at the age of 26 in 1905, and became governor of Maine in 1920. He was a man ahead of his time on many issues. As governor, he devoted time and energy to a wide range of causes from women's suffrage to the development of a state park system.

In addition, he politically and financially enabled the construction of Baxter School for the Deaf, donating the 100-acre Mackworth Island to that end. The perimeter of the island is open to the public as a nature preserve. Please be considerate of school activities when you visit.

The area is open from sunup to sundown. Parking for about 20 cars is available on the right directly across from the school gatehouse at the end of the causeway.

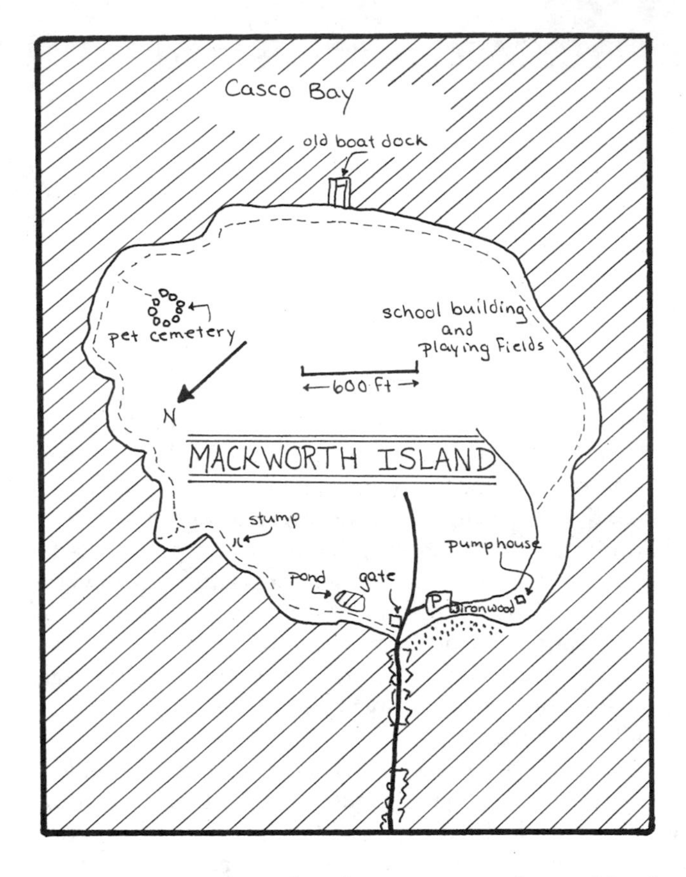

On our visit we started at the entrance to the parking lot and hiked counterclockwise around the island. The **path is flat and wide with views of the ocean its entire length.** It is used by parents with children, runners, racewalkers, birders, and romantics. Its easy accessibility from Portland, unparalleled beauty, and gentle slope make it very popular. **Access to the beach is provided at regular intervals** via stepped walkways.

Pass the edge of the parking lot and a large red oak on the right (this tree has a numbered tag with its Latin name inscribed). Just beyond, a set of stairs leads down to the beach passing through a small grove of **eastern hop hornbeam.** This tree is also called ironwood because of its unusually tough, hard, heavy wood. The branches of the tree are slender and droopy, its bark is ribbed with long flat scales, and the trunk is no wider than 10 or 12 inches in diameter. The fruit of the hop hornbeam is a cluster of bladderlike sacs, each of which encloses a small, flat, smooth seedlike nutlet. In mid-August the gray squirrels make quick work of the year's produce—they look like a line of beachgoers at a Ben & Jerry's stand as they hungrily tear through the fruit.

The beach grades to small gravel and then to mud. Everywhere there are bits of blue mussel shell. The mud is covered with worm castings, which look like mud squirted out of a toothpaste tube. These are the indigestible remains of the burrowing worm's dinner. Along the shore-forest margin, mugwort, beach rose, and mustards thrive.

The trail continues along the edge of a mowed field on the left. On the right are bittersweet vines, raspberry bushes, touch-me-not, woody nightshade, and tree-height staghorn sumac. Taking advantage of this area are some of the biggest, fattest **groundhogs** in southern Maine. In August they are putting on a few extra pounds for a long winter snooze. Imagine not being able to eat for months at a time.

Many of the plants along the walk are not native species and may be unfamiliar. Pass the brick pump house and a large stand of Japanese knotweed. The flowering knotweed has a strong scent and is often covered with honeybees. The stems are very similar to bamboo—hollow in the center with enlarged joints at regular intervals. When the shoots are less than a foot high they can be harvested, steamed for five minutes, and eaten like asparagus.

At 0.2 mile the trail branches to the right, leaving the dirt road, and within 300 feet enters a wood. On the

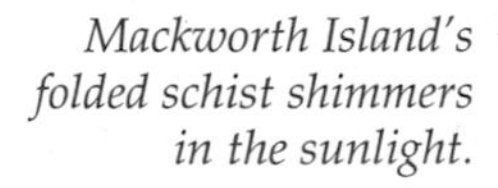

Mackworth Island's folded schist shimmers in the sunlight.

left is a stand of Scotch pine easily distinguished by its scaly bark. The bark at the crown of the tree has a conspicuous orange brown coloration.

On the right is a bench overlooking extensive beds of blue mussels and rockweed. As you look over the bay from this bench, Fort Gorges immediately catches the eye. Behind it and to the right is the flashing of Portland Head Light. Directly opposite Fort Gorges on the right is Spring Point Light. The large tankers unloading at the wharf are carrying oil that will be pumped by pipeline to Canada. Great Diamond Island is on the left.

At 0.4 mile there is a large patch of daylilies on the left followed by playing fields. In 400 feet the trail reenters the woods. Norway, or red, pine are on the left. The needles of this tree grow in clusters of two like the Scotch pine but are four to six inches in length. The color of the bark is consistent the entire length of the trunk. The tree is not from Norway. The name refers to its original discovery near Norway, Maine. Nearby is the Norway spruce, distinguished by its long sweeping branches and shorter, prickly needles. This tree is not a native of Maine or New England but of Europe.

The trail reaches the jetty at 0.6 mile. A former boat dock, this is the **perfect place for a picnic.** There are sweeping views of Casco Bay and stairs leading down to the beach. The exposed bedrock has been oxidized to the color of brass and shimmers in the sunlight. Herring and greater black-backed gulls trumpet their greetings.

Rounding the point of land, and continuing beyond another collection of benches and views, the trail is intersected by a path to the left. Set in a grove of tall white pines is the Percival P. Baxter **Pet Cemetery.**

Unlike the Stephen King namesake, this cemetery has an air of contemplative solitude. It is a monument to the care and affection Baxter had for his most loyal companions, his horse, Jerry Roan, and his Irish setters. A plaque in the center stone declares "The State of Maine by Legislative Act Chapter I, Laws of 1943, accepted the gift of Mackworth Isle, and covenanted to maintain forever the burial place of my dogs with the stonewall and the boulder with the bronze marker thereon erected in their memory."

Along with the cemetery there is one more odd memorial on the island. At 1.1 miles there is a huge, old, decayed red oak stump. Completely hollow on the inside, the tree's skeleton has been carefully protected by a painted wood fence. A row of hosta borders the enclosure. Take a moment to inspect the inner surface. Three carved faces will greet you in return. No bronze plaque sheds light on the mystery.

Continue over a path of crushed stone past a small pond on the left before returning to the gatehouse. Pass a clump of wild asparagus and walk under the shade of a basswood (linden) tree before reaching the parking lot. The basswood is frequently planted as a shade tree on lawns and along city streets. The asparagus probably escaped from an old garden. Basswood flowers and leaves steeped in hot water and consumed as tea are a traditional home remedy for colds, coughs, and sore throats. The inner bark makes a soothing application for skin irritations and burns.

Returning to the parking area completes the 1.5-mile walk.

Getting There

From I-295 in Portland, travel north to Exit 9 (Route 1, Falmouth). Go north over the bridge and take the third right, Andrews Avenue. This distance from Exit 9 to Andrews Avenue is 1.2 miles. Go east along Andrews Avenue and across the causeway to the gatehouse. The visitor's parking lot is on the right.

For more information call the Maine Bureau of Public Lands at 207-289-3061.

20. Falmouth Nature Preserve

Falmouth
34 Acres

Estuarine Uplands
1.4 miles
1 hour

Falmouth was one of the first European settlements established in Maine. It sat on the edge of a large wooded frontier. During the many Indian wars and the American Revolution, it was burned to the ground, but the residents returned. Today it remains a desirable place to live. Indications of the wilderness, however, have all but disappeared. Two other Falmouth nature walks have been included in this book: Gilsland Farm (see p. 134), which preserves the flavor of a working saltwater farm; and Mackworth Island (see p. 145), which, though developed, gives a palpable impression of a Casco Bay island. The Falmouth Nature Preserve has a different goal—it recaptures a tiny part of a once vast wild land.

The entrance to the preserve is tucked between two private residences on Route 88. The only indication that the narrow dirt road leads to a wildlife sanctuary is a sign at the corner of the drive stating No Motorized Vehicles. The park opens at 7:00 A.M. and closes at dusk. The trails show some evidence of use by mountain bik-

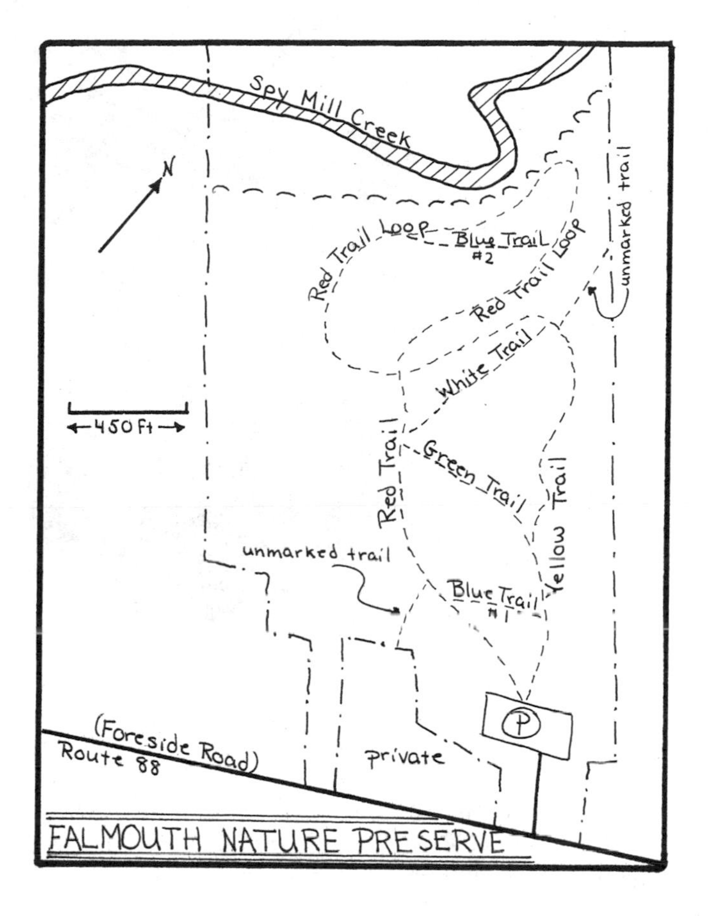

ers and runners, but midday, midweek, midsummer, you are likely to have the place to yourself. At the end of the short dirt road are parking spaces for five or six cars and a map board describing the area.

Large white pines overhang the edge of the marsh.

The two main trails are blazed in red and yellow. The trails connecting them are blazed with blue, green, and white. The Yellow Trail begins to the right of the map board in a grove composed of white pine, red maple, balsam fir, red spruce, hemlock, and birch. Standing in this space and identifying the trees provides a good cross section of the most common species native to Maine.

In 0.1 mile, Blue Trail No. 1 enters on the left at a small clearing of bracken ferns and blueberry bushes. Bracken is the most common fern in the eastern U.S. and is quite easy to identify. It has large, upright, dark green, leathery fronds divided into three parts. It is edible as a fiddlehead (unfurling bud) but must be harvested in the spring before it reaches a height of six inches (and of course shouldn't be harvested in protected areas such as this). Mature fronds are toxic. Unlike other ferns that are curled in a tight spiral when they first emerge, the bracken's unfolding frond looks like the poised talon of an eagle. Rub off the woolly covering and boil for 30 to 45 minutes before serving with copious quantities of butter. Canned **fiddleheads** purchased in supermarkets are likely to be ostrich ferns instead of bracken.

Blue Trail No. 1 is only 200 feet in length but has a good selection of spring wildflowers. They include partridgeberry, wild oats, bunchberry, and Canada mayflower (false lily of the valley). From mid-August to October, the berries of these plants are almost as pretty as the flowers: bunchberry and partridgeberry are bright red and the Canada mayflower is speckled platinum.

Return to the Yellow Trail. An additional 220 feet along will bring you to the junction with the Green Trail. This path continues straight ahead, while the Yellow Trail swings right. The Green Trail is only 235 feet, but it also leads to some interesting plants. On the right, beneath a standing dead white pine riddled with woodpecker holes, are **starflower, partridgeberry,** and **Indian cucumber.** Although the cucumber produces deep blue berries, these are inedible, as are the two whorled sets of leaves. The root, however, tastes mildly like cucumber and can be eaten in salads or pickled. The plant is scarce in Maine and is protected from the curious by a hefty fine. Observe its beauty, but do not pick it. The starflower has a single set of whorled leaves and twin white, star-shaped blossoms. It is shorter than the wild cucumber, reaching a height of six to eight inches.

The Yellow Trail turns left in 400 feet, at the same place the White Trail enters from the left. This junction is a bit confusing as a third unmarked trail continues straight ahead. The way is ill-defined for 30 to 50 feet, with much crisscrossing of various paths.

The White Trail passes through 240 feet of hemlock forest before intersecting with the Red Trail. Hikers should veer left with the Yellow Trail.

The Yellow Trail enters a wet area with an old well or cistern on the right, then climbs a small knoll to a stand of older white pine and hemlock. Keep to the left as an unmarked trail enters on the right. The Yellow Trail ends at a four-way intersection with the Red Trail and Red Trail Loop, 0.3 mile after leaving the parking lot.

Follow the Red Trail left to return to the parking lot or take the half-mile Red Trail Loop by continuing straight ahead from the Yellow Trail. Seventy-five feet down the loop on the right notice a large old red maple. Some years ago it sustained a major injury to the length of the trunk. Notice how the edges of the bark have healed, but the injury was too big to mend and the core of the tree has rotted. Scan the top branches, though, and you will still see leaves. This shows that the cambium layer—the part of a tree just underneath the bark that is alive and transports food and water to the leaves and roots—is still intact. That is why the tree can survive even when its center is gone.

(A friend claims this is nature's proof that you can survive a broken heart.)

The Red Trail Loop descends past a huge white pine on the left, then passes through a blackberry patch. Watch for poison ivy here. At 0.2 mile, the Blue Trail No. 2 enters on your right. This Blue Trail is 740 feet in length, parallels a deep draw lined with hemlock, and harbors resident ruffed grouse. It also has a 150-foot stretch of poison ivy that overhangs the trail on both sides. If it is summer and you are wearing shorts, this trail is not recommended. Cross-country skiing should be fine.

Advancing on the Red Trail Loop, descend to a wooden footbridge over a draw and climb to the open understory of an evergreen knoll. **Spy Mill Creek flood plain and salt marsh** are visible on the left through the trees. Descend to a more spacious glimpse of the estuary. At the top of the sandbank ahead is a dirt road. Follow it to the left for the best views of the tidal creek and its environs. To the right the loop continues past sweet fern, juniper, and honeysuckle.

At 0.4 mile the Red Trail Loop takes a sharp right, leaving the dirt road but continuing on an old woods road for the rest of its length. Listen for the call of chickadees and the scolding of blue jays and red squirrels. Blue Trail No. 2 enters on the right just before a shallow draw. From here it is only 0.1 mile to complete the loop and rejoin the Yellow Trail at the four way intersection. To return to the parking lot proceed straight ahead on the Red Trail at the intersection.

As you make your way back, scan the ground for signs of unseen wildlife. The tracks of white-tailed deer

Evergreens border Spy Mill Creek.

are plentiful and cut a narrow V into the wet soil. The scat of red fox may contain berries in summer but is often bound by the fur of small rodents it has consumed. Red squirrels leave piles of evergreen cone scales.

The White and Green Trails enter on the left. In another 0.1 mile the Red Trail takes a sharp left and an unmarked trail continues straight ahead. If you miss this turn you will find yourself in a neighbor's back yard. Blue Trail No. 1 enters on the left a few hundred feet before the trail reaches the parking lot.

The preserve welcomes walkers, runners, skiers, and birders. No motorized vehicles are allowed.

Getting There

From the north, the preserve is off Route 88 (Foreside Road) about 0.7 mile southwest of the Town Landing Market (the intersection of Johnson and Foreside Roads). The dirt road leading to the preserve is directly opposite 177 Foreside Road.

From the south, take Exit 9 (Route 1) off I-295 in Portland. Travel 2.1 miles to the intersection of Routes 1 and 88. Bear right. Continue 1.7 miles to 177 Foreside Road. Turn left down a narrow dirt road between two houses.

For more information contact the Falmouth Conservation Commission, Falmouth, ME 04105.

21. Royal River Park

Yarmouth
10 Acres

Woodlands

1.0 mile round-trip

0.5 hour

Wheelchair accessible: level 1–3 (see p. xiv)

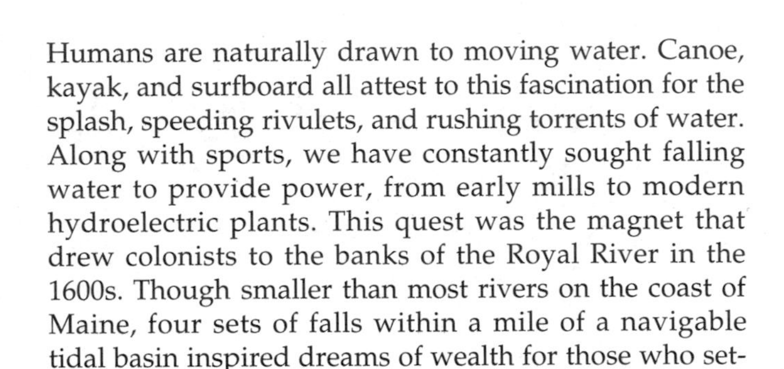

Humans are naturally drawn to moving water. Canoe, kayak, and surfboard all attest to this fascination for the splash, speeding rivulets, and rushing torrents of water. Along with sports, we have constantly sought falling water to provide power, from early mills to modern hydroelectric plants. This quest was the magnet that drew colonists to the banks of the Royal River in the 1600s. Though smaller than most rivers on the coast of Maine, four sets of falls within a mile of a navigable tidal basin inspired dreams of wealth for those who settled here.

The trail begins at the parking lot on East Elm Street. To the left of the parking lot, a **footbridge** spans an old sluiceway. Here is a small island park with a dam and **fish ladder** on the far side. After viewing the fish ladder, return to the trailhead at the parking lot. In front of the cars, a blacktop path slopes down toward the riverbank. A broad stretch of grassland park, peppered with picnic tables during the warm months of the

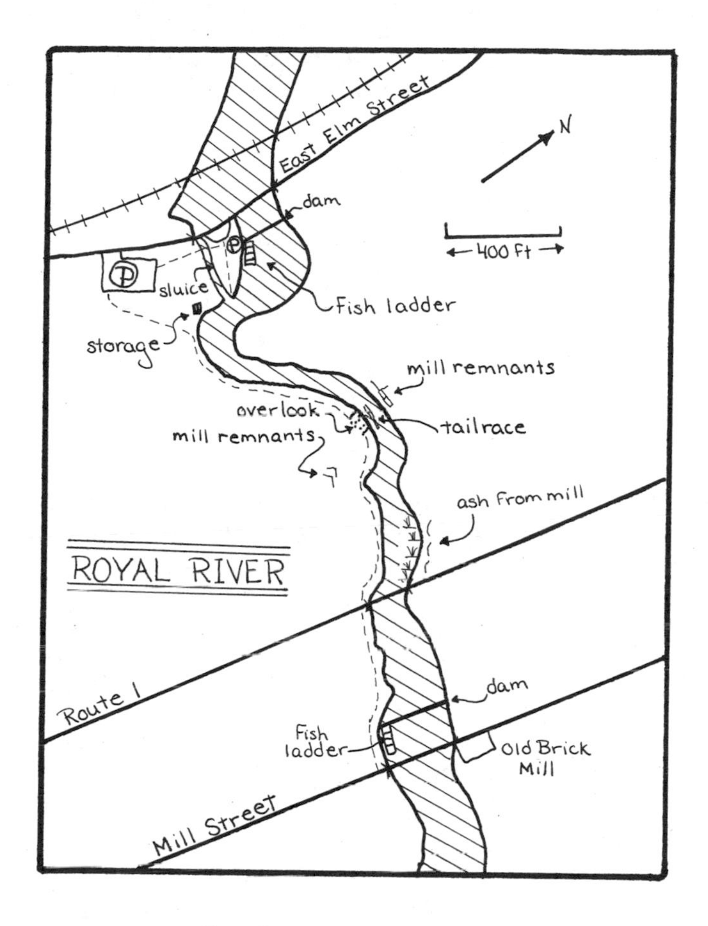

year, sweeps off to the right, while on the left is a winter storage building. It is a friendly spot for grown-ups, kids, and family pets (on a leash). The path carries the hiker within 10 feet of the river for much its 2,500-foot length. Here the sight and the sound of water works its magic. It is best to make this a round-trip walk (1.0 mile) as there are no parking spaces available at the far end.

About 700 feet from the parking lot, the trail comes to a graveled overlook where some of the first large remains of **millworks** come into view. Stone, brickwork, and reinforced concrete give evidence of attempts to control the flow of water over the natural ledges of the riverbed. During the early years, almost every kind of manufacturing could be found along these banks, making use of the falling water. Sawmills and gristmills were built here as early as 1674. Pottery kilns, brickworks, fuller's earth works (a mineral used in textiles), clockworks, cotton and yarns, potash, pulp and paper, tanning, ancient masts, modern machine works, and more found their place along the falls of the Royal.

A foundry and forge, powered by the river, and a touch of invention led one John H. Hall to invent a breech-loading rifle. It was good enough to be accepted by federal troops prior to the Civil War. His success carried him to locate his arsenal at Harper's Ferry in West Virginia, where it was raided in 1859 by one John Brown. He was hanged and memorialized in song for the deed.

From the overlook the trail again descends, this time to a small bridge with a brick rectangle on the right. The stone and brick formations are the remains of the Forest Paper Company, a large pulp mill. In the river, on the left, are the remains of a channeled **tailrace** below the mill complex.

The trail continues down a slope and levels out where the river widens to a pond area almost 300 feet across. Marsh grasses on the far side provide feed for some of the ducks that frequent the river. The path passes along the bank under a canopy of mixed hardwoods and evergreens, including aspen, willow, pine, and hemlock. To the right, large white pines press up the slope to create a shaded summer grove and protection from the cold winds of winter. They are descendants of the giant **mast trees** harvested between the Royal and Androscoggin Rivers and shipped to England in the 1700s.

The pond itself is the result of the low dam on the second set of falls along the river. As the trail passes under the Route 1 bridge, the dam is easily seen. The trail ends a couple of hundred feet beyond the dam at Mill Street. At the near corner of the dam there is another fish ladder, companion to the one near the parking lot at the trailhead.

Fish ladders play an important part in the **ecology** of rivers and coastal waters. Their presence on the Royal River is an encouraging sign. The early settlement of New England ensured disruption of the breeding areas of migratory fish. Humans have made heavy use of the rivers over the last 300 years. Salmon, alewives, shad, and even the American eel have all but disappeared from native streams. These were important food sources for Native Americans, settlers, and many indigenous animals. Where they thrive, such fish are important to the economy for commercial, sport, and tourist business. Unfortunately, these species were

Quiet water behind the dam and fish ladder provides a respite for migratory fish.

almost eradicated from the Northeast before their full value was realized. Early settlers fished the rivers heavily. Dams prevented the reproduction of the species, as adults could not make it into shallow streams to deposit eggs. Now there is a concerted attempt to reverse the accumulated damage of 300 years. Fish ladders on the Royal River are an indication of the present effort to make the rivers accessible to migratory fish, an effort to use the river while maintaining the wildlife.

Return upriver to complete the one-mile walk or have someone pick you up at the bridge on Mill Street. Most of the time you will share this shaded walk with townspeople. Consider visiting in July when the well-known Yarmouth Clam Festival draws visitors from all over New England.

Getting There

From Route 1 north or south where it cuts across Yarmouth, take the exit for Route 115. This brings you to Main Street and a right turn. Drive as far as the railroad tracks on Main Street. Make a right onto East Elm Street at the next intersection. Continue 0.3 mile to an open area on the right before the bridge, where you can park in the lot.

22. Wolfe's Neck Woods State Park

Freeport
233 Acres

Rocky Coast

up to 2 miles

2.5 hours

0.5 mile wheelchair accessible: level 1 (see p. xiv)

Wolfe's Neck Woods State Park sits near the tip of one of many peninsulas along midcoast Maine. These fingers of land are the result of rising sea levels following the sinking of the **continental crust** under the weight of the Ice Age. These peninsulas and many offshore islands give Maine a length of coastline second only to Alaska.

Within the park are reminders of a time greatly predating even the last Ice Age. With a little geologic help from the park ranger, you can be transported back to the formation of the Atlantic Ocean and the North American continent. The shoreline **layers** of pegmatite, metamorphic ledge, and basalt hold clues to the mountain building resulting from collisions between North America and Africa. A rifting process began opening the Atlantic Ocean 60 million years ago. The widening process continues today along the **Mid-Atlantic Rift,** stretching almost pole to pole beneath the sea.

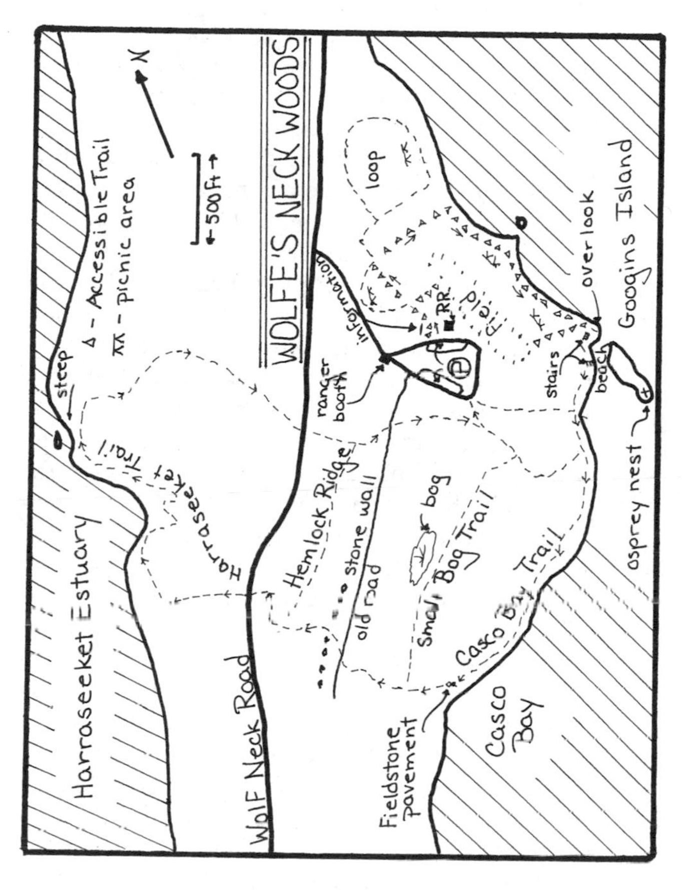

The ride through Wolfe's Neck, a subdivision of Freeport, is a pretty one. Large farms and older homes speak of a time when people were **homesteaders.** In the 1800s these were saltwater farms, so named because much of their sustenance came from the surrounding marsh and bay. One active farm, part of the University of Maine, raises organic beef from black angus and provides beautiful campsites on its bay-side property.

Wolfe's Neck Woods, named for an early settler (not the animal) stands out as a forested area beyond fields dedicated to the black angus. Once you pass the ranger's tollbooth, there are several areas that draw your attention. The trail description begins at the large information board explaining the white pine grove near the rest rooms and the **wheelchair-accessible trail.** The trails are open and clear; some are well marked with informational signs, others are clear but unmarked.

After absorbing the map information and the history of Wolfe's Neck from the board, walk toward the field on the right. Before entering the field, the designated Accessible Trail turns left behind the signboard. Follow this path into the woods. At the next intersection you have a variety of choices. On the left is a picnic area under the imposing white pines. Straight ahead an unnamed trail leads to a half-mile rustic loop with a few isolated picnic tables along the margin of the bay. Follow the Accessible Trail to the right. Enter an area of oak, pine, and hemlock. Farther along you will see one of the more attractive picnic areas in southern Maine. The tables are widely spaced and are surrounded by hemlock, pine, and some spruce. The left side of the same trail begins as a fern-lined gully leading down to Casco Bay. About 300 feet from the intersection, the path takes a sharp turn to the right and, depending on the tide, looks through trees to water or extensive mudflats.

These **mudflats** represent an important resource. They are composed of a fine, soft mix of clay and organic matter. While not impressive to humans, such muck is home to a large number of sea creatures. Chief among these is the soft-shell clam, or steamer. This mollusk passes its adult life, quiet as a clam, unmoved in this mire. Its neck, composed of two siphons, draws in water containing food and oxygen and carries away bodily wastes and sex cells for procreation. We, and the Native Americans before us, have cherished this animal for its nourishing flesh. Some bays are overfished, but most shore areas are exposed to **sewage**, making the animal dangerous to consume. These wastes, acting as fertilizer, have increased some of the less desirable algae in coastal water and abetted the red tides that make the meat of the soft-shell clam toxic to mammals (that includes us) and birds. In summer, you may see a few of the lucky diggers who have permits to harvest these clam flats. In other seasons, only tracks and mud piles remain, symbols of their manual labor.

Continue along the Accessible Trail. It wends back and forth, tracing the lip of the land across two small railed bridges. There are informational signs at strategic points describing the plants and animals of the area. On your right, through the trees, is the field between the trail and the parking area. Several short paths lead to tables in this direction through red spruce and hemlock. About 100 feet beyond the last right-hand avenue to the field and picnic grounds, the Accessible Trail dead-ends at the **overlook** viewing the osprey nest on Googins Island. You can return as you came or take the path from the point at Googins Island back across the field, about 1,500 feet to the parking lot.

Many people return each year to follow the pair of **osprey** that have claimed Googins Island as their home. A tall shaft of dead pine on the near side of the island, snapped at the top, is the site of a nest destroyed in a hurricane. Undeterred, the pair reestablished a nest on the south side of the island. They successfully raise one, sometimes two, chicks each year. In summer, the anxious cries of the young reach across the bay if a parent is in sight or slow with the supply of fresh fish. Watch an adult as it hovers a moment, folds its wings, and plummets into the bay. The bird often disappears in a tremendous splash. Then, with several broad wing

Googins Island harbors an osprey preserve.

beats, it lifts its dripping body and its prey clear of the water. It will carry the fish headfirst in its talons, back to the aerie for its young or mate.

When you've seen enough of the aerial display, backtrack 100 feet to the main portion of the trail. From this point you may follow the Accessible Trail into the field and the parking lot or turn left to a set of stairs. If you are still adventurous, follow the stairs leading from the Accessible Trail to the ledges of the **beach.** Here, separated layers of ancient metamorphic rock angle up like gaping mouths. The layered effect is broken in places by intrusions of light-colored lumps of pegmatite. This is composed of large crystals of feldspar, garnet, and flakes of mica. No rock hammers, please—this is a park where you need to leave the beauty for all to see.

As you leave the beach ledges, turn left and meet the Casco Bay Trail. This walkway, while bedded with wood chips, is on a heavy clay soil with the ledge breaking the surface occasionally. The thin dense soil forces tree **roots** to the surface, so keep an eye out for them as you hike any of the trails in this end of the park.

The Casco Bay Trail follows the shoreline for about 1,800 feet. At its southern junction with the Harraseeket Trail, there is a fine overview of the bay and its islands. A sign describes the offshore scenic **vista.**

From the fieldstone pavement that marks the beginning of the Harraseeket, begin climbing the inland leg of the hike. A little more than 400 feet into the woods is the southern end of the Small Bog Trail. In spite of the name, this is a high and rather dry path for most of its 1,200 feet. You are more apt to spot a toad hunting one of the 300 insects it consumes in a day as opposed to a frog, which requires a moist environment. The actual bog, a shallow depression in the underlying rock holding water and decaying vegetation, parallels part of the trail on the landward side. There are ledge, metamorphic rock, stunted trees, and many lichens on this trail. In contrast with the bog, the higher, drier ledges have reindeer moss (lichen) and several species of encrusting lichens helping to form soil.

From its junction with the Small Bog Trail, continue to follow the Harraseeket uphill parallel to the border of the park. About 600 feet beyond the Small Bog Trail, the path opens out into a level open area marked by an old road/power line intersecting the trail at a right angle. Continue on to step through an old stone wall, a remnant of a long-gone pasture or property line.

Arriving at the southern end of the Hemlock Ridge Trail, you are at the high point of the Harraseeket Trail. A sign notes it is 0.5 mile if you choose to return to the parking lot via the Hemlock Ridge Trail on the right and 1.2 miles if you choose to use the Harraseeket Trail.

Take a moment to look about at the **understory plants.** Like several nature walks listed in this text, the area supports teaberry, partridgeberry, and wild sarsaparilla, plants associated with the mixed forest dominating Wolfe's Neck Woods State Park. In the autumn when mushrooms begin to fruit, this area of the trail may show the unusual coral fungus. From the forest floor it appears as thin fingerlike protrusions three to four inches tall. The bright yellow-to-white clusters look very much like their namesake coral heads. This fungus and its many relatives grow underground, dissolving and feeding on dead and decaying plant matter. They

Wild sarsaparilla grows in the understory at Wolfe's Neck.

recycle nutrients into the soil for all plants. In late summer and fall, the fungi reproduce by pushing spore-laden heads aboveground. We call these heads mushrooms, some tasty and some toxic.

Continue along the Harraseeket Trail. The path takes a sharp right turn downhill and parallels the Hemlock Ridge Trail, now 15 feet above your head. Many roots, rocks, and high spots are covered in cone scales, attesting to a well-fed population of **red squirrels** in this area. The path soon turns away from the Hemlock Ridge Trail and drops steadily amid large trees whose growing roots press the rocks above the soil.

In a couple of hundred feet, the Harraseeket Trail meets the Wolf Neck Road. Cross the road carefully, and enter a grove of mixed trees. About 300 feet into the forest is a young stand of white pine on the left. Their even size shows they were all seeded at the same time, possibly part of forest reclamation. Five hundred feet from the road the trail bears right sharply, and you begin a route that parallels the Harraseeket River estuary. The land behind the boat moorings is South Freeport. A tower among the trees on the opposite bank is a remnant of the Casco Castle. This was an early hotel designed along the lines of an English castle. Unlike the Casco Bay side of the park, the trail on this side climbs higher until it is about 40 feet above the water. Most of the time, the trail is well away from the edge of the estuary. After it descends to planks over a stream, the path rises again and approaches a **steep edge** overlooking water. Along the path, a tremendous rock has split away from the margin of the trail leaving a 20-foot gap some 40 feet deep. This point provides a photogenic overlook, but watch the vertical drop. Shortly beyond this aberrant **boulder,** the trail turns back toward the road, through some of the larger hemlocks and white pines in the park. The pines are more than 2 feet in diameter, approaching the size of trees used as masts. Hemlock, which splits easily, was not utilized in ship construction.

Too quickly the trail returns to the Wolf Neck Road. From this point it is a little more than 0.3 mile to the parking and picnic areas.

Wolfe's Neck Woods State Park, on land donated by a Freeport family, is an ideal day visit. Tall trees and water on both sides of the park keep it particularly cool in the summer. Even harsh Maine winters do not keep visitors away. Many people park along the road and roam the area on cross-country skis.

Getting There

From Exits 19 or 20 on I-95, or from Route 1, drive to the center of Freeport. Right in front of the L. L. Bean complex, take Bow Street directly off Main Street (U.S. 1). Follow Bow Street down through the Mast Landing area for 2.3 miles. A large sign announces Wolfe's Neck Woods State Park to the right on Wolf Neck Road (without the *e*). Follow this route 2.1 miles to the park on the left.

For information call 207-865-4465.

23. Mast Landing Sanctuary

Freeport
186 Acres

Estuarine Uplands
up to 2 miles
1.5 hours

Mast Landing is a quiet backwater today. It sits on the margin of Freeport, one of Maine's contemporary business centers. Very little about the present appearance of the landing gives any hint of the early commerce carried out within and about its borders. A series of mapped/marked trails are maintained by the Maine Audubon Society, covering estuarine marsh, slow streams, old fields, and young forest. Mast Landing can be a **peaceful,** contemplative walk for a family among a wide variety of plant communities.

Plants have shaped the history of Maine and the distribution of its people. Today, we easily perceive the potato and blueberry as economically important to the state. Even though the Maine state flower is the **white pine,** most of us do not realize that much modern geography is based on Maine trees. Mast agents for the king of England lent their names to the town of Westbrook and to Waldo County. Machias was settled in 1763 by families escaping the fiery destruction of masting and lumbering operations in Scarborough. The settlement at

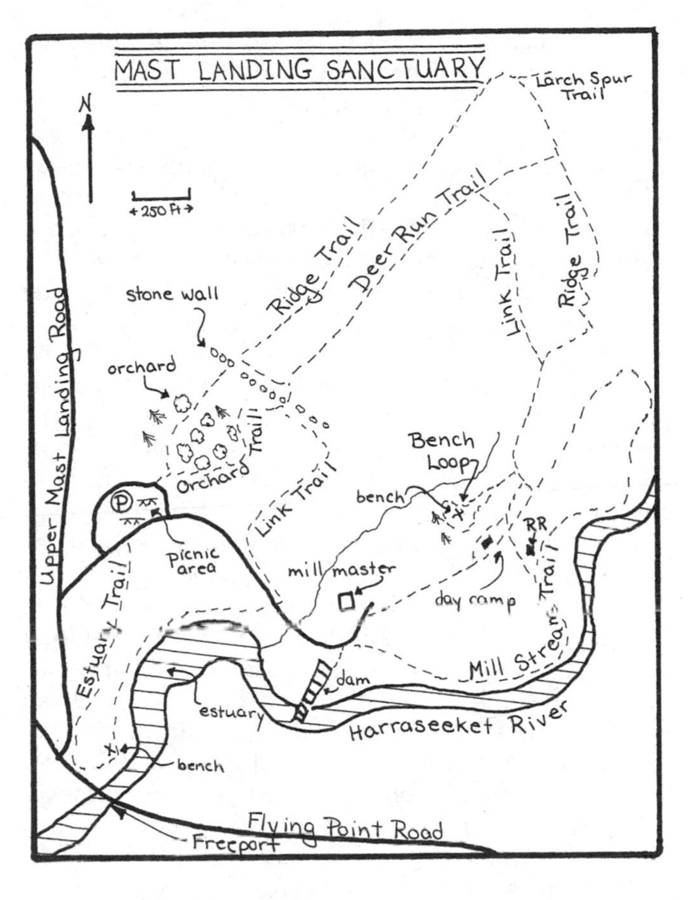

Falmouth (now Portland) lost 400 buildings to a British cannonade by refusing to give up masts on the eve of the American Revolution. Modern roads leading into coastal towns follow old logging paths swamped out for the transport of mast trees and lumber products. Every shoreline nook or cranny had a settled "**landing**" where trees were transformed into ships that sailed the far corners of the world.

Maine's affair with trees and ships began as early as 1607 when the pinnace *Virginia* was hewn from native wood. She plied Atlantic waters for 20 years, but the Popham colony that built her lasted only one. The hunt for ships' timbers expanded. The hull of a single seventeenth-century vessel might require 3,000 **oak trees,** and Britain was trying to sustain a 600-ship navy. Scandinavian supplies for masts were cut off, and England looked to the New World for the giant trees required for British shipbuilding. The Revolution shifted ship construction to the emerging states, and the Americans took over where the British left off. Individual entrepreneurs built ships in their back yards at places like Clay Cove, Richmond Island, and Agry's Point. The ring of the caulking hammer called out from landings with names like Mast, Porter's, Kennebunk, and Pipe Stave. These locations are not as familiar as Bath, Kennebunkport, Falmouth, and Kittery, which we easily connect with ships even today. In fact, many early shipyards cannot be found on today's maps. When the trees were gone or too distant to be cut cheaply, jobs ran out and people drifted away. Much of this part of our history is buried in the soils of Mast Landing and hidden by a veneer of time.

At the intersection of Main and Bow Streets in the heart of Freeport is a strange corner, a reminder of bygone days. Busy tourists do not take notice. On the west corner of Bow Street, older curbing, embedded in the modern brick, makes a 45-degree angle to Main Street, runs for 60 feet, and abuts Bow Street. This truncated corner preserves the **path** made by trains of oxen as they moved 90-foot mast timbers onto Bow Street 200 years ago, when the area was part of the shipping industry. The trees were hauled down Bow Street, then rafted to the mast agent at Fore River in Falmouth. From there they were shipped to ports in England.

A short drive east from Freeport brings you to Upper Mast Landing Road and the entrance to Maine Audubon's Mast Landing Sanctuary. The loop parking lot has a shaded picnic area and parking for 15 to 20 vehicles. A note board gives directions, and maps showing the blazed trails are available. The area is accessible throughout the year barring deep snow. Rest rooms are located in the corner of the field near the day-camp buildings.

The longest path, the Ridge Trail, practically circumnavigates the entire **sanctuary.** To begin the hike, step from the parking/picnic area into the cool shade of the white pines and walk to the junction of the Ridge and Orchard Trails. Either track will take you through ample evidence of an extensive old orchard mixed into the pines. Follow the Ridge Trail into an overgrown field that makes fine fodder for deer, especially with the lure of apples in season. Deer move about in early morning and evening. They are shy and elusive. Only the very quiet hiker will chance to see one. This field demonstrates the process where nature begins to recapture an area once cleared by humans. There is a great mix of tall grasses and shrubbery—dogbanes, goldenrods, steeplebush, and sumacs grow over the old fields, paving the way for birches and aspens. Much later the larger "climax" species for this area—oaks, maples, and evergreens—clothe the land as before and the marks of humanity are eased away. The process of reclamation over a period of time is called **succession.** It is a natural process much like we encounter when "weeds" invade our carefully planned gardens.

About 700 feet into the mix of old fields and burgeoning new forest is a stone wall, probably the boundary of an early pasture. On the other side of the stone wall is the Link Trail, which cuts across the width of the sanctuary toward the Harraseeket Estuary.

A hundred feet beyond the Link Trail, you enter an older evergreen forest. The succession seen earlier in the field has progressed much further here. A heavy pine canopy permits only some younger balsam and witch hazel in the understory. In this area you can see the origin of the trail name. The path follows the apex of a ridge for hundreds of feet. To the right an open ledge parallels the trail for 200 feet. The heavy cover in this area will cool you on a warm day.

About 0.5 mile from the trailhead, intersect with a short dead-end trail, the Larch Spur. The Ridge Trail continues right and 700 feet past the spur joins its parallel partner, the Deer Run Trail. The sanctuary here boasts mature trees, some possibly 100 years old. It feels as though the area has never been disturbed by humans, although that is unlikely in our world.

Continue the pleasant walk through this secondary forest and across the open area created by a telephone line right-of-way. Six hundred feet farther a second Link Trail crosses back to the Deer Run Trail. The next junction, 300 feet farther on the right, will be the Bench Loop. This is a worthwhile side trip. The Bench Loop leads into an airy, but shaded, area of young aspen and pine. On the right side the land drops steeply away to the fern-covered beginnings of a stream. This slope has widely dispersed mature red oak, hemlock, white birch, and white pine. About 300 feet into the loop you come to the namesake bench. It is poised at the top of the steep slope and offers a **panoramic view.** Sitting here quietly you might get a chance look at the pileated woodpecker or hear its chickenlike call among the trees.

A few hundred feet beyond the bench, the trail begins its return, following the crest that drops away to the right. Severe **erosion** at one time left the sharp slopes bordering the Bench Loop Trail. Now extensive root systems of the mature trees protect and conserve the topsoil.

Having traversed about 0.2 mile, you will close the loop and return to the Ridge Trail. Turn right; 200 feet farther the path opens into a field merging with one end of the Mill Stream Trail. The Ridge Trail turns right from this point, past buildings where day-camp activities are offered to youngsters of the area. From this junction hikers can choose to extend the walk and follow the Mill Stream Trail as it snakes along the banks of the stream. The alternative is to follow the Ridge Trail through the field toward the caretaker's residence, once the home of the miller at Mast Landing.

Either trail will bring hikers to the gravel drive leading from the miller's old home. In doing so, take time to walk out on the dam at the headwaters of the Harraseeket River. This was an active **waterpower site**

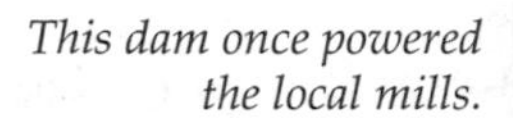

This dam once powered the local mills.

from the very early 1700s until the mill burned in 1861. The hand-hewn quarry stones on the top guide you to the sluiceway where water poured through, powering the wheels of the lumber and gristmills. Below is the spartina marsh of the estuary. You may see the great blue heron, white egrets, or a vagabond raccoon searching the tidal waters for a meal.

Located on the gravel drive back to the parking lot is another attractive hike. The Estuary Trail follows along the edge of the salt marsh at the base of the dam site. At the farther reaches of this trail there is a bench in a quiet pine grove. Like the site on the Bench Loop, it's just the right place for a brief rest or a picnic. Follow the Estuary Trail back to the gravel road and the parking area.

Since 1967 the Mast Landing Sanctuary has provided a place for youngsters. The area is a haven for plants, animals, and people. It is a credit to the Maine Audubon Society and the volunteer stewards who help maintain it.

Getting There

From I-95 take either Exit 19 or 20 to Main Street, Freeport. Turn right from either exit toward the center of town. Directly in front of L. L. Bean, turn onto Bow Street, which will become Flying Point Road. Follow this road for 1.0 mile to the left turn onto Upper Mast Landing Road (just beyond Lower Mast Landing Road). At 0.1 mile on your right will be the sign and gravel drive to Maine Audubon's Mast Landing Sanctuary.

For information call 207-781-2330.

24. Bradbury Mountain State Park

Pownal

500 Acres

Foothills

0.3 mile–2.0 miles

up to 2 hours

We are a society tied into the freeways, interstates, and turnpikes of life. There comes a time when we need to turn onto one of the back roads and take time to see the world around us; to slow down and focus on our surroundings. Whether you are a local or "from away," you can see the real Maine only if you get off the turnpike and onto a **slow lane** surrounded by the pastoral beauty of Maine.

One of the finer back roads for such a venture is Route 9. For much of its length, it traces the Post Road, or King's Highway, of colonial times. Along this road you can find churches, homes, and farms that date back to the beginnings of this nation. Only in this way do you get a taste of Maine, past and present. Clothed in the muted white of winter, summer's green, or swathed in autumn's color, the gently rolling land speaks of life in many ways. There are fields with hol-

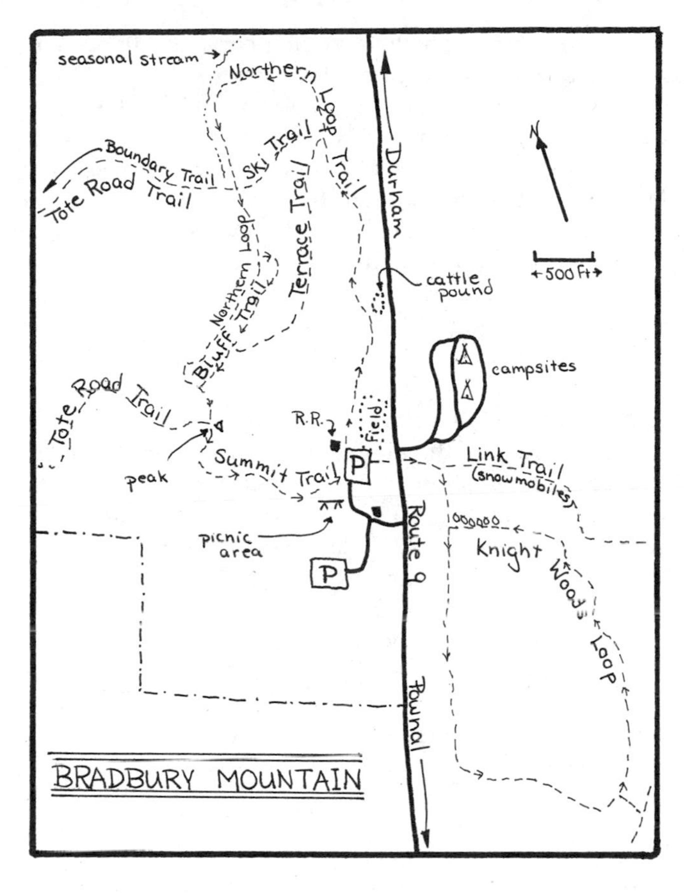

steins and belted galloways. People work their hay mows (wagons) and tedders, tend their crops, or make cider and maple syrup. Folks from away wonder, "What do they do in winter?" History books and highways can't bring you close to the people of Maine. You have to discover them along the back roads.

Tucked in the hills along the Old Post Road is Bradbury Mountain State Park. It is fixed in the rustic scenery of the countryside, comfortably removed from larger suburban areas. Here the trails cut across many **stone walls** built by people almost lost in time. The view from Bradbury Mountain, which rises only a few hundred feet above the surrounding landscape, remains virtually unchanged by the years. You can't see the turnpike or I-95, and metropolitan Portland stands far on the horizon.

The ranger's station, at the entrance to the park, provides a map of the area. Most trails are marked with signs or a blaze; a few are unmarked but well mapped. Beyond the ranger's booth are two large parking areas with adjoining picnic and play areas for young families. If you are inclined to stay overnight, there are 40 **campsites** where the park extends across Route 9.

The most popular point in the park is the summit of the mountain. From spring through early fall the trails of the area rustle with the sounds of small animals and the footfalls of **hikers** young and old. If you are still in the freeway frame of mind (tsk, tsk!), the 0.2-mile Summit Trail is a quick up and down. The trailhead is located at the rear of the upper parking lot. It is steep enough to require the stone steps built into several areas. This helps the hiker and slows the loss of topsoil.

If you are in a more relaxed mood, the 1.0-mile Northern Loop Trail is another way to the top. This trail begins at the far end of the upper parking lot near the rest rooms. It parallels a softball field and volleyball area. The stone walls woven through the woods are an immediate reminder that we are not the first people to walk here. Much of the present forest was pasture once. Just 800 feet from the trailhead is a high rock enclosure between the trail and Route 9—a 200-year-old **cattle pound** where stray animals were kept until bailed out by their owners.

The trail angles away from the road around the shoulder of the hill and begins up a moderate grade where it meets the Terrace Trail, a more direct, steeper route to the top at 0.4 mile. At this same intersection,

Nature reclaims the work of humans: lichen-covered rocks of the old cattle pound.

the Ski Trail, an extension of the Tote Road Trail, also joins the Northern Loop.

To continue a leisurely approach, veer to the right and slightly downhill to remain on the Northern Loop as it swings through the young forest. About 500 feet from the Terrace Trail, notice the orange blaze of the Boundary Trail tracing the limits of the park. From this point on, the Northern Loop cuts left and, following a seasonal stream on the right, crosses the Tote Road Trail. The vegetation along the trail is still young forest. Gray birches, only a few inches in diameter, with shiny leaves shaped like toothed arrowheads, are a common sight. Moosewood (striped maple) produces a greenish bark with the namesake vertical stripes. Its leaves, which turn a bright yellow in fall, have three large pointed lobes shaped like a goose foot. Areas where the canopy opens produce common juniper, a low-spreading evergreen with half-inch pointed needles and blue green berries used in making gin. Whorled wood aster, with its large, toothed leaves and delicate white flower heads, is found in the more open areas.

About 700 feet beyond the Tote Road Trail junction, the Northern Loop Trail enters a grove of young beech. The smooth gray bark of these trees contrasts with the coarser surface of the surrounding oak and pine. The leaves are strongly serrated and remain on the branch through the winter. On the left, a 100-foot unmarked trail leads up to an open patch of ledge. This is the beginning of the red-blazed Bluff Trail, with its pleasant view of the countryside. (The blaze consists of faint red marks on the open areas of ledge.) There is a 60-foot drop from the ledge, so keep a hand on young ones. The

Striped maple is also known as goose-foot maple for the shape of its leaves.

Bluff Trail parallels the Northern Loop Trail. Apart from the initial danger of the high area of ledge, this trail is easy for all. Halfway along this avenue, on a steep hemlock-covered slope to the left, the Terrace Trail joins the Bluff Trail.

The Bluff Trail rejoins the Northern Loop Trail and the terrain levels out. From this point there is only a small gain in elevation to reach the **summit.**

The peak opens onto a large granite **ledge** facing east toward the sea. Visible from here are Harpswell, Freeport, Wolfe's Neck, and Portland on the southern horizon. The spot is large enough for several families to picnic comfortably. There is a significant drop from the ledge. Keep a close watch on younger hikers. The most direct route back to the parking lot is the 1,000-foot-long Summit Trail.

For a **secluded,** quiet walk, try the Knight Woods Loop. The trail leaves the upper parking lot, crosses Route 9 and separates from the Link Trail (used by snowmobiles in winter), and heads right. The Knight Woods Loop is a bit narrower than the Link Trail and is marked with a white blaze. The path meanders through a young mixed forest. It quickly brings the hiker across a stone wall on the left that marks the other branch of the Knight Woods Loop. Go straight ahead. This path parallels Route 9 off to the right and snakes along the forest floor. Rotting stumps indicate the area was heavily logged in the past. **Glacial** activity has scattered large rounded boulders through the region. The rich, soft ground cover is springy to the step and understory plants abound. Early spring and summer show a variety of true mosses, ferns, and club mosses. Wild lily of the valley, with its two bright green leaves, supports a small head of white flowers in spring and speckled red berries in late summer and fall. This lily is normally accompanied by the wood anemone, a five-petaled nodding bloom with three deeply cut leaves.

The trail slopes gently downhill along Route 9. As it turns away from the road it levels out. At the point where it joins a short spur to the Snowmobile Trail, the Knight Woods Loop begins to work up a gentle gradient, regaining the elevation lost on the initial portion of the trail. A left turn and a fieldstone wall mark the end of the loop walk. It is 200 feet to the parking area.

When the urge to get away from life in the fast lane has the upper hand, Bradbury Mountain State Park offers a prescription for peace and tranquility. The picnic, hiking, and camping facilities provide a wonderful place to slow down and relax.

Getting There

A pleasant way to get to Bradbury Mountain State Park is Route 9. Pick up Route 9 east in Portland and follow it about 17 miles to the park entrance. Travel Route 9 west from Lisbon Falls (10 miles) and Durham (6 miles). The quicker, less scenic route is from Exit 20 on I-95. From this exit follow the signs for Pownal, about 200 feet to a stop sign. Turn left and follow Pownal Road (Elmwood Road) to Pownal Center. At the only light, turn right onto Route 9. The park is 0.3 mile on the left.

25. Austin Cary Lot

Harpswell
200 Acres

Estuarine Uplands
2–4 miles
2–4 hours

At first glance on a map of this region, it is difficult to distinguish between peninsulas and islands. Both send fingerlike roots into the dark cold waters of the Gulf of Maine. Roads run north-south only to dead-end on rocky ledges, brought up short by an unbroken horizon of blue against blue.

The town of Harpswell, set off from North Yarmouth and incorporated as a separate town in 1758, is more water than solid earth. Connected to the mainland by bridges and a narrow strip of land, Harpswell's political boundaries encompass about 40 islands. Although lumbering, shipbuilding, and subsistence farming were practiced by early inhabitants, bedrock protrusions form the spine of the islands and topsoil is limited to a few inches or less in most places. Now the mast trees are gone and farming must be supplemented with more practical pursuits. Fishing is still an important part of the economy—the older homes are fronted by docks and at least one boat—but today many people leave each day for mainland jobs in Bath and Brunswick.

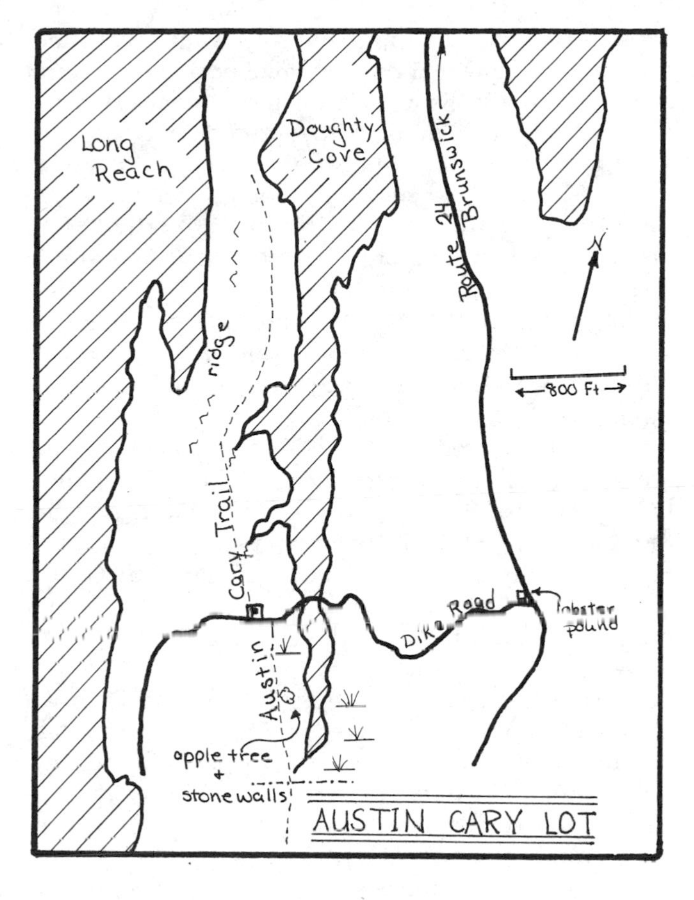

This hike is the least: the one you are least likely to find on first try, least likely that you will keep to the trail, least likely to see another person traveling. The property—a gift of former governor Percival Baxter to the people of Maine—appears to receive little real attention or management and is reverting back to its natural state. Traces of previous inhabitants—**stone walls, cellar holes,** and **remnant orchards**—guard the walk.

The southern section of trail leaves Dike Road on the left, 500 feet past the end of the earthen causeway over Doughty Cove. Travel an additional 200 feet beyond to the parking area on the right. The northern section of trail begins here.

Heading south, the path enters the woods in a grassy area bordered by **sensitive and spinulose wood-ferns** beneath a stand of white pines. The trail continues through a cluster of sprouting balsam fir intermingled with red spruce, red maple, and red oak. Although the footpath parallels Doughty Cove, you do not glimpse the marsh until 0.3 mile. At 0.4 mile there is a vague fork to the left, while the main path swings right, passing a large divided white pine on the left. In 200 feet cross a stone wall in its southwest corner. Climb to a high point, pass through the stone wall again, and descend slightly.

The open area before you is probably the site of an old homestead. The apple tree on the left is completely hollow except for a shell of bark, yet it still sustains leaves and produces fruit. It brings to mind the protected hollow tree at Baxter's other southern Maine preserve on Mackworth Island (see p. 150). Watch for woodchuck holes in the tall grass.

From the clearing, the trail makes a sharp right in a stand of white pine. The bank slopes steeply to a wash on the left. Flat areas in the open area below might be a good spot for picnics. Keep an eye out for

Doughty Cove, a portion of the productive Harpswell Sound.

the exposed roots crossing the footpath. These indicate shallow soils.

At 0.8 mile the trail crosses into private land. The owners have posted the area open to hiking and cross-country skiing but do not allow fires, hunting, or off-road vehicles. You may continue another 0.4 mile across their property and the northernmost section of Doughty Cove, but please be respectful of the kindness of these landowners.

Return to Dike Road and walk west 200 feet to the parking area. Directly across from the parking area is a **sphagnum bog.** Although not large in size, this bog is not likely to fill in anytime in the near future. Unlike other shallow wet areas that tend to undergo succession fairly rapidly as shrubs encroach along the borders and leaves and other sediments collect along the bottom, sphagnum creates self-perpetuating conditions. The plant is a virtual sponge. More than 90 percent of its mass is water. In some places it forms thick floating mats that can help slow evaporation. As the plant dies it produces an acid too strong for most other organisms to survive, including bacteria that aid decomposition. Often the only plants that tolerate the harsh environment are cranberries, a few sedges, insectivores (sundew and pitcher plants), and black spruce. Over hundreds of years the bogs can become several feet thick with repeating layers of dead but never decomposed organisms. The accumulated material is called peat.

Following the northern section of trail, pass to the left of the earthen berm blocking vehicular passage. Proceed under large white pines, noticing northern sarsaparilla, violets, brambles, and an understory of balsam fir. The violets and sarsaparilla are early spring flowering plants. After its blooms are past, the violet is seldom noticed, as its small cluster of heart-shaped leaves blend in with other ground plants. The **sarsaparilla,** one to three feet high, is much more noticeable. Each of its three leaves is divided into three-to-five-toothed leaflets. Although the root was used as an ingredient in root beer, the berries are poisonous.

The path here is a wide, old woods road sprinkled with pine cones. Watch for shelf fungi and mushrooms in the wet cool of autumn. This is an ideal environment in which to study **fungi.** Much of the trail is shady and wet, ocean breezes moderate temperatures, and decomposing leaves litter the ground. You may see bright orange jellies, sulfur yellow slime molds, amanitas with red and white warts, tiny cups of bird's nests, or blue-staining boleti.

Although the moisture is great for mushrooms, you may prefer to keep dry. After a rain, this trail may have several inches of water in some places. Come prepared with rubber-bottomed boots.

Game trails join from the left, just before the path enters a hemlock stand and descends to an intermittent stream at 0.2 mile. You may glimpse an inlet of Doughty Cove through the trees on the right. This trail never sidles up to the edge of the cove. It was originally constructed as an access road to private camps built on the north end of this peninsula. The camps have been abandoned for decades, but the road remains relatively high and dry. If you would like to get a closer view of the water and the wildlife that may be feeding there, it is necessary to **bushwhack.**

Because it is very difficult to get lost on a narrow strip of land bordered on three sides by water with a woods road running down the middle and dirt road at the other end, this is probably one of the safest places imaginable for trail-less walking. But there are some precautions you should take. Watch where you step. Unlike trails or roads, the footing in open woods is uneven and marked with small animal burrows, some covered and some not. Especially near water, be on the lookout for the eggs of ground-nesting birds, such as mallards, black ducks, and common eider. Try to walk quietly so as not to disturb dabbling ducks or darting herons. Feeding time is precious, particularly during migration when birds must conserve precious fat

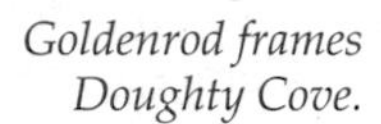

Goldenrod frames Doughty Cove.

reserves, and animals are a lot more fun to observe when they are unaware of your presence.

In tidal areas, there are two additional concerns: slippery mud on exposed banks at low tide and rocky outcrops that create sudden drop-offs or are covered with slippery algae. This is a very isolated trail that does not receive lots of use. Although that is particularly nice if you prefer solitude and a wilder environment, it means you are much less likely to receive help from a passerby if you should sprain an ankle, especially if you are not on the trail.

With that in mind, occasional short jaunts to the water's edge are recommended as the best way to see what this parcel really offers. Consider bringing field glasses and sitting quietly there.

At 0.4 mile, a game trail leads to the right from the main trail to the water's/estuary's edge. Look for tunnels in muddy banks indicating the excavations of wildlife. Watch quietly from a distance, but do not approach too closely.

The trees in this section of trail are the same age, indicating recent logging. In addition, you may note decaying stump remains and log piles that were never removed. In time, these decomposing remnants will provide nutrients for new growth. Some fallen trees actually serve that purpose before they are completely decomposed. Seeds lodge in the rotted wood and sprout new life. When this happens the dead tree is referred to as a nursery log.

Barberry plants on the left indicate that you have traveled approximately 0.6 mile from your car and are nearing the boundaries of this public parcel. The barberry is an introduced species that has escaped from gardens and become naturalized in fields and woods. This woody shrub grows 3 to 10 feet in height. It can be identified by its uncommon habit of growing leaves in tiny rosettes along the arching branches. Scarlet berries droop beneath each rosette. There are no signs to indicate private land.

This is a good spot to try one more go at bushwhacking. If you climb to the top of the ridge at sunset, you will receive a spectacular view of the quiet waters of Long Reach and the isolated lands along this peninsula.

Getting There

From the intersection of Routes 1 and 24, drive 5 miles south along Route 24 (1.25 miles south from the bridge crossing Gurnet Strait between Brunswick and Harpswell). The entrance to Dike Road (also called Long Reach Road or Chatigie Road) appears to be the driveway of a lobster pound. Continue beyond the pound and two homes, keeping to the right. Within a half-mile, the dirt road descends to the marsh at the south end of Doughty Cove. One-tenth of a mile past the far side of this short earthen causeway, the trail leaves the road on the left and travels in a southerly direction for more than a mile. Parking for two cars is available on the right 200 feet beyond.

For more information call Baxter Park Authority at 207-723-5140.

26. Popham Beach State Park

Phippsburg
600 Acres

Sandy Beach

2.9 miles

3 hours

In 1607, two ships, the *Gift of God* and the *Mary and John,* set sail from Plymouth, England, for the northern Virginia Colony. Their mission was to establish the first permanent British settlement in the New World. Funded in part by Sir John Popham and commanded by George Popham, the undertaking became known as the Popham Colony. They chose a site at the mouth of the Sagadahoc River, now known as the Kennebec, and began erecting a fort, storehouse, and living quarters. The intention of the founders was to establish a plantation, begin trading with the native people for furs, harvest timber for shipbuilding and fish for export, and explore for minerals.

Unfortunately, the colony failed in little more than a year. When both Pophams died and the second in command, Raleigh Gilbert, returned to England to attend to his late brother's affairs, the colony was left without leadership. In addition, the remaining colonists

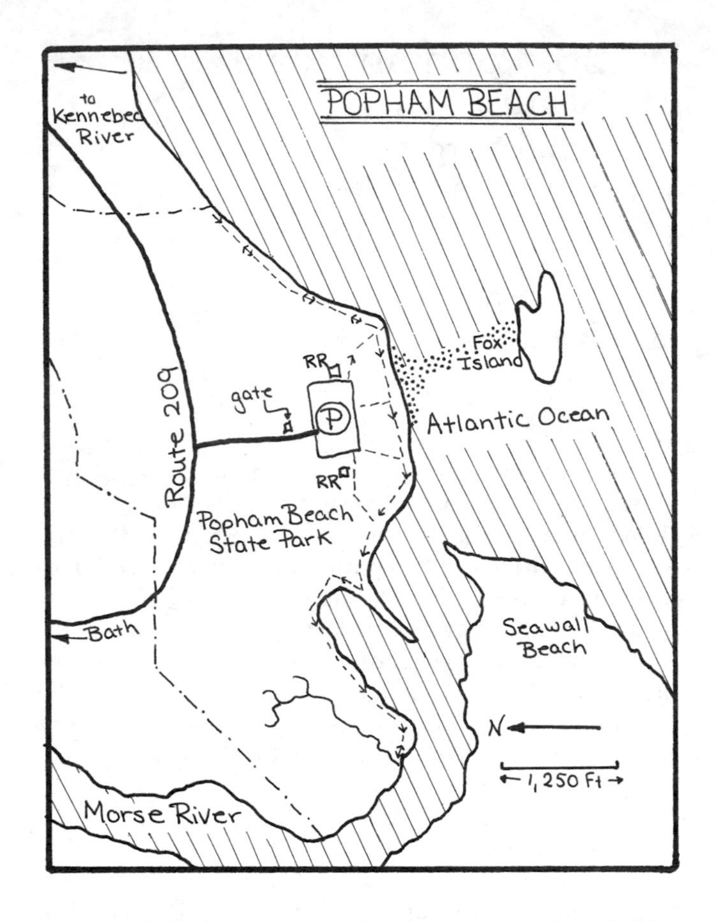

were unskilled, vagrant, and corrupt—not a bunch likely to take well to difficult conditions and hard labor. When the going got tough, they opted to board ship and head back to England.

The Popham name remains to mark this early attempt at colonization. The preservation of large tracts of land on the Phippsburg Peninsula, including acres of marsh, more than a mile of undeveloped shoreline, and expansive island views, reminds us of the beauty that existed when they came to this strange new land. Today it would be difficult to imagine abandoning this place.

Excluding the paths leading from the parking area to the water, there are no trails at Popham except for the one made by the rising and falling of the tides. It is easily maintained by the traffic it receives and endangered only by too many footfalls. The view from the length of the sand beach is punctuated by islands. From east to west the smaller near islands are Pond, Wood, Fox, and Heron. Seguin Island and its lighthouse mark the entrance into the Kennebec and the access for ships making passage up the river to Bath Iron Works (BIW). BIW is one of the largest contractors for navy destroyers and one of the largest employers in Maine, a fitting tribute to the boatbuilders of Popham Colony.

The **sand beach** runs east-west, then turns north at the mouth of the Morse River. The distance from the eastern boundary of the park to the marsh grasses of the Morse River estuary is approximately **1.5 miles.** At low tide this hike may be extended to include the rocky headlands via an exposed sand spit. At high tide the last stretch along the Morse River may be impassable.

The best time to visit Popham is during the week or after Labor Day. On hot sunny days the beach can be crowded. A modest fee is requested at the gate of the large parking lot. Bathrooms and bathhouses are available at the far right and far left corners. There are four trails to the beach. Three are about 500 feet in length and the fourth (far right) is 1,050 feet. No dogs are allowed.

Beginning the hike from the east, leave the parking lot on the left, pass the bathhouses, and keep right. There will be several picnic tables on your right before you reach the beach. Stepping out onto the wide expanse of sand and breathing in the marine horizon expands the soul. Here at the edge of the land, you may dream about distant voyages, choices not yet explored, and future possibilities.

Bring a field guide, such as Judith Hansen's *Seashells in My Pocket: A Child's Nature Guide to Exploring the Atlantic Coast* (AMC Books), to the seashore and head east. Beaches are for discovering small treasures, and there are many to be found here. Some of the shells may even tell the silent story of their owner's demise. Occasionally you may turn over the shell of that tasty Maine delicacy, the **steamer clam.** These shells are rough, oblong, and chalky white. If the shell has a perfectly round quarter-inch hole grazed in it, the steamer was eaten alive by a **moon snail.** This snail uses the rows of sharp teeth on its tongue to slowly rasp away at the steamer clam's shell. Having breached the protective covering, it then uses those same teeth to rip flesh from the live clam.

Sometimes the shells of **blue mussels**—dark blue to bluish black on the outside, white on the inside with violet margins—also show evidence of predation. In this case, the holes are symmetrical, but they are considerably smaller. The culprit this time is the eastern **dog whelk**, or winkle. Shells of both the predator and prey are common along the beaches of southern Maine.

The sands of Popham Beach have a pinkish hue when compared to many other Maine beaches. The strong currents of the Kennebec River carry the erosion products of bedrock granite, depositing them in the quiet waters of the ocean's shallows. Flecks of mica catch the sun and shimmer. Tumbled grains of **garnet** collect in the ripples. Mixed with quartz particles, they paint the beach a reddish color.

The eastern boundary of the park is reached 0.3 mile from the access trail. Beyond this point are private homes. Turning toward the western boundary, continue to scan the sand for shells. False quahog are common; the true quahog would be a rare find. This once plentiful bivalve was used as a medium of exchange during the colonial era (hence its Latin name *Mercenaria mercenaria,* meaning "money money") but is now scarce due to overharvesting.

Three hundred feet beyond the first path to the beach is the second path, now on your right. Directly across from it on the left is a **sand spit,** called a **tombolo,** which at low tide connects the mainland to the rocky headland of Fox Island. This is a great place to explore with children or to spend a few hours reading a good book. The distance to the island is 0.2 mile. Rockweed, barnacles, and blue mussels climb the rock marking the water depth at high tide. Clinging to the shallow soils are salt-tolerant seaside goldenrod and seaside plantain. Beneath them note the twisted spine of the bedrock. Course granite intrudes into vertically folded schist. Return to the mainland before high tide, as the narrow water passage makes for dangerous currents.

A tombolo leads to Fox Island at low tide.

Note two more paths leading down to the beach from the parking lot. One is 450 feet beyond the sand spit and the last is another 300 feet farther. The final trail also leads behind the sand dunes to a shaded picnic area nestled under pitch pine.

As you return to the water's edge, the shoreline curves north along the Morse River. Erosion is evident in the dunes on the right. In places, there is a three-foot drop from the base of the grasses to the sand below. Here their deep-branching roots are exposed to the sometimes gentle, sometimes fierce, wind. The breeze sweeps away the firmly held sand collected over years, maybe decades, of slow, creeping growth. Even on a relatively quiet day you can observe the formation of pyramidal piles of sand collecting along the base of the bank. Occasional streamers, like the sand in an hour-glass, cascade downward. This is powerful evidence of the importance of the netlike roots to erosion control. In calmer years, or in sheltered spots, sand is deposited and the plants creep forward to reclaim the beach. They will continue their seaward march if they are undisturbed.

As the beach narrows and the tall grasses approach the water, scan the marsh for the characteristic low flight of the **northern harrier,** or marsh hawk—a bird the size of a crow. It barely skims the tops of the grasses as it searches intently for rodents and small birds. Males

Dune grasses are an important defense against beach erosion.

are pale gray and females are streaked brown. The females prefer mammals and the males prefer birds. Both sexes are strong enough first to drown, then take small waterfowl. If you are unsure of their identification, look for a white patch on the rump. In addition, feathers around the eyes form a shallow dish, similar to an owl's, which funnels sound. Like an owls, the ear openings are in the feathers just behind the dish.

Backtrack along the beach. As you return, any of the four trails to the left through the dunes leads back to the parking lot.

Getting There

From Bath, take Route 209 southeast 15.4 miles from its intersection with Route 1. This will be 3.5 miles southeast of Route 209's intersection with Route 206. The well-marked gate is on your right.

For more information call 207-389-1335.

27. Reid State Park

Georgetown
766 Acres

Sandy Beach
2.0–4.2 miles
4 hours

Reid State Park was donated to the people of Maine in the 1940s by Walter Reid and his family. Reid, a native of Georgetown, purchased the land in smaller parcels and then consolidated them. He first gave Griffith Head, then Todd's Point. His intent was solely to provide access for all to the beautiful sand beaches of mid-coast Maine.

The park has several ecological niches. The **sand beaches, rocky headlands, sand dunes, marsh,** and **upland woods** provide habitats for a variety of different species. Most visitors to the park come to enjoy the surf and are unaware of the rich mélange just beyond the sand dunes.

There are two walks. The first stretches the 2.1-mile length of the park's three beaches, beginning at the northeast boundary with East Beach and terminating at the southwest boundary, the Little River. The second walk is designed as a 2.0 mile ski trail but can also be hiked in summer.

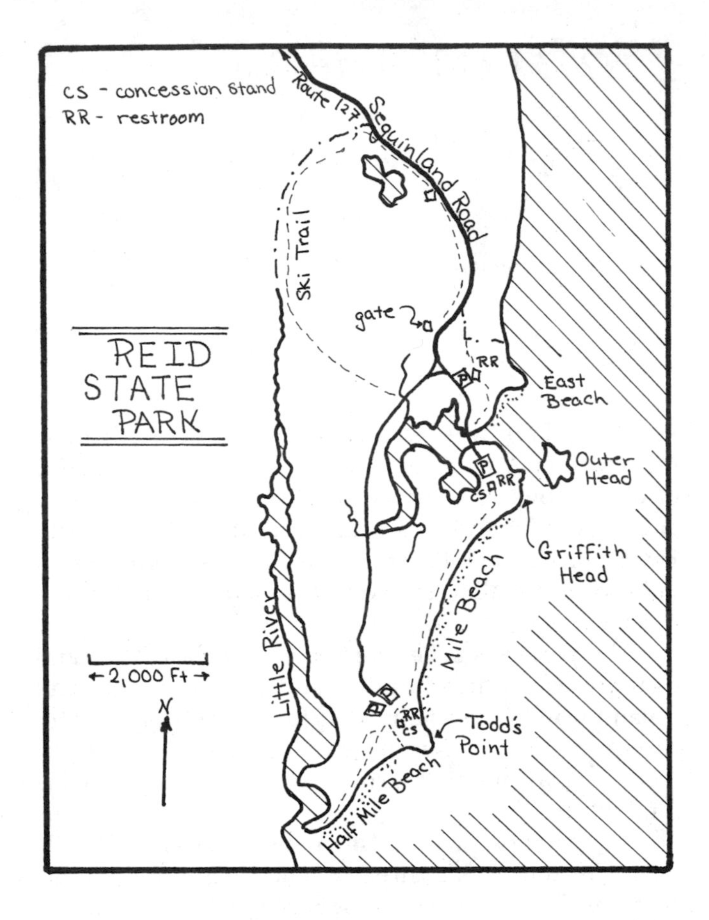

The beach walk can be reached from any one of the three parking and picnic areas: East Beach, Griffith Head, or Todd's Point. Each has rest rooms, and Griffith Head and Todd's Point have concession stands and bathhouses. To begin at East Beach, take a right at the junction just after the toll gate (fee is levied per person), and park in the first parking lot on the left. The offshoot trail on the left, through the woods to the eastern boundary, is 0.2 mile in length, passing the rest rooms and four secluded picnic tables in the woods. To reach the beach, go to the far end of the parking lot. The view is striking. There is little hint on your approach of such expansiveness. The rocky heads on either end of the beach add visual relief to the curve of sand and seemingly endless stretch of water.

Turn right, passing several picnic tables and barbecue pits. It is 0.1 mile to the stream exiting the marsh and lagoon. Cross on the bridge or ford the stream. The water here will be significantly warmer than the open ocean as it has been warmed in the shallows of the wetlands. The stream is a good place to look for tide pool organisms. Hum to the periwinkles if you want them to open their trap doors and come out. Turn over seaweed to expose **green and hermit crabs** at low tide. Be careful of their claws, and never attempt to pull a hermit crab from its recycled snail shell. The shell is its only protection from predators, it will allow you to tear it limb from limb (thus killing it), before it will let go.

From the bridge, there are great views of the marsh. Cormorants sit low in the water with only their necks and head showing, dive for fish, or rest on a rock drying their wings. **Great blue herons** and **snowy egrets** stand motionless in the shallows waiting for the right moment to strike at unsuspecting fish and crabs. Mallards, red-breasted mergansers, scoters, and common loons appear more plentiful in the fall as they arrive here from their freshwater breeding grounds to winter in the relative safety of the open, iceless waters of the ocean.

On the far side of the stream is a 0.1-mile sand spit that extends out to a small island, Outer Head, at mid- to low tide. This is a favorite spot for many visitors to the park who have harbored a dream of escaping to an island off the coast of Maine or who feel comforted by being surrounded by water on all sides. It is a place to catch the sun, picnic, read a good book, or dream. Remember to keep an eye on the tide to avoid being stranded when it comes in.

Follow the beach or the path along the road to Griffith Head, a high knob of coarse-grained white granite. The wood is a community of pitch pine, white spruce, large-toothed aspen (poplar), and staghorn sumac. Cross the 750-foot length of the parking lot. Notice the **lagoon** down the slope from the bathhouse. This quiet spot behind the dunes is perfect for those who cannot tolerate the cool temperatures of Maine's coastal waters. The lagoon's water is usually 10 degrees warmer than the surf. For those with small children, there are benches, picnic tables, and a lifeguard. On the far side of the lagoon, waterfowl will continue to make a living diving and dabbling while bathers splash.

To reach Mile Beach (really 0.75 mile in length), follow the path at the far right of the parking lot through beach rose's summerlong, large, fragrant, five-petal blossoms; meadowsweet's pink spire of tiny August blossoms; blackberry and raspberry brambles; and the tiny, waxy blue berries of the bayberry. On the ocean side of the dunes, you will immediately experience a drop in air temperature. Heed the signs indicating the importance of the sand dunes and walk only on the beach. Without the fragile plants and their root systems, the dunes would be swept away by storm erosion and the marsh would be breached. The grasses, mustards, and beach pea are responsible for anchoring the sand and making this beach possible. The dunes also provide nesting habitat for endangered bird species, making it doubly important not to trespass.

At the end of Mile Beach, follow the trail to the right, crossing Todd's Point, or climb around on the rocks to the left. Facing the ocean in front of the bathhouse, take the trail to the right for Half Mile Beach. Pass picnic tables and grills on your left.

In 0.1 mile the trail forks. To the left is a short trail to the beach. To the right the trail takes you behind the dunes for a view of the marsh before crossing to the ocean side in 400 feet. These are the northernmost dunes in Maine. Notice how thin the barrier is between the marsh and ocean. The sand on Half Mile Beach is finer than the coarse grains of Mile Beach. This indicates it has been carried farther. Scuff your feet as you walk, and the dry finer-grained sand will sing to you.

Sanderlings are the little birds chasing the retreating waves. They are searching the sands for invertebrates—tiny "shrimp" and worms that come up to feed when the water covers them. The birds feed in small flocks that seem to be coordinated by a master brain. When approached they fly off as a group in the same direction. How do they know which way to go? Why don't they scatter in all directions like a flock of chickens? Another curious habit you may observe is the one-

Estuaries are a productive and vitally important part of the seaside ecosystem.

legged stance. Constantly running in and out of the frigid surf leads to cold feet. Taking a short break in the sun and tucking one foot up next to the body can do wonders for the circulation.

During migration the sanderlings are often joined by plovers and ruddy turnstones. All of these birds are busy trying to eat enough to stay alive and continue their journey of hundreds or thousands of miles. The more time they must spend scattering before intruders, the less time they have to feed. If you can avoid walking in their path, please do so.

Half Mile Beach is truly a half-mile in length at high tide. At low tide it is a little bit longer, as the sand spit at the end of the Little River is exposed. The total length of the hike from East Beach to the Little River is 2.1 miles. Double that if you are backtracking to the East Beach.

The two-mile loop of the Cross-country Ski Trail can be accessed from behind the toll gate at the park entrance. It is marked by orange blazes on trees or by metal markers painted with orange diamonds inside a black border and nailed onto the trees. The trail goes north through the woods paralleling the entrance road. In 0.4 mile it passes behind the park office on Seguinland Road. For the next 0.6 mile it is within sight of the road skirting the edge of two large beaver ponds. The expansion of these ponds may make it necessary to walk along the shoulder of the road for a few feet. Notice the **turtle crosswalk** painted on the pavement between the ponds. This is a dangerous spot for turtles making the arduous springtime journey back to water.

Beaver ponds often seem like a nuisance to humans, but they are of great benefit to wildlife. All animals need water, and wetlands are especially productive. Fish, amphibians, reptiles, waterfowl, and the mammals that pursue them are all found in abundance here. Maine's native peoples considered beavers sacred and never hunted them except during the harshest winters. They were the ace in the hole if no other food could be found and, therefore, were not to be killed unless starvation threatened. The beaver lodge of woven branches advertised their presence and made them easy prey if it became necessary. The coming of European fur traders changed all that. When top hats of beaver skin became fashionable beaver became scarce. In many New England states, beaver were hunted to extinction. It is only in the last 50 years that they have staged a comeback and are now considered abundant.

On the far side of the second beaver pond, the trail enters the forest on the left along an old woods road. Pine needles cushion the forest floor and ferns edge the trail. This road is the park's northwest boundary. It continues along the back side of the ponds for approximately 0.5 mile before connecting with the dirt maintenance road. Bear left. In 0.4 mile the trail meets the paved road to Todd's Point. Turn left, passing an excellent view of the marsh on your right. Follow the pavement 0.1 mile back to the toll gate.

Reid State Park is open from 9:00 A.M. to sunset daily, year-round, and encourages winter visitors.

Getting There

Take Route 127 south from Route 1 in Woolwich 10.6 miles to the junction with Seguinland Road on your right. An American flag painted on a rock marks the turn. Travel 2.0 miles to the park gate. From the gate it is 0.2 mile to the parking lot for East Beach and 0.4 mile to the parking area for Griffith Head. Keep left for both. It is 1.25 miles to Todd's Point. Keep right.

For more information call 207-371-2303.

28. Josephine Newman Sanctuary

Georgetown

119 Acres

Estuarine Uplands

2.5 miles

3 hours

The Josephine Newman Sanctuary is a mixture of forest, estuary, and rocky coast, melding with remnants of mid-coast working farm fields and stone walls. The history of the place begins long before the arrival of Europeans.

Both the **Anasagunticooks** and **Kennebecs** (also called Canibas) lived, played, worked, and worshiped along the shore of midcoast Maine and plied their canoes within the bountiful waters of Merrymeeting Bay. By 1724, following the massacre at Norridgewock, they were a beaten people. They had been stripped of their land, livelihood, and dignity. The colonial English government had placed a bounty on their heads, and they were hunted down and killed for their scalps like animals. Those who could escaped to safety in Canada. A few survived in the upper tributaries of the Androscoggin River. By 1797, they no longer made the annual pilgrimage to consecrate the graves of ancestors on the lower reaches of the Androscoggin River. Too few remained to honor the dead.

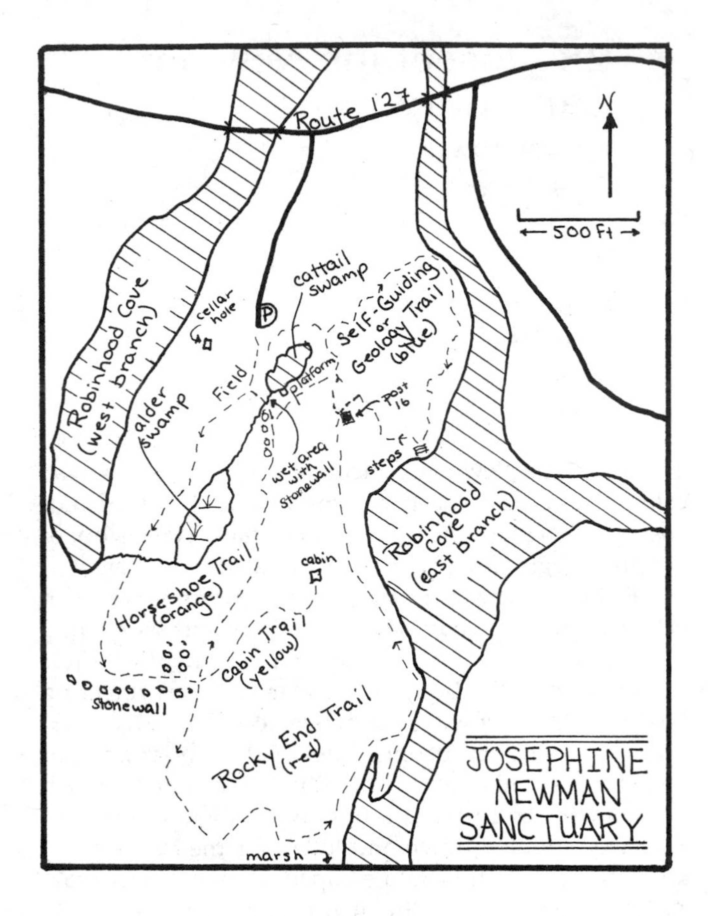

In a 1760 land deed that included portions of the Josephine Newman Sanctuary, Georgetown Island is referred to as Ruscohegan, alias Parker's Island. John Parker was the proprietor of the local trading post from

1650 to 1676. In the interim between 1676 and 1760, much of Georgetown Island and Arrowsic Island were abandoned. The repeated wars between the Europeans and Native Americans had made it impractical to attempt farming or maintain a trading post. With the defeat of the Indians and the cessation of hostilities, the Plymouth Council began to encourage resettlement in the area. Joseph Bubier received a grant of 214 acres bounded on one side by the east branch of Robinhood Cove and the other by the Kennebeck (sic) River on condition he reimburse the council 35 pounds in one year's time. Although a hefty sum for that era, it is the equivalent of 30 cents an acre today. At the time, the Massachusetts government (which included Maine in its jurisdiction) was offering 100 pounds for the scalp of an Anasagunticook brave.

This sanctuary has special meaning for me, as I am a descendant of the Anasagunticook and of Joseph Bubier. Although the Bubiers had only a brief occupation, it is here that two contrasting lines of ancestry are reconciled.

Josephine Oliver Newman, for whom the sanctuary is named, moved here as a young girl. The daughter of a Georgetown native, she became a respected naturalist specializing in mosses, liverworts, and lichens. In 1968, she willed the 119 acres that comprise this sanctuary to the Maine Audubon Society.

The trails of the Josephine Newman Sanctuary often parallel the old stone walls built by the first European settlers. Each rock was set in place by hand. As you follow a path, consider the number of times someone bent to scrape the dirt from around a rock, hefted it to their shoulder, walked to the stone wall, and carefully lowered it into its proper place. Then look around to see how many stones are still left on the ground. Each winter the frost forces rocks from beneath the soil and lays them on the surface. The winters are bitter cold. On a blustery February day, the wind sweeps across a field, turning granules of snow into sandblasters that pelt every square inch of exposed skin. The spring brings mud as the shallow soil easily becomes saturated with melting snow and rain. The bedrock holds pools of water in puddles, ponds, and lakes. Soon the black flies hatch and mosquitoes follow on their heels.

The Maine Audubon Society publishes an excellent guide booklet, *Forest, Fields, and Estuaries: A Guide to the Natural Communities of Josephine Newman Sanctuary,* which is available at its office in Falmouth. The guide is loaded with details about the site's ecology.

The sanctuary has three main trails. Each is a loop beginning and ending at the entrance to the field. The Rocky End Trail, blazed in red, is the longest at 1.3 miles and is also the most scenic. Start by crossing the near left (northeast) corner of the field. Along with the expected grasses and wildflowers, you will find naturalized flowers from the Newman garden. The house foundation is hidden in the northwest edge of the field. In early to mid-August the phlox begin to bloom, their pink heads contrasting with the more plentiful white and gold of the late-summer wildflowers. Pass through the poplar and alder border and into a mature forest.

For the first 400 feet, the Geology Trail or Self-Guiding Trail (blue blazes), the Horseshoe Trail (orange blazes), and the Rocky End Trail (red blazes) all follow the same path. As you enter a wet area and cross the first stone wall, the Geology Trail branches left, while the Horseshoe and Rocky End Trails continue right. As judged by the size of the trees, the forest is approximately 100 years old. The stone wall paralleling the trail on the right marks the border of an abandoned field. Tall branches of red oak and red maple filter the sunlight. Watch the upper branches carefully for the flight of a barred owl. In Native American mythology the owl sees what others cannot. It is believed that the bird sees through deception and receives wisdom through silent observation.

An owl is indeed silent in flight. Its feathers are edged in soft down. It has no abrupt edges to cut the wind. Active primarily at night, the owl has excellent hearing and eyesight. It waits quietly for any movement, then swoops down. By the time the unsuspecting prey is aware of its presence, it is too late. **Barred owls** feed on small rodents and some birds, particularly crows and blue jays.

Approximately 0.3 mile from the beginning of the walk, the Horseshoe Trail branches to the right. To the left is the Cabin Trail (yellow blazes). The Cabin Trail is 0.2 mile in length. It begins by cutting along the side then climbing a knoll through a red oak forest. Farther along it passes through a stand of mixed evergreen before ending at the tumbled remains of an old cabin. Retrace your steps to the intersection.

The Rocky End Trail continues straight ahead at the intersection. In 400 feet, it curves left. On the right is a small clearing of 100-year-old red oak, with smaller spruce, fir, and pine surrounding them.

At 0.1 mile from the clearing, the trail begins to climb over a ridge. There is a sturdy stone wall on your right composed of large angular blocks of schist. The age of the stone wall can be determined by identifying the species of lichens growing on the rocks. Most lichens grow at an established rate, some only a fraction of an inch in 100 years. One of the slowest growing lichens, the apple green map lichen, grows 0.4 inch in 1,000 years.

The crest of the ridge is the highest point in the sanctuary. Here the trail swings left and the east branch of Robinhood Cove appears through the trees on your right. Descend gradually for 0.2 mile to sea level. At this point, the trail curves right with faint hints of a game trail straight ahead. In 100 feet the path branches. Take the right fork 350 feet down a peninsula to the best picnic spot in the sanctuary. The bedrock peninsula extends into the cove, lending an air of quiet solitude. A cool breeze rustles the leaves and riffles the water. This is a good place to spot osprey and snowy egrets.

In August, **horseshoe crabs** molt. The tall grasses of the marsh catch the paper-thin sand-colored shells at high tide and hold them as the waters recede. Meanwhile, the former owners are rummaging through the bottom muck for worms and snails, their primary food source. These creatures and their molted shells are easily identifiable. The outline of their body is U-shaped with a long spinelike tail. Despite their tail and clawed feet, these arthropods are harmless. **Their ancestors were around long before the dinosaurs.** From fossil records, we know they are kin to the extinct trilobites that once roamed the seas. Although we call them crabs,

Shed shells of the horseshoe crab.

they are more closely related to spiders. Generally rare in Maine, horseshoe crabs are locally common in a few midcoast estuaries where hundreds of them may be seen mating in late June. Horseshoe crabs are also very important to the ecology in more-southern states like Delaware. In spring, millions of horseshoe crab eggs are eaten by migrating shorebirds in Chesapeake Bay. The eggs provide protein and fat reserves essential for refueling the birds on their energy-intensive journey.

Backtrack along this rocky spur, noticing the juniper, blueberry, white pine, and red oak. The shallow soils of the peninsula limit their stature. Returning to the main trail, continue straight ahead, keeping the cove on your right for 0.1 mile before curving to the left and leaving the water's edge. The trail begins to climb, steeply in places, over rocks and roots. Pass a vertical rock outcrop whitewashed with lichen before turning to the right onto a well-graded, old woods road.

At 1.25 miles, the Rocky End Trail intersects with the Geology Trail at post 16 of the Audubon self-guided tour. They travel together for 100 feet before the Geology Trail leaves to the left. After 200 feet they once again rejoin and continue together, returning to the sanctuary entrance. Cumulative length of the Rocky End Trail is 1.4 miles.

To begin the Horseshoe Trail cross the field, passing through hawkweed, goldenrod, and meadowsweet. After 650 feet it enters the woods. To the right, through the trees, the west branch of Robinhood Cove is visible. Approximately 0.4 mile from the trail's start, the path makes a sharp left turn—don't be confused by an unmarked trail that continues straight ahead. Cross a stone wall with a huge old maple on the right and continue to the intersection with the Cabin Trail (yellow blazes). Turn left, joining the Rocky End Trail. It is 0.3 mile back to the field paralleling the stone wall on your left through a forest of red oak and red maple. The total length of the trail is a little more than 0.8 mile.

The Geology Trail (blue blazes) is a self-guided nature walk with 20 points of interest. The descriptions are included in *Forest, Fields, and Estuaries.* Although it is the shortest of the three loops (less than 0.7 mile), it is also the most challenging as it climbs up and down the rocky ledges of Robinhood Cove in the northeast quadrant of the sanctuary. Facing the field, the trail begins on your left. It quickly enters the woods, passing a marshy area on the right. Piles of pine cone scales grace

Quiet waters of Robinhood Cove.

the bog bridges where red squirrels have lunched. The Rocky End Trail intersects on the right 250 feet from the trail's beginning, but follow the blue blazes.

At 0.2 mile, the trail turns right in a grove of hemlock overlooking the cove. Nearby are the **reversing falls.** When the tide is low, the stream drops down to the cove and you may hear water tumbling over the rocks. At high tide, the water in the cove rises above that in the stream and flows in the opposite direction. As you proceed, notice a vertical outcrop on your right. When this slab was first formed, these layers were horizontal. Four hundred and fifty million years ago, the continents of Europe and Africa collided with North America, forming the Appalachian Mountains, crushing and folding these rocks with enormous pressure and heat.

Watch the ground to see how many varieties of cones you can identify. Study the trunks of the trees. Can you tell the different kinds apart by the color and texture of their bark? Find two trees that appear the same. Look up to see if the needles also match. Do they have the same cones? The evergreen trees found along the trail include eastern hemlock, balsam fir, red spruce, and white pine. **Hemlock** have flat needles a half-inch in length and produce the smallest cones of the group. **Balsam** fir also have flat needles, but they are one-half to one inch in length. Their cones, two to three inches in length, have the unusual habit of growing upright near the tips of the branches. **Red spruce** have pointed angular needles that are prickly to the touch. Spruce cones are one to two inches in length and hang down from the branch. **Pines** have the longest needles, from three to four inches long, and the longest cones, six to eight inches.

The trail climbs through evergreens to a dry rocky ridge, then descends to the cove about 0.4 mile from the hike's start. On the left are wooden steps leading down to the water's edge at high tide or the mudflats at low tide. Sitting quietly you may be able to observe **wading birds** feeding along the margins, **ducks** dabbling in the weeds, or **cormorants** diving for fish in open water.

From the steps, it is less than 0.2 mile to the junction with the Rocky End Trail. After the junction go right 90 feet, then left following the blue blazes, skirting the edge of the **cattail swamp.** On your right is a wooden platform for viewing the marsh without getting wet feet. Large lily pads block a view of the water directly in front.

At the end of the marsh, rejoin the Rocky End Trail, turn right, and emerge into the field.

Getting There

Follow Route 1 to Route 127 south in Woolwich, just east of the Woolwich/Bath bridge. Travel 9.1 miles. The sign announcing the entrance to the sanctuary is on the right just after the Georgetown post office and the bridge over Robinhood Cove. Turn right and follow the dirt entrance road to a small parking area (space for 12 to 15 cars).

For more information call the Maine Audubon Society at 207-781-2330.

29. Steve Powell Game Management Area—Swan Island

Perkins Township/Richmond
175 Acres

Estuarine Uplands
0.5–10.7 miles
0.5–8 hours

Spending an overnight on Swan Island allows the best opportunity to relax and truly enjoy the gift of the Steve Powell Game Management Area. **Adirondack-style lean-tos for sleeping** border a large field overlooking the waters of Merrymeeting Bay. Bring a folding chair and sit in the sun, a cool breeze feathering wisps of hair, setting the grass to dancing, and muffling the distant call of crows. In August, fall dandelion is in bloom, purple clover bends unsteadily before the wind, and the grasses are alive with the chatter of insects. Crickets chirp feverishly, locust wings clatter, a dragonfly pursues a panicked butterfly, and evening brings the occasional high-pitched drone of cicadas.

Choose your lean-to carefully because acorns falling from overhanging oaks sound like pelting rocks—a startling occurrence as you're dozing off to sleep. Drinking water and firewood are provided. There is a fee for

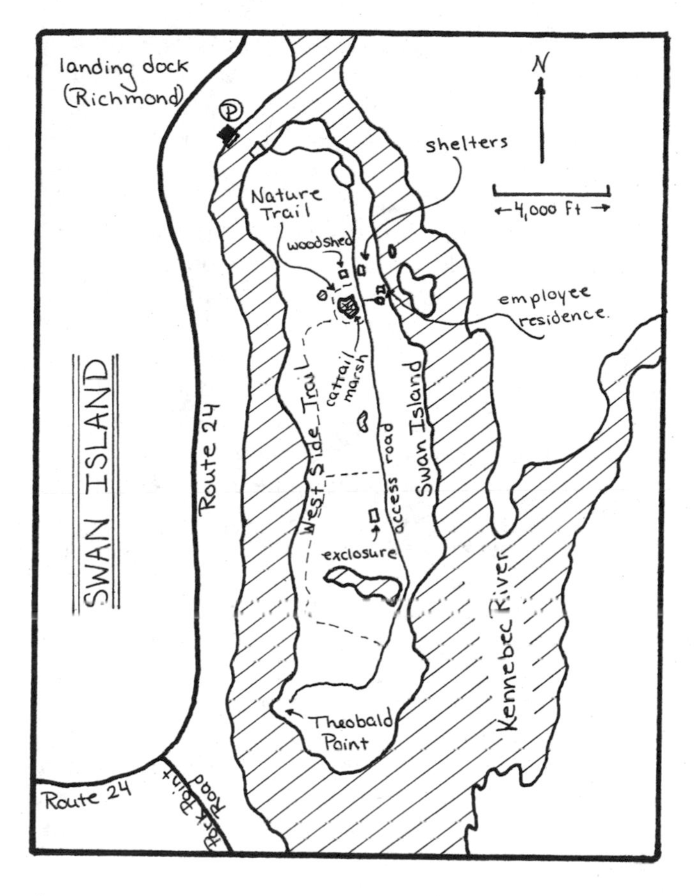

day and overnight visits, and bookings must be made in advance. The ferry to the island runs by reservation only. If you miss your appointed time, there may not be another one.

When making reservations, request a copy of *Steve Powell Wildlife Management Area: A History and Self-Guiding Tour.* This brochure discusses the rich chronicle of the island and its ecology. In addition, conservation technicians give daily tours for interested guests. The Maine Conservation Corps has built two trails on the island. The first, the Nature Trail, departs from the island's access road just beyond the woodshed across from the campground. This hike, blazed in yellow, is 0.6 mile in length. The West Side Trail, blazed in red, branches from the Nature Trail. The West Side Trail traverses 2.9 miles of the island's length and terminates on the southern end of the access road. Walk the dirt track back at dusk for great deer-watching opportunities.

The access road is also the route of the self-guiding tour. **Native Americans** resided on this island long before Europeans arrived. They called it Swango, Island of Eagles (today there are two active eagle nests). Europeans visited in 1607 and Captain John Smith stopped here in 1614. Although the island was purchased from the Kennebecs in 1614 and again in 1667, there is no record of Europeans actually living on the island until 1730. The community grew to a population of 95 by 1860. Residents worked at farming, fishing, lumbering, shipbuilding, and ice cutting. By 1900, many of these industries were in decline and the population shrank. The Department of Inland Fisheries and Wildlife began to purchase land as residents left in the 1940s. The island's **tidal flats** are rich feeding ground for **wild ducks.** The open fields provide food for migrating Canada geese, and the forest floor, showered with acorns and beechnuts, is ideal habitat for the reintroduction of **wild turkey.** By the 1950s the only remaining piece of private land was the cemetery. The family plots around the island had been dug up and the remains reinterred in the community site. In 1971, the Swan Island Game Management Area was renamed to honor the memory of one of its first biologists and benefactor, Stephen E. Powell.

Some of the island's historic landmarks and many of its game management practices are outlined in the self-guiding tour. This walk is highly recommended, as is the pickup-truck tour provided by the department's personnel. Consider packing a lunch to take with you on the tour and walking back along the West Side Trail.

The yellow-blazed Nature Trail is a wide path and easy to follow. Leaving the woodshed the trail dips slightly, passing thistle, speckled alder, and raspberry bushes. Behind the shrubs is a forest of red oak, white ash, and hemlock. In 0.1 mile, on the right, you will notice a strange setup of benches and logs. This is the test camp for Junior Maine Guides, a program that teaches teens to navigate and survive in the deep woods. Continue to the edge of a field, then follow its border on the left. As you reenter the woods notice the brush pile on your right. It may look unsightly, but it provides important shelter to wildlife. Hares, squirrels, grouse, and small rodents are protected from wind, heavy snows, and predators under the woven branches.

At 0.3 mile, cross a footbridge over a draw with a cattail marsh on your right. Notice the duck boxes (large bird houses) on poles or dead trees. These artificial cavities are provided for common goldeneyes, hooded mergansers, and wood ducks, and are placed

Aluminum tree bands keep marauding predators from ducks that nest in tree cavities.

over water to protect the nesting duck and her eggs from predators. In a wilderness setting, woodpeckers excavate large old trees to feed on wood-boring insects, creating nesting holes for birds and mammals. As humans harvest mature trees, there are fewer and fewer nesting sites available to ducks. Without these natural or artificial homes, reproduction fails and duck populations decline. The Department of Inland Fisheries and Wildlife maintains 21 duck boxes on the island.

In addition to duck boxes, the department has also placed a number of bluebird houses throughout the area. These birds were also in decline throughout much of their range due to a lack of nesting sites and competition from introduced species. Although many of these houses are occupied by tree swallows, four **bluebird** pairs successfully fledged young in 1994.

Pass a rustic wooden bench on the left, followed by hay-scented fern, sweet fern, and pearly everlasting (pearly everlasting has long, thin, white, woolly leaves, spiraling up a stem, crowned with a yellow tufted flower cradled in pearly white, petal like bracts). Descend slightly and cross an earthen dam separating the wood duck marsh on the left from an alder thicket on the right. In August, the bright yellow and black stripes of the **monarch butterfly** caterpillar will catch your eye immediately if you inspect the milkweed plants growing here. The bright coloration is a warning to any would-be predators that this insect is inedible. The milky juice of the milkweed plant is bitter and mildly toxic. When the caterpillar ingests leaves, it retains the same quality. This characteristic is passed on to the adult monarch, but the warning colors change from yellow to bright orange red. The message is the same, "Eat me and you'll regret it."

On the far side of the earthen dam, the West Side Trail diverges to the right. The Nature Trail continues left and skirts the edge of the marsh. Benches are provided for observation of wetlands wildlife. Listen for the wood duck whistle or the rattle of a belted kingfisher. Watch the ground for the iridescent feathers of wild turkeys.

At 0.6 mile regain the dirt access road. Turn left. It is less than 0.1 mile back to the campground.

The West Side Trail was completed in 1994. Aside from being a serene walk in the woods, it illustrates one of the island's greatest wildlife management dilemmas. The trail swings right, away from the Nature Trail and along a ridge bordering a wet draw. Travel 0.2 mile on the West Side Trail before reaching another wet area crossed by puncheons (log bridges). Climb slightly. Glimpse a view of Merrymeeting Bay through the trees. It is at this point, or perhaps earlier, that you may notice the parklike appearance of the forest. There is no understory. Small shrubs of varying heights do not block the view. If you were to opt for bushwhacking, you could easily set a course without tearing your clothes to shreds on brush or being whipped in the eye by an errant branch. Until recently, the island's deer population was so high (200 or more individuals) that every green shrub within reach was eaten.

A range is saturated when the deer population reaches a concentration of 20 per square mile. The island is almost 2 square miles in area, so the carrying capacity of the locality should be 40. In a natural setting, **deer** will scatter to maintain a manageable feeding area that regenerates itself annually. Unfortunately, the deer here were being fed. The intention was kindhearted, the result was devastating. They flocked to the site for the apples and hay provided, concentrating their numbers. Unable to digest the hay shafts, some starved to death with full stomachs. Others found nourishment by pawing through the snow for the buds of young shoots. In an attempt to limit the herd size, the supervising department suggested a hunting season open only to wheelchair users. Area towns defeated the plan. Finally, in the 1980s the feeding program was stopped and deer began to disperse.

Today the management area harbors between 25 and 50 deer. The undergrowth is beginning to establish itself again. Deer exclosures along the access road demonstrate how dense the shrubbery would be without deer. The comparison is stark. As you walk the West Side Trail watch for signs of regeneration—tiny red oak and white pine seedlings sprouting on otherwise barren ground. Without the new growth, there would be no replacement for mature trees as they grow old, die, and fall to the ground.

Notice the signs that these woods were once cleared for fields. At 0.4 mile, pass a row of trees with the remnants of a barbed wire fence embedded in their trunks. The path crosses stone walls several times. You will advance through mature, even-aged stands of red pine and descend through hemlock before skirting the edge of the mudflats, exposed at low tide. Seeded with wild rice, this is a very important feeding ground for migrating geese and ducks that pass through in early May.

At 1.4 miles, enter a large open field. To the left along the edge is a side trail leading back to the access road. If you are following the self-guiding tour book, you will find yourself at number 20, the corn crib. Turn left upon reaching the access road to return to the shelters.

To continue on the West Side Trail, traverse the field diagonally to the right. In summer, follow monarch butterflies through the mowed path of milkweed and goldenrod. Regain the woods by crossing a puncheon bridge and climbing rock steps up the far bank. In 0.3 mile, you will enter a large area bordered

Vast fields on Swan Island slope to the banks of the Kennebec River.

with hay-scented ferns on either side. Straight ahead are beautiful sweeping views of Merrymeeting Bay.

The last half of the journey is forested, passing through some wet areas where footbridges are always provided. Listen for the thrushes, black-capped chickadees, and red-breasted nuthatches. Due to the lack of cover, the density of songbirds is much lower than might be expected. The chatter of squirrels is conspicuously absent. In spring you may hear the occasional peep, trill, or ga-rumff of frogs.

The trail ends by skirting a wooded stone wall, then crossing the edge of a field. At dusk you may see several deer feeding in this and other fields along the road. If you take the road to the right, it is 0.8 mile to

Theobald Point, the southwestern tip of Swan Island and the end of the road. To the left, it is approximately 2.0 miles back to the campground, a beautiful walk with plenty of open views across fields to the waters of the Kennebec.

Getting There

Exit I-95 at Bowdoinham. Then travel east on Route 125, turning left (north) on Route 24 in downtown Bowdoinham. Follow Route 24 into the village of Richmond. The Department of Inland Fisheries and Wildlife provides transportation to and from Swan Island from its landing on the right just after the town's riverside park. **Reservations are required.** The daily operating season runs from the first Monday in June through Labor Day, with **additional weekends only** from the last weekend in April to the first Monday in June. A small fee is charged. Write: Swan Island Reservations, Maine Department of Inland Fisheries and Wildlife, RFD #1, Box 6378, Waterville, ME 04901, or call 207-547-4167.

Northwest

30. Lord Hill
Stoneham/White Mountain National Forest

Foothills
2 miles
3 hours

Although New Hampshire is nicknamed the Granite State, Maine certainly has its share of this bedrock material. The hike to Lord Hill Quarry provides an opportunity to do some rockhounding and to enjoy scenic views of Horseshoe Pond and the surrounding hills and mountains.

Lord Hill was **once an active commercial quarry;** it is presently part of the White Mountain National Forest and open to the public for collecting with hand tools. As a commercial site it yielded **milky** and **smoky quartz, topaz,** and **beryl crystals.** At least one of the topaz crystals is now part of the Harvard University mineral collection. You can collect one-inch crystals of quartz by sifting through the cast-off debris, or tailings, by hand. A rock hammer (for safety's sake please do not use a carpenter's hammer) will allow you to break off pieces of the exposed bedrock. Power tools are pro-

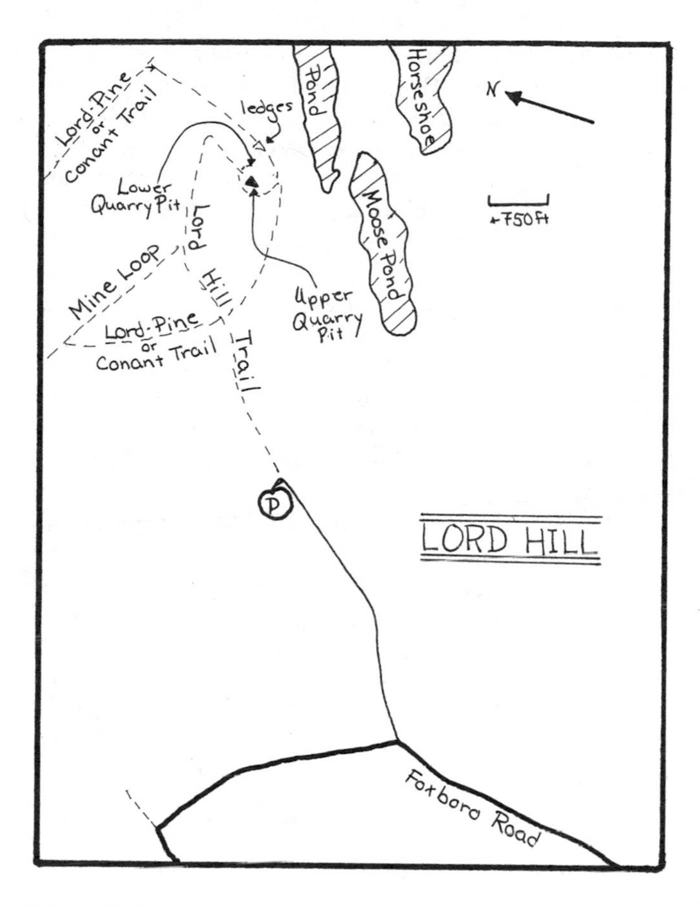

hibited. In this way, you may uncover minerals not available at the surface and select minerals you might like that are embedded in the rock. Always use safety goggles.

The type of rock formation observed at Lord Hill is called **granite pegmatite.** Pegmatite refers to the size of the crystals, which range from inches to feet in length. This makes them quite unlike the barely visible grains found in some fine granites. Large crystals were formed when fissures opened in already cooled granite, permitting magma to inch up through the cracks. This new molten material had a high water content, which allowed minerals of like chemistry to attract each other and collect over time. The longer it took the magma to cool, the larger the crystals. The entire process happened miles beneath the earth's surface. Millions of years later, after much erosion and uplift, the granite bedrock is exposed at the surface for us to view and puzzle over.

Along with the more eye-catching crystals of quartz, topaz, and beryl, Lord Hill also displays small crystals of **garnet** and **pyrite** and larger crystals of **feldspar** and **mica.** Mica was used for house windows before glass became widely available in this country. It was also used for the clear panels in kerosene stoves until a few decades ago. At Lord Hill, mica crystals are plentiful and a lot of fun. Children often spend hours trying to peel off the thinnest layer possible—not easy to do without breaking it into tiny pieces.

Although it takes a good deal of time and energy to locate complete crystals of quartz, irregular pieces of milky quartz, mica, and feldspar are available from the moment you step out of your car. You may hesitate when driving into the parking area as the ground appears to be covered with pieces of broken glass, but on closer inspection, the "glass" is really mica flakes.

Books of mica crystals punctuate the quarry walls at Lord Hill.

Park your car on the right, where the stone wall forms an open gate and the dirt road branches left into a field, or park in the field. If you have a four-wheel-drive vehicle or a high undercarriage, you can continue an additional 1,400 feet through the gate before stopping. If you are walking, watch for mica and quartz chips along the dirt road.

The end of the road is blocked by four large boulders on the left. Pass through these stones to begin a gentle climb. From here it is just under a mile to the quarry. The Lord Hill Trail is an old road that passes between **hemlock, speckled alder,** and **beech.** By the age and size of the trees, it appears the area has only recently grown into woods. The stone walls may have bordered open fields less than 50 years ago.

These three species provide food and shelter for many animals. Hemlock buds are a favorite winter food of white-tailed deer. Where the speckled alder grows in profusion, American woodcock thrive. Black bears love the fruit of the beech tree and will scale the trunk to gather mouthfuls of the nuts. Inspect the smooth, gray bark of larger trees for claw marks.

Along the path beneath these trees, you will discover bracken fern, sweet fern, wild sarsaparilla, and wild raspberry. In mid- to late-July the raspberries will be ripe and ready to eat. Both **sweet fern** leaves and the root of the wild sarsaparilla can be dried and used for tea. **Sarsaparilla** can also be used to concoct a root beer—the drink the good guys always ordered when they sidled up to the bar in the cowboy movies. The sarsaparilla plant is about one foot in height. Each of its three leaves is divided into three-to-five-toothed leaflets. Beneath the leaf, the flower or fruit forms three spherical clusters. Sweet fern is not a fern at all but a small herbal-smelling shrub. It is about two feet in height with long, narrow, dark olive green leaves. The large-toothed margins give the leaf a zigzag appearance.

At approximately 0.4 mile, a trail marked in blazes of yellow over white bisects the old road you are traveling on. This is the Conant Trail (Lord-Pine Trail), maintained by the Chatham Trail Association (CTA). The Conant Trail (Lord-Pine Trail) begins at Deer Hill Road, ascends Pine Hill and Lord Hill, passes a side trail to

Horseshoe Pond, and completes the 5-mile loop after slabbing Harndon Hill. Continue straight ahead.

In 0.2 mile, the CTA Mine Loop to Conant Trail (Lord-Pine Trail) joins from the left with blazes of yellow over yellow. Travel straight ahead on the woods road.

The forest type begins to change at about 0.8 mile from the bouldered start of the hike. Here red spruce and white pine mix with the hemlock. The long clusters of needles on the white pine soften the wind. You may find a daring **American toad** camouflaged and awaiting its next insect meal in the dry leaves next to the trail. Or you may discover a brown-and-green garter snake awaiting its next meal of fresh toad. Toads tend to be rather laissez-faire about self-defense. Just behind their ears are two poison glands that make them very distasteful to most animals. Usually the extreme irritation to mucous glands experienced by predators who attempt to swallow a toad is enough to make their first try their last. Not so for garter snakes. They have evolved an immunity to the poison and find the toad a delicacy.

The trail branches at 0.9 mile. Seventy-five feet to the left is the smaller, more recently excavated Lower Quarry Pit. This is the best spot to comb through the mine tailings for quartz crystals, but be patient because it may take an hour to find a single one-inch crystal.

Straight ahead 50 feet is the larger Upper Quarry Pit. Most collecting activity with rock hammers is done here. The clean rock faces on the right bare mute testimony to past collecting. On the left, above the excavated crystal pocket, there are good examples of large (one-foot-by-one-foot) feldspar crystals and books of mica several inches across.

To the right it is 0.1 mile to the intersection of the Mine Loop Trail (Lord Hill Trail) and the Conant Trail (Lord-Pine Trail). Continue 100 feet straight ahead along the Lord-Pine Trail. An additional 100 feet brings you out onto the ledges overlooking Horseshoe Pond. This is the perfect picnic spot. At the end of July, the ledges are covered with plump, juicy blueberries, a delicious dessert. The views north are toward Evans Notch and include West and East Royce and Speckled Mountain. Retrace your steps on your return trip. As you leave the ledges look for signs of moose. Their scat resembles piles of very large Cocoa Puffs. Watch your step!

Getting There

From the junction of Routes 5 and 93 in Lovell Village, drive north 2.4 miles on Route 5. Turn left onto West Lovell Road and proceed 2.75 miles to a fork in the road. Keep left at the fork (this is Foxboro Road) and continue northwest for 1.5 miles. Turn right onto a paved road that becomes gravel (go straight where the main road curves to the left), and drive north 1.0 mile to the junction with the woods road on the left. Park here.

For more information contact District Ranger, Evans Notch Ranger District, WMNF, RR2, Box 2270, Bethel, ME 04217, or call 207-824-2134.

31. Jockey Cap
Fryeburg

Foothills
0.3 mile, 130-foot elevation gain
0.5 hour

The hike to the top of Jockey Cap is similar to that of Douglas Mountain (see p. 268). The reward is a tremendous **view** with relatively little climbing effort. This kind of walk is great for stretching muscles after a long drive. It provides a short break to loosen up, relax, and resume the trip. This hike also begins in the back yard of a small grocery store, so it's easy to pick up a drink or snack.

Driving up to a store and motel seems like an unlikely way to start a hike. Between the two buildings that share the name "Jockey Cap" is a white fence with an arcade announcing the trail. Eighty feet into a young mixed forest, turn right onto a dusty path about 5 feet wide. The trail then angles to the left, away from the sounds of the roadway. About 500 feet into the woods the footpath becomes a wash from the base of a cliff. Large blocks of **granite,** some 20 feet high, are scattered about in the sandy soil.

Local history notes the last of the Pequawket tribe, Moll Ockett, made a home among these rocks and, after her death at age 90, was buried in Andover, Maine. Some of the granite chunks are the remains of a rock lip that gave Jockey Cap its name. Gravity and time got the

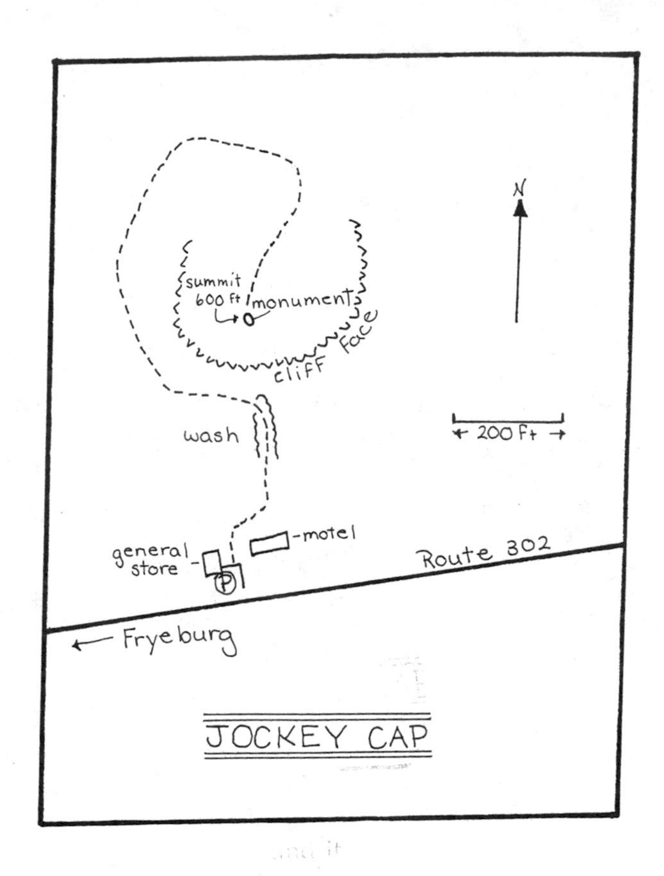

best of the cap visor, and it gave way many years ago. Behind the crumpled granite is the cap proper—a towering 100-foot dome. There are small trails that braid up through the brush along the base where more daring folks have challenged the vertical stone face. The main trail bears left along the foot of the wall and out into the woods along the west side.

The trail begins to climb through young pine and oak and mounts the western shoulder of the granite monolith, for the most part hidden in trees to the right. About 800 feet from the start, the trail gets a bit more demanding with exposed rocks and roots. The path comes out of the woods onto a steep, rounded slab that makes up the back of Jockey Cap. The last 300 feet of the trip are across this roughly textured surface. Some of the broken areas may come from the fact that the local artillery company raised during the War of 1812 used Jockey Cap as a target!

Unlike the surrounding peaks, whose open areas often harbor a lush supply of grass and blueberries, the vegetation on Jockey Cap is sparse. Most green patches are stubby pitch pine, also found along the coastal dune areas of Maine. Another lowbush on the top is scrub (bear) oak, looking somewhat like malnourished white oak but for the bristles at the tips of the lobes and the tiny (three-eighths of an inch) acorns. This oak is more like a shrub than a tree. It is three to five feet high with light gray bark and small three-inch leaves. Between these islands of green is a rough gray mineral surface with plenty of room to sit and rest. Beware the long drop off the south face. It could provide a needlessly quick way back to the parking area for the unwary!

Most visitors to Jockey Cap don't take time to sit. They are too busy turning, absorbing the fine 360-degree **panorama** (some trees obstruct) of peaks stitched along the horizon. The view extends from nearby foothills in Maine, across the valley into New Hamp-

The bronze rim of the monument at Jockey Cap mimics the peaks on the surrounding horizon.

shire, to the peak of Mt. Washington, nestled between Mt. Kearsarge and Wildcat Mountain.

At the summit is a unique marker/monument—a four-foot granite column topped with a compass plate of bronze—commemorating the survey work done by Admiral Robert Peary during his residence in 1878–79. The margins are turned up like a pie plate and the mountains on the horizon are replicated in the vertical metal edge. Line up a peak on the horizon with its outline on the plate lip and read off the name. The novel and effective monument identifies a total of 50 peaks. Included in this horizontal geography is the spire of Fryeburg Academy, established in 1792 and home to onetime headmaster of note Daniel Webster.

The elevation also gives a good view of Lovewell Pond. This is the site of the last major resistance by tribes along the Saco River valley. A battle on May 8, 1725, pitted 80 members of the Pequawket tribe against 34 Massachusetts Rangers. Both sides suffered heavily and the ranger leader, John Lovewell, was among the casualties. There are many stone markers and statues raised in the memory of the **conquerors** of these lands. Only place names of rivers and hills commemorate the past presence of the Native American. Learn the names and use them with respect. Soothe the spirits and memories of a people that linger still among these timeworn hills.

The return trip to the parking area is less than 10 minutes. Along with the brief exercise, this hike also provides a unique way to obtain an overall view of peaks you might wish to visit in southern Maine and New Hampshire.

Getting There

From the junction of Routes 5 and 302 in Fryeburg, follow 302 east for 0.9 mile. On the right is the Fryeburg Plaza and on the left are the Jockey Cap Motel and Jockey Cap General Store. Pull into the yard in front of the store and just to the right is the trailhead. If it is crowded, you can also park off to the left of the store along a dirt road under the power lines.

32. Mount Tom
Fryeburg

Foothills

3 miles round-trip, 600-foot elevation gain

2 hours

The words mountain and climb are often used in the same sentence. In reference to Mount Tom, walk is the operative word. The elevation gain, stretched over a 1.5-mile jaunt, holds no steep pitches to trouble the inexperienced hiker. The trek through heavy forest affords little hint of altitude until the grassy crest opens on a vista of the surrounding countryside. It also gives a sense of **isolation** or escape as little sign of roads, homes, or power lines is visible after leaving dwellings near the trailhead.

The beginning of the trail is several miles off Route 302 along a paved fire lane. The very old homes and stone walls confirm this now dead-end street was a main thoroughfare in the mid-to-late 1700s. Finding the trailhead requires attention to detail—the beginning is not a wide-open path. Follow Fire Lane 31, 2.4 miles to a small granite-walled **cemetery** on the right. Park in front. If history and headstones are an interest, there is a second cemetery about 300 feet behind the first. Headstones of original settlers date to the 1700s, including members of the Frye family.

From the roadside cemetery, walk an additional 400 feet down the blacktop to the rear of a large barn

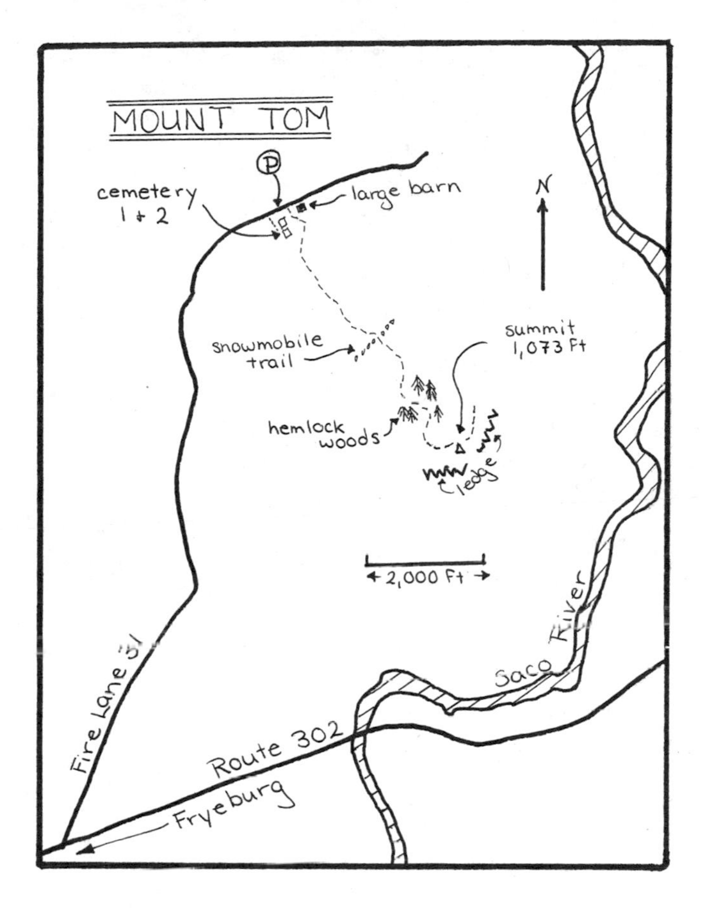

(Inglenook Farm) on your right. The trail cuts immediately behind this barn. The owner occasionally clears the path through to the road. It does look like you are walking into a back yard, but some 60 feet from the pavement the trail is guarded on both sides by old stone walls. The path cuts behind the Inglenook Farm buildings and takes on the appearance of the old carriage road it once was, making its way up Mount Tom. The trail, and the protecting walls, continue for 1,000 feet between a few homes and camp buildings. Then you are alone with the forest.

For almost 3,000 feet the trail remains a road about 15 feet wide, then narrows to a single-lane jeep path. It is bordered by evergreen forest and young American beech. Interrupted fern, goldenrods, asters, and a variety of tree seedlings grow in the sunlit areas. The only break in the woods lining the path is a **snowmobile trail** entering from the right about 3,200 feet from the trailhead.

About halfway to the top the trail grade increases gradually. The number of American beech increases, with an **understory** of hobblebush, goldthread, teaberry, and wild sarsaparilla. There is beech fern in the woods with bracken fern and sweet fern along the open area of the trail.

The ferns seen in this area are easy to classify. The 18-inch bracken fern has a single leaf stalk divided into three triangular parts, each looking like an individual leaf. The interrupted fern forms a three-foot-tall circle of green leaves. The central section of each frond forms spores interrupting the outline of the leaf, hence the name. The beech fern is about a foot high, and the lower leaflet on each frond projects down from the rest.

The forest growth changes dramatically along the northwestern brow of Mount Tom. Step into a **Mirkwood** right out of the world of J. R. R. Tolkien. This

The ledge face of Mount Tom overlooks the Saco River.

cool, dark hillside environment is created by the dense cover of eastern hemlock and a few white pine. The ground cover becomes a blanket of brown needles, mosses, and a variety of fungi. Notice an immediate temperature and light reduction stepping into this new habitat. Not too far into this shaded wood the trail takes a sharp right and again increases its uphill angle. At the time the climb levels out there is another change in the surroundings. Grasses, whorled wood asters, white and red oaks, and an increase in the light level announce the summit of Mount Tom.

The trail now cuts left (east) toward some ledges that face Pleasant Mountain. Look down on **Kezar Pond** and the extensive marsh system of a serpentine Saco River. The parklike vista of the summit affords comfortable picnicking. In addition to the pleasant view, summer may provide a snack for the weary hiker. Raspberries and blueberries grow here and there, and the ledges support some sheep sorrel for a tangy trail nibble. The three-inch-long basal leaves of this plant have lobes giving them the appearance of small arrowheads or spear points.

All things considered, this lesser-known area is one of several **genteel walks** in the Fryeburg area. Kids, cats, and the family dog can all make it with ease to the top of Mount Tom along the leisurely path.

Getting There

Follow Route 302, 1.8 miles east (right) from the junction with Route 5 in Fryeburg. Watch the left for Fire Lane 31.

From the east on Route 302, the fire lane is on the right 1 mile past the bridge over the Saco River. As you cross this bridge, look right for a glimpse of the ledge face of Mount Tom. Follow the fire lane 2.4 miles to the graveyard on the right. Walk 400 feet farther to the trailhead behind the barn, also on the right.

33. Mount Cutler
Hiram

Foothills

1.6 miles round-trip, 800-foot elevation gain

1.5 hours

This relatively short hike gives a rich view up and down the Saco River valley. The color scale of the landscape ranges from subtle greens of spring and summer to the more varied palette of ochres and crimsons in fall.

The trail begins in the parking lot at the old **rail siding** in Hiram. As you approach the tracks, the trailhead is about 80 feet to the left along the rails. At this point, the path cuts right, crosses the tracks, and slopes up through a grove of white pine. The trail is 10 feet wide and bedded with pine needles. Two hundred feet farther, the path forks with a white **blaze** bearing to the right. There is only one route to the top but the blazes are hardly color coordinated. They vary from white to the more common red or tan. Regardless of blazes, the tramped earth is clear enough to mark the way. At the top of a rise, the trail levels and enters a tranquil clearing beneath tall, slender pines.

Off to one side, an old **stone wall** provides shelter for the eastern chipmunk. Bulging cheek pouches serve to remind us of the industrious nature of this animal. The chippie is, along with the gray squirrel, the most commonly identified small mammal ranging

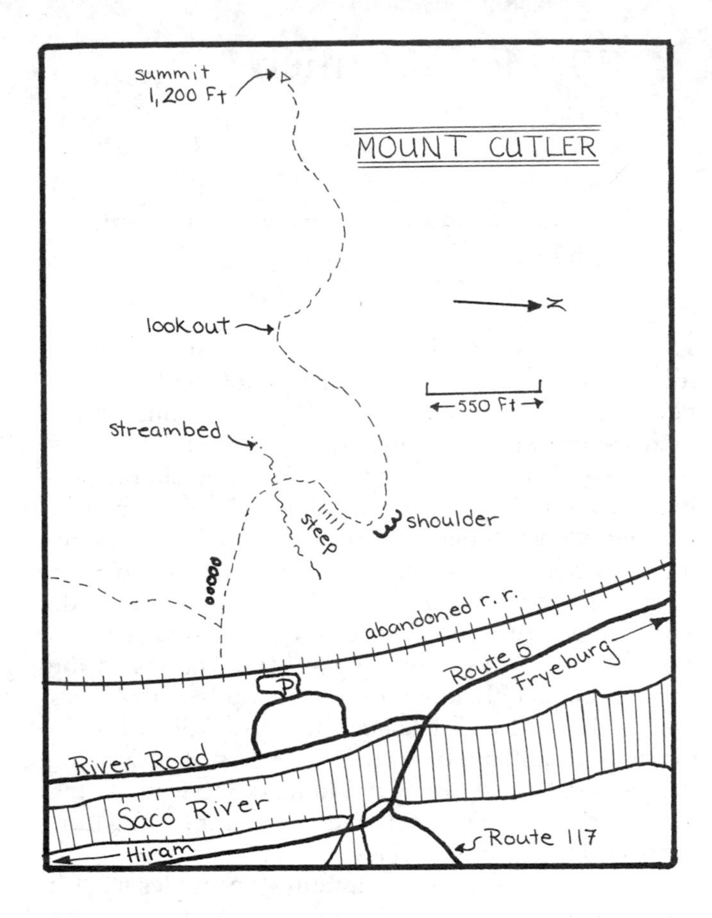

over eastern North America. The bright-eyed face, straight bushy tail, and striped body are all readily recognized by youngsters. It is one wild creature that has prospered in spite of human progress. The chipmunk is common to campgrounds and bird feeders, and is sometimes an unwelcome visitor rooting in a favored garden site.

On the far side of the wide, quiet grove, the trail narrows quickly and begins to climb over rounded stones and roots. The gradient increases as the path approaches an elongated **ledge** arrayed in Christmas ferns, lichens, and mosses. In a tangle of roots and rocks, the path mounts the right corner of the ledge and quickly gains elevation. The trail snakes, rises about 40 feet, levels out, and then angles down to a small rocky valley. Here, a stream flows in the spring or after a heavy rain, sluicing around the boulders. The far side of the watercourse is a **steep embankment** with large rocks sprinkled through the trees. The trail crosses the streambed and moves directly up into the precipitous face of the boulder field. At this point the path rises about six inches with each step. As the climb approaches the base of a 40-foot wall, it forms a Y. The more accessible approach is the right path, which climbs to the foot of the cliff and takes an immediate right along its base. Much of this section is a **scramble,** requiring two hands and two feet.

The trail next becomes a 200-foot-long narrow path with a **steep drop** to the right. There are plenty of rock and root **handholds,** but keep kids close by. Once past this precarious area, the trail emerges onto a ledge with an aerial view of the village of Hiram, the Saco River, and the Route 5 bridge. The beaten path follows the mountain around its shoulder, to the west (upriver), and then cuts left through a field spotted with some red and white oak. Climbing during July ensures a plentiful

Mount Cutler rises over marshes along the Saco River.

supply of early lowbush blueberry spread throughout the grass.

While there is still a grade, the hardest part of the climb is past. Young beech, red and white oak, and red cedar grow here, providing a rich supply of seeds for the birds and mammals of the area, especially those scampering chippies. Filtering through the trees to the left is a view of the Saco River valley toward Hiram Dam. It becomes more dramatic as you step out of a thick grove of young eastern hemlock onto a wide, flat **ledge** providing a comfortable overlook for the valley. There is a clearing about 60 feet across and more than 100 feet long, plenty of room to rest and picnic. Below, a rusting **trestle** crosses the Saco River, and large areas of bog behind the Hiram Dam are evident. Distant hills, pressed skyward, then rounded by glaciers and time, block a view of the Atlantic. This one **picturesque** area is the main reason most people make the climb on Mount Cutler.

For those wishing to explore farther or achieve the summit, there is another 0.3 mile of trail and about 300 feet of elevation to conquer. The path leaves the ledge and cuts back into the woods, following the crown of the mountain. Rock cairns replace the paint blaze in open areas of ledge. Along the trail, there is evidence of short- and long-term changes. Bits of **charcoal** speak of a fire in the recent past and possibly explain the thin soil and young trees covering the mountain's crest. Sections of the **granite** have been lifted and split by years of frost. Parts of the exposed ledge show large crystals

The ledge area overlooks the Saco River valley.

of feldspar, milky quartz, and mica created as magma slowly cooled. Much of the open ledge area has large patches of lichen, giving an alpine appearance to the mountaintop. The actual summit is marked by a cairn in a grassy area that lacks the spectacular view to the south from that first ledge. Retrace your steps carefully. Jamming joints and toes in the steep areas makes descending tougher than climbing.

Getting There

Follow Route 5 east from Fryeburg or west from Saco. Either direction brings you to a bridge over the Saco River in Hiram. From the east, you approach the bridge at the junction of 117. Cross the bridge and immediately turn left (River Road). From the west, approach the bridge and make a sharp right turn just before the abutments. River Road goes past a construction company and a five-story building with a sharp roof peak. Turn right just past this building. Some 200 feet beyond is a sharp left. Make this turn and the grassy field of the railroad is on your immediate right. There is parking for 15 cars across the first set of tracks.

34. Hiram Nature Study Area

Hiram

60 Acres

Woodlands

1 mile

1 hour

For thousands of years, the Saco River ran, unfettered, 150 miles from Saco Lake in Crawford Notch, New Hampshire, to sea level on the Maine coast. During this time the **Native Americans** used the river to travel and to fish. The first Europeans to arrive viewed the river as a source of power and soon used its waters to move the blades of sawmills and grind grains into meal. Dams were built to control the movement of timber down the river. Ultimately the water was impounded, as we see it today, for the production of electricity.

On the upstream end, the first of eight dams creates a 10-foot cascade at Swans Falls in Fryeburg. The last is a 45-foot drop, the Ram Cat Dam, at tidewater in Saco, Maine. Between these two, an additional six dams control the flow of the river and hydroelectric power. The most massive dam on the river is Skelton in Buxton, at Union Falls, and the highest is **Hiram Dam** at the Great Falls.

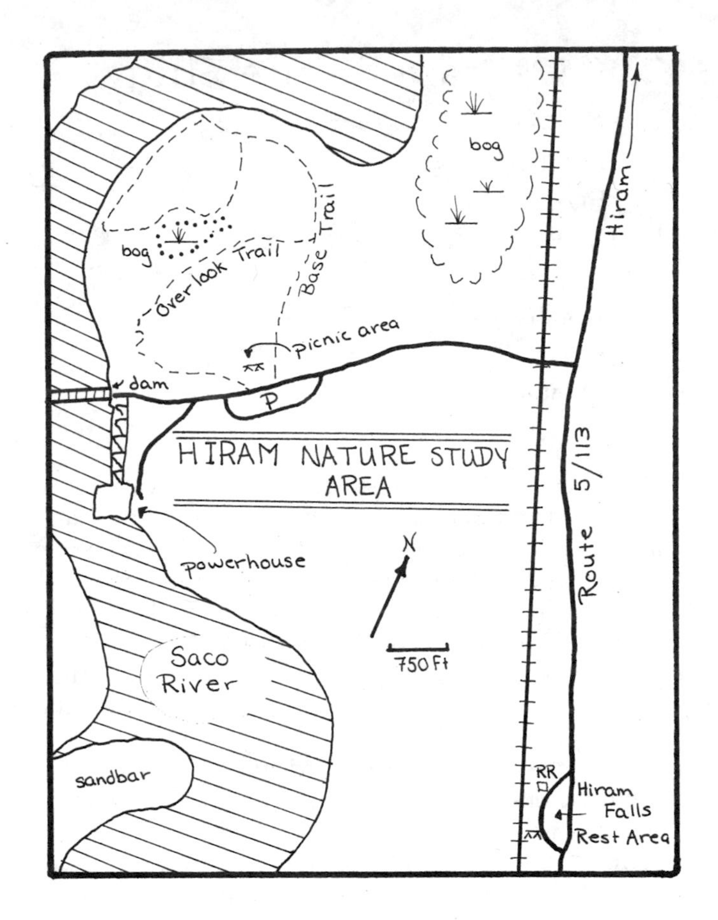

A 75-foot nightmare cascade greeted the weary salmon on their journey upriver to spawn even before the construction of Hiram Dam in 1917. It is not a massive concrete structure. Mother Nature made the original wall; mortals just had to control the flow of water over it. There is no huge lake backed up to provide power; a 10-foot tube delivers much of the river to a set of turbines at the base of the falls. You can hear the turbines hum with the energy of the falling water and see the spent water roil out beneath the powerhouse on its way to the next dam.

The eastern border of the dam has been set aside by Central Maine Power as a natural area. Along with a substantial parking lot there are three picnic tables, two of which are nicely roofed in case of rain. With the aid of the University of Maine and the extension service, two loop trails have been created that do an excellent job of displaying the diversity of plants in a relatively compact area. Dozens of plants are displayed and labeled along the paths.

The hikes are set in two loops as pictured on the information bulletin in front of the picnic area. The **Base Trail,** the easier and longer of the two, swings right down to the riverbank. It crosses through white pine and pitch pine as it moves down at a slight angle. The trail is about five feet wide and bedded with evergreen needles. You will begin to notice metal stakes with large labels naming the various species along the path. There are several dozen such stakes scattered in the study area. The designated plant, depending on the season, is not always in bloom.

The Base Trail bears left through hemlock and white pine. Eight hundred feet down the Base Trail, a second, smaller trail, part of the **Overlook Trail,** enters from the left. There is a post showing the late lowbush blueberry at this junction. Continue on the Base Trail as

Dams, a resource for humans, can limit the reproduction of migratory fish.

it angles down a bit more steeply. To the right, through the trees, you can see part of the backwater behind the dam. Erosion on a 50-foot section of the trail has left some rounded stones six to eight inches above the path. Watch your step. Almost 2,000 feet from the picnic area, the trail reaches the river. The banking is about 4 feet high, and the tree-lined opposite shore is about 150 feet away.

The trail now turns left. Feel the coolness from the adjacent water as you walk through a mixed-age growth of white pines and a few young red pines with their distinctive rusty colored bark. You will come upon highbush blueberry. If the late lowbush blueberry seen earlier had any edible berries, you will see few berries left on the highbush because they ripen earlier. With this difference in ripening between the two varieties, you can nibble blueberries for the better part of the summer: pick highbush in mid-July and lowbush in late July and early August.

The trail turns hard left away from the river and a slough appears on your right, with the yellow bullhead lily breaking the surface in open water. Several species of fern are noted here along with **lycopodium,** or ground pine. Actually, the three species of lycopodium common to Maine are all present on this tiny preserve. Two species look like large moss plants two to six inches high growing from horizontal stems. They hold tiny half-inch pine cone–like spore cases raised above the forest floor. A third species, looking like a series of small lacy umbrellas, also snakes along the ground with similar spore cases arching over it like a little brown candelabra. They are living botanical fossils. Their growth and history predate birds, dinosaurs, and many of the well-known seed plants. Of the 400 known species of this lowly plant, none is found in the western U.S., and many in the east are endangered due to habitat destruction and their use in Christmas decor. It is nice to see all three here.

The trail passes the slough, winds to the left, and joins the Base Trail about 200 feet from the riverbank. You can retrace your steps to the picnic area or move onto the next trail by following the Base Trail 0.4 mile back toward the picnic area.

The Overlook Trail enters from the right It is narrow and has steeper inclines than the Base Trail. From the junction with the Base Trail the path quickly begins to climb at a 10-degree angle. About 500 feet in, it

Still waters of the impoundment at Hiram Nature Center.

emerges onto a ledge area with reindeer lichen, moss, bracken fern, white oak, and red maple. This portion of the trail also marks a swing to the sunny southwest side of the hill, with markedly fewer pine and hemlock. The change in vegetation reflects the new variations in environmental factors: thin soil, less moisture, increased light and heat. At the summit of the hill the trees are less dense, allowing more light to reach the ground. This is in stark contrast to the shady cool climb through the dense conifers on the initial part of this trail.

Descending from the summit of the Overlook Trail, you can see the river at the base of the falls. There is a large sandbar on the opposite side of the river where people soak and sun themselves on warm summer days. This area can be reached by a road from Hiram a few miles above the falls. Watch your footing among the numerous rocks on this descending path. This trail is about half the length of the Base Trail, so you quickly regain the picnic area.

You can explore closer to the dam if the gate at the parking lot is open. Walk the 1,000 feet of gravel road to the control gates at the top of the dam. From this viewpoint you can see a canoe takeout (opposite bank) and a log boom guarding the spillway. The lower tarred road leads down to the powerhouse.

The Hiram Nature Study Area is just that. It is a quiet retreat where you can enjoy some of the botany of southern Maine and the scenery of the Saco River valley.

Getting There

The access road to the Hiram Nature Study Area is Route 5. If you follow it south from New Hampshire and Fryeburg, Maine, you will enter Hiram at the junction of Routes 5 and 117. From this point travel south 1.9 miles to the dirt entrance on your right. There is a small sign on the same side just before the road. Traveling north, stay on Route 5 as you make a left turn joining Route 113. From this junction, the Nature Study Area will be 2.9 miles on your left through West Baldwin. As you approach from the south, you will first reach the Hiram Falls Rest Area on the left. The entrance to the nature area is 0.3 mile farther on the same side.

35. Douglas Mountain Preserve

Sebago
169 Acres

Foothills
0.3–1.5 miles
up to 2 hours

Those who like the idea of a maximum reward for minimum effort will enjoy Douglas Mountain. You can hike a 1,000-foot path and get a fantastic panoramic **view** from the White Mountains in New Hampshire to the Atlantic coast of Maine. You don't have to hike uphill for hours to get a view worthy of peaks several thousand feet high—15 minutes from the car and you are there.

Douglas Mountain Preserve is a property of The Nature Conservancy. Industrious **volunteers** keep trails marked and clear. Purchased in 1971, this popular viewing spot remains open to public use. It was originally farmland and was later heavily logged. The last major landowner in the area, Dr. William Blackman, purchased the parcel in 1890 and helped to construct the stone **tower** on the summit in 1925.

Like many small preserves, there is limited parking and adjacent private landowners to consider. When you arrive at the end of Douglas Mountain Tower Road, there is a small parking area (8 to 10 cars) on your left. The road

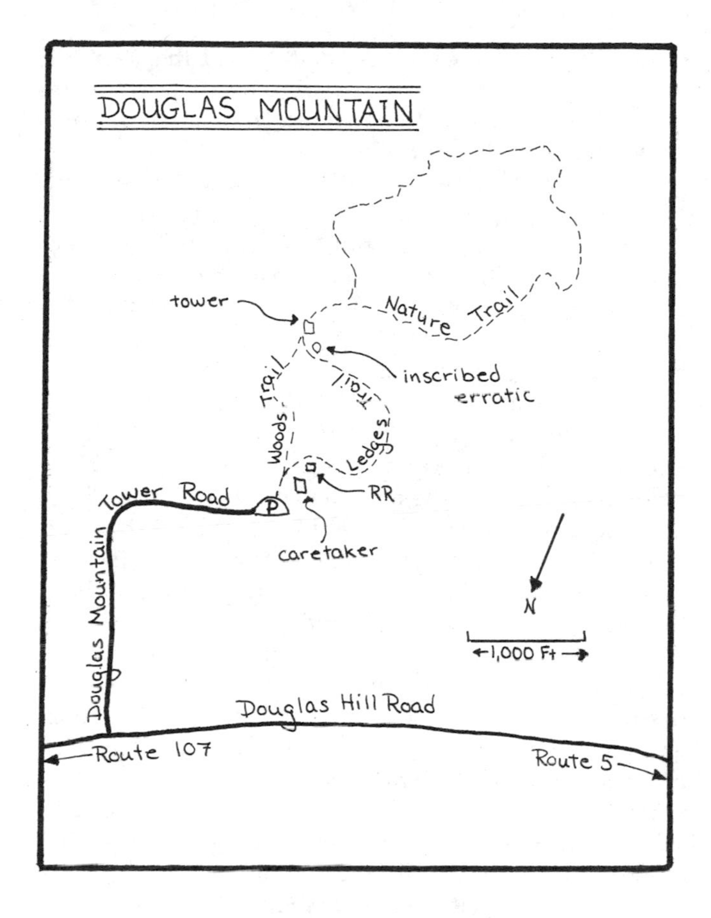

that continues beyond the parking area is a private drive. In winter, be cautious of snow and ice on the roads.

In the woods, above the parking lot to the right of the trailhead, is a rest room next to an equally small caretaker's storage cabin. A small box at the trailhead offers returnable maps of the preserve. The trails are marked with small lettered signs. The nature trail has an orange blaze in addition to signs.

Begin your hike at the parking lot. Climb steeply up steps, over some rugged roots, and through two stone **pillars** onto the Woods Trail. It is easy to see where many feet over the years have worn the soil away to expose bedrock. Stay on the path to prevent further erosion. The trail rises sharply for the first 300 feet, then levels out. Six hundred feet from the stone pillars is a fork in the trail. The left-hand fork, Ledges Trail, is the steeper, shorter (about 1,000 feet) path to the summit. The Woods Trail, dropping slightly to the right, is more gradual and reaches the top after about 1,800 feet.

Take a moment to notice some clues about the **habitat.** You may have been scolded by a red squirrel by now. Several species of warblers, easy to hear and hard to see, flutter through the evergreens. You see red spruce mixed in with the white pine and hemlock. The spruce has short prickly needles around each branch, the pine has three-to-five-inch needles clustered in groups of five, and the hemlock has flattened half-inch needles on each of the branches. One particular tree, the striped maple or (moosewood), stands in the thin acid soil amongst the mosses. This tree is a sign of increasing elevation (foothills) and that you are at the edge of a boreal environment. The tender tips of this tree are a favorite nibble of rabbits, hares, the white-tailed deer, and even moose.

In the spring along the Ledges Trail, you can see a heavy concentration of Maine's common **orchid,** the lady's slipper, another sign of acid soil. The bright pink oval blossom droops from the top of a 10-inch stem growing from two large oval leaves at the base. This flower is under pressure from habitat destruction and is protected by law.

The trail angles to the right, passing tree roots and large **glacial boulders.** About 1,800 feet from the trailhead you break out into relatively open ground. There are lowbush blueberry, wild sarsaparilla, and bracken fern scattered across the more exposed areas of ledge.

The peak is a level area of bedrock. Look carefully at the ledge under your feet. It is composed of distinctly layered schist sitting almost on edge. This ancient sea sediment was heated, compressed, and dramatically twisted some 400 million years ago. Contrast this with the large boulder bearing the Latin inscription *Non sibi sed omnibus* (Not for one but for all). The boulder is good Maine granite and is not part of this schist mountain. While set in place by humans, it was not brought here by the hand of humans. It is a **glacial erratic.** As the last glacier retreated, it left large boulders all over Douglas Mountain and much of Maine. The bulldozing ice carried rocks—some house-sized—hundreds of miles from their northern point of origin and into the foothills of Maine.

A square fieldstone tower 15 feet high, with a protective chain-link fence around the top, marks the summit of Douglas Mountain. The tower entrance, opposite the incoming trails, has 17 steps to its top. The commanding view, on a clear day, is described by a pictorial key. The closest landmarks are Sebago Lake and Frye Island 9 miles away to the east. The looming mass of

"Not for one but for all" reminds us that some areas must remain accessible.

Mt. Washington, 30 miles northwest, is unmistakable. Small bumps and dips in the wide horizon are noted on the key along with several lakes. The tower platform is small, but the base and ledges below are great for lunch and relaxation.

As you step out of the tower door, an orange-blazed trail leads off to the right. The Nature Trail follows a loop almost three-quarters of a mile long. It drops more than 100 feet from the summit, and you must regain this altitude on the return trip. The outgoing portion of the loop leads right, across an open ledge, and you will quickly notice the first in a series of small, hand-lettered informational signs along the path. The trail leads past several clumps of witch hazel into a rather dense growth of eastern hemlock. The trail angles down, and there is very little undergrowth in the heavy shade of the hemlock. A few of the trees have large rectangular holes drilled by the pileated woodpecker.

Take a close look at the witch hazel. It is usually a 10-to-15-foot arching shrub. The leaves have wavy edges and very uneven bases. It carries small yellow flowers in the fall and seedpods most of the year. Witch hazel is still used in as an over-the-counter **treatment** for hemorrhoids, skin irritations, and itches.

The ground levels out in the stand of hemlock. Some of these trees were too young to be harvested in the last round of lumbering— now they are close to two and a half feet in diameter. There are small beeches, yellow birch, hay-scented fern, and more glacial erratics scattered through the forest. The trail continues in an up-and-down, zigzag fashion and works its way along the eastern shoulder of the mountain. It then begins to turn back toward the top. The eastern slope shows a slight change in climate. It is brighter, lighter, and drier. There is a heavy growth of American beech and yellow birch. The understory contains a lot of viburnum, hobblebush, and more witch hazel. Through the beeches, the trail is steeper, climbing about six inches with each step up over a slope of small rounded rocks. You will soon return to the ledges behind the tower.

The Ledges Trail, quickest way up and down, is steep enough to warrant caution in dry weather with its coating of slippery pine needles. In wet or icy conditions it should be avoided. The upper part of the trail, the source of its name, is open, and the angled ledges continue the fine view seen from the tower. Just after the trail bears left, it drops back into the forest, becomes the standard rock and root trail, and is not as slick as the top portion. In a few minutes, you are back at your vehicle and ready for a cool sip of water.

Getting There

Douglas Hill Road stretches between Route 107 in Sebago and Route 5 in West Baldwin. From Route 5 in West Baldwin turn onto Douglas Hill Road and travel 5.0 miles to Douglas Mountain Tower Road, on your right. If you come from Route 107, 3 miles north of East Baldwin look on the left for Douglas Hill Road, Fire Lane 52. Turn onto Douglas Hill Road and Douglas Mountain Tower Road will be your next left at 0.8 mile. For information call 207-729-5181.

36. Pleasant Mountain
Denmark

Foothills
4 miles round-trip, 1,600-foot elevation gain
3 hours

This granite massif separating the Saco River watershed from that of the Bridgton-Sebago region is aptly named. The drive to it, the walk, surrounding forest, and scenery all are most pleasant. It is a big brother hike to Mount Tom—longer, a bit steeper, with an increased elevation gain and a more expansive view of the surrounding landscape at the summit.

The walk, on a path called the Firewarden's Trail, begins in a **rural** agrarian scene on an isolated gravel road. The trailhead is between a roadside parking area and a large yellow Victorian farmhouse with matching outbuildings. Step around the gate to reach the well-traveled Firewarden's Trail. The dirt road angles slightly left, away from the farm, through young maple and evergreen trees growing over cinnamon and interrupted fern. You are soon aware of the sound of **running water** off to the left. There are a couple of level areas where you can wander off and look down on gently gurgling water. The most advantageous spot is 1,200 feet from the start where the road crosses the stream on a timbered **bridge.** Upstream the water courses down a narrow chute, between ledges, into a large reflecting

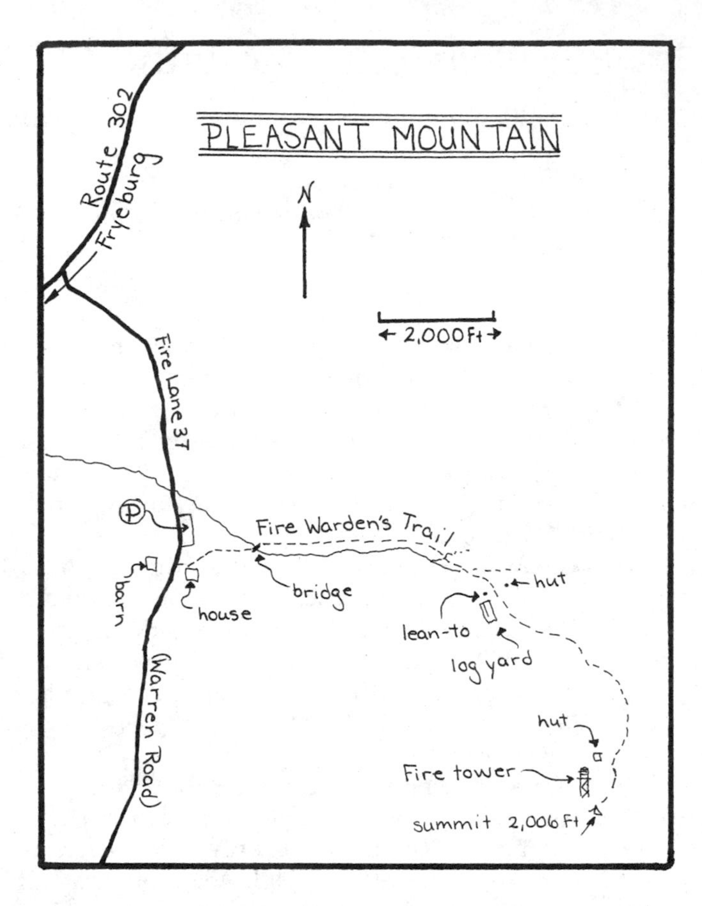

pool. In the fall, maple leaves run the chute and swirl on the surface of the pool like children at a water park. In a spring freshet, this same area can be a 15-foot-wide sheet of water cascading down over the broad, flat granite. The downstream side of the bridge shows more rounded mossy boulders with smaller pools.

From the bridge, the road now parallels the stream on its right bank. In some spots, the streambed is 30 or more feet below road level, but the trill of water over rock reminds the walker of its constant company. Many areas along this section of the road beckon you to step off to the right, under soaring pines and hemlocks, to rest and listen to the music of the woods and water.

For the first 4,000 feet, the road is fairly level and smooth. There are some cutoffs and an open area where logs are yarded alongside the main trail. A few glacial erratics, white pine, large eastern hemlock, striped maple, American beech, maple-leaved viburnum, red maple, teaberry, and many understory plants create a parklike atmosphere for the first half of this walk.

About 200 feet short of a mile, the trail takes a sharp turn to the right and cuts back across the tiny head of the stream. There is a long low lean-to ahead and a small shack to the left. Straight ahead is a large clearing in the woods that looks like a dirt parking lot for 50 or more vehicles. This is another yarding area for logs. The trail moves up through the trees just to the left of this cleared area. It narrows and steepens, gaining some 200 feet in the next 1,000 feet of trail. Underfoot it is cobbled with **stones** and **ledges,** so walk carefully. Along this narrow section, the trail is often forked and may be confusing. These trail divisions are generally less than 100 feet apart. They rejoin a couple of hundred feet farther along. If there is any doubt, look for the telephone wire that follows the trail among the trees and leads to the fire tower at the summit.

About 4,000 feet from the lean-to area, the trail begins to level as it runs south. The footing is almost all solid ledge. Some sections of granite are weathered and soft, crumbled and broken, while other portions are worn smooth with the tramping feet of early loggers and hikers. The surrounding **horizon** peeks through red oak and red pine stunted by thin soil and elevation. The trail makes a sharp right at an old hut and then another sharp cut to the left. From this last turn, the fire tower should be visible through the trees.

The **summit** of Pleasant Mountain is worn granite capped with red pine, red oak, gray birch, white birch, cherry, and a variety of other undersized trees. The ledges are lined with blueberries and their huckleberry relatives. Cracks in the boulders often house a small evergreen—three-toothed cinquefoil. The real attraction is the sweeping view of the horizon and the valley below.

The eastern slope looks immediately down on Moose Pond. The most obvious hill, 18 miles to the northeast, is Streaked Mountain (with fire tower), named for the rock slides scarring its sides. Directly to the east is a relatively low plain with few notable features. The **western view** is more outstanding. The bald pointed head of Mt. Chocorua is visible to the southwest; the rounded dome of Mt. Kearsarge with another fire tower is almost due west. To the right of Kearsarge is the dominant mountain of New Hampshire, Washington. With binoculars the buildings and towers on its peak are easily distinguished and a deep incision, the headwall of Tuckerman Ravine, carves into its slopes.

In the valley at the western edge of Pleasant Mountain are many landmarks of the Saco River valley. You

The western view from Pleasant Mountain.

can look southwest across Pleasant Pond to Lovewell Pond and on to the town of Fryeburg. The rounded knob of Mount Tom with its mantle of ledges rises almost due west. In an arc to the north of Mount Tom and cutting along the base of Pleasant Mountain is the Saco River itself. Most of the river's course in this area is man-made. To reduce the flooding of farmland, a decision was made in the early 1800s to cut a new channel for the river. The new course drained a lake as large as Lovewell Pond and moved the main channel several miles closer to the base of Mount Tom. Man created a 17-mile meandering arc where the native river once snaked through 33 miles of the valley. This reduced loop remains today as the most heavily used portion of the river. Thousands of canoeists annually make the trek from Swan's Falls in Fryeburg to the takeout on Route 302 below Mount Tom or the Route 160 bridge near East Brownfield. Even the native Pequawkets made use of this long loop in the river. They could leave their main **encampment** near Fryeburg, then hunt and fish for more than 30 miles along the river. They would then turn up into Lovewell Pond and be within 2 miles of their camp. One of the main roads follows the portage trail toward their homesite. How often did the Pequawket come to this pleasant peak and gaze over their valley, river, and hunting grounds?

There are several trails to the summit of Pleasant Mountain, but none afford the ease and access of the Firewarden's Trail. Return as you came, carrying the memory of the scenic view across these hills of southern Maine. Bring back the image of a distinctive flower or shrub. Hold a special thought for those who stood here first.

Getting There

Traveling west on Route 302, pass Moose Pond on the left and watch for Mountain Road and a sign advertising a local ski area. Continue past it another 2.3 miles to Fire Lane 37 (Warren Road) on the left. Traveling east from Fryeburg on Route 302, look for Denmark Road in East Fryeburg. Fire Lane 37 will be on the right about 0.9 mile from Denmark Road. Follow Fire Lane 37 for 1.1 miles of blacktop and later some gravel. As you approach a large yellow barn on the right, there will be parking on the left just before an equally yellow farmhouse also to the left. The trail begins just before the house on the left behind a barred gate.

37. Sebago Lake State Park

Naples

1,300 Acres

Woodlands

0.5 mile–3.0 miles

0.5 hour–6 hours

Nestled along the northern shore of Sebago Lake is the park that shares its name. It rests on aged glacial till and the floodplain of the Crooked and Songo Rivers. Sand grains ground by ancient glaciers and sorted by the melting waters of the **retreating ice** created a forested delta. The margin of this delta is several thousand feet of magnificent beach now incorporated into the park. Acres of picnic grounds and almost 300 campsites attest to the popularity of this area. The Songo River has formed a remarkable set of meanders and oxbows within the park borders producing a spacious wetland habitat for a variety of plant and animal species.

Sebago Lake State Park appeals to all types of outdoor enthusiasts. The layout of the park, designed by Myron Lamb in the 1930s, concentrated people into the camping and picnic facilities located close to the water, leaving much of the acreage as close to **wilderness** as possible. Those wanting to swim or snack or enjoy a crackling campfire with friends have one part of the park. Boaters and fishermen have access to the Songo

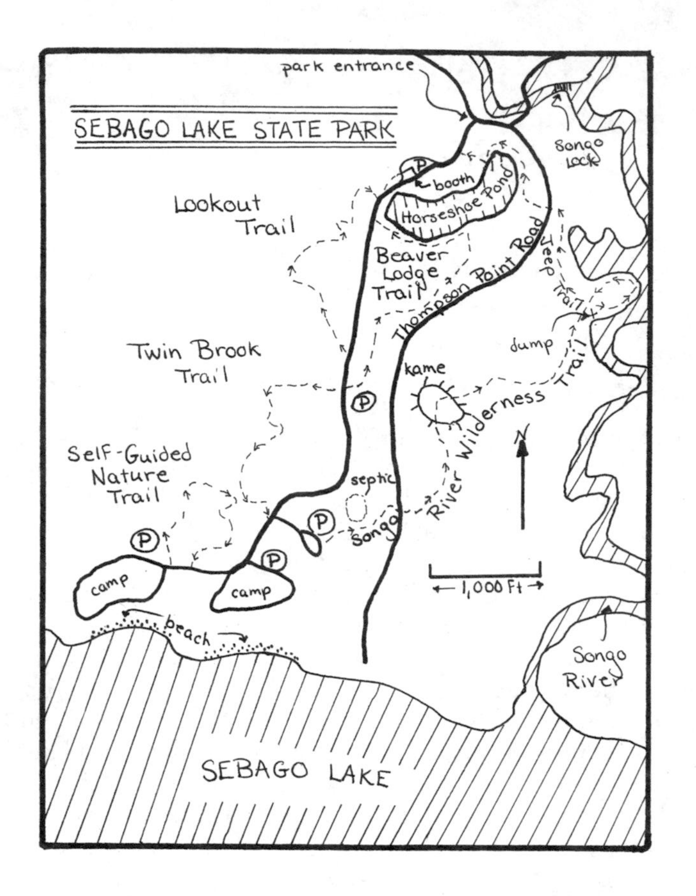

River and Sebago Lake, one of Maine's largest. Hikers seeking isolation can retreat to the five trails laced through the backwoods.

Four of these five **trails** are relatively short hikes, blazed in white, about 30 minutes each. The longest, the

Songo River Wilderness Trail, is three miles long. The closest to the camping area is the **Self-Guided Nature Trail.** You can walk it in either direction, but beginning in the parking area near campsites 120 and 121 allows for easier access. A white diamond on the pavement marks the entrance to the woods. The path enters the trees and immediately gains elevation, snaking up and around granite boulders spotted with common polypody ferns. The six-inch evergreen fronds of this fern commonly grow on boulders in moist forest. They are almost leatherlike, and the individual leaflets on each frond are not subdivided as are many lacy woodland ferns.

The trail continues uphill around and beyond the boulders covered with a black lichen called rock tripe. The initial section is steep, but the path soon levels out about 80 feet above the campground. The surrounding forest is the usual northern mixed hardwood and evergreens with a scattering of American beech and quite a bit of witch hazel. Glacial erratics seen along the trail were left as the giant ice sheet retreated. The soil is thin and acid, covered with mosses and the leathery oval leaves of the six-inch-high teaberry. Farther into the woods the path drops into some low spots with cinnamon fern, goldthread, and sphagnum appearing. The trail loops around a bog and heads back toward the road. It emerges onto the blacktop at another white diamond across from campsite 57, a couple of hundred feet from the starting point.

The one-mile (one-way) **Twin Brook Trail** begins about 0.5 mile down the entrance road from the ranger booth, across from the trailhead to the Beaver Lodge Trail. All are marked with signs and the familiar white diamonds on the blacktop. Twin Brook Trail moves through a mixed forest with some hemlock and a heavy dose of wild sarsaparilla. It is a fairly flat trail initially. As it cuts left, a beautiful **brook** comes into view. It is a green mossy stripe in the floor of an already verdant forest. The water gurgles and ripples about the base of countless small glacial boulders. About 700 feet farther, the trail follows a shoulder along another, less striking stream in a parklike area with a thick canopy of young white pine. This trail heads back toward the road and cuts through American beech and striped maple just before it comes out to the macadam and the white diamond marker.

The **Beaver Lodge Trail,** like the Twin Brook Trail, begins on the entrance road 0.5 mile from the ranger booth. There is a brown sign on the left and a diamond marker on the road. It has more deciduous trees—oaks and maples—mixed in with evergreens. It parallels the road for a few hundred feet, drops along the very steep slope of a glacial **terrace** and moves right across sandy soil deposited by the Songo River. Overall, it has the fewest hills and slopes of all the paths in the park. As the trail cuts back to the left, a pond with an intense growth of water plants comes into view. You have to strain to see high hummocks marked with peeled sticks —the active home of a North American beaver family. The quiet waters and lush vegetation of the Songo River make a perfect habitat for this animal.

Much of the early fur trade across our continent was based on the **beaver.** Once seriously depleted, it is making a comeback. While still legally trapped and considered a bit of a novelty in Maine, it is known for its persistence, damming waters in areas humans prefer to keep clear. The beaver has great value, though, for its dams and impounded waters create precious habitat for birds, fish, other mammals, and a variety of plants.

The last of the short hikes is the **Lookout Trail.** It requires more exertion with an elevation gain of around 300 feet. It begins on the right side of the entrance road almost 0.5 mile from the ranger booth, just before the trailheads for the Beaver Lodge and Twin Brook Trails. It follows a steady climb through primarily deciduous forest. The **summit** is a flattened ledge covered with grasses, oak, and pine and looks down on the road leading into the campsites. From the peak, the trail drops and winds down through a heavy growth of beech and striped maple. Near the base of the trail is a dark moist area with eastern hemlock, a perfect habitat for amphibians. Stay on the trail. Tread carefully, as some of the plants in this area are Maine's protected orchids. One example is the dwarf rattlesnake plantain. It has a rosette of basal leaves with white-checkered veins on a dark green background. It shows a spike of white flowers in July and August. A few hundred feet from the boggy spot, the trail emerges from the woods just below the ranger's registration booth and its parking lot.

The real **star** of the trail system is the **Songo River Wilderness Trail.** Including the roadway, it is a three-mile loop carrying the walker well away from the sounds on the lake and the campfire smell of wood smoke. The trailhead is somewhat inconspicuous, tucked away on the blacktop drive in the service area on the left, three-quarters of the way down the campground road.

This is the only trail with a blue blaze. It must be watched initially as the trail crisscrosses several other paths in the first 600 feet. The surrounding forest is, like much of the park, young deciduous trees, red and white oaks, red maples, and some conifers. A close look at the ground forecasts a change coming in the canopy. Hundreds of small white pine **seedlings** are thrusting through the ground cover. If most make it to maturity, this natural succession will create a different forest in 50 years.

The trail swings northeast, past large septic fields serving the park. Here it follows the rounded shoulder of a glacial terrace. As it begins to drop and cut right over this shoulder, Thompson Point Road comes into view. A blue diamond and arrow direct the walker to the left and a couple of hundred feet down the road, a matching marker points you back into the woods on the far side of the road. Here, 2,000 feet into the walk, the hiker comes to the most isolated portion of the park.

A cautious, quiet person may glimpse a doe and fawn or young buck grazing on tender shoots in the spring or masticating on acorns in the fall. Hunting is not allowed in this park, and the white-tailed deer take advantage of the protection. The trail is quite even here and walking quietly is easy. Droppings, tracks, and the occasional deer are here for the observant eye.

About 1,000 feet in from the road, the flat trail hits another section of glacial deposit (a **kame**) that rises 40 to 50 feet above the surrounding material laid down by the Songo River. Beech, gray birch, eastern hemlock, and striped maple are growing along the top of the rise. Many of the younger gray birch, with arching white trunks marked with gray patches, will be overgrown by the taller trees. Even in winter the beech trees are easy to spot. They retain most of their oval toothed leaves, which are a light brown color as opposed to summer green. The young beech also have a light gray, smooth bark. Watch for the larger cobbles that make up the kame showing through the trail on the downhill side.

Now 3,800 feet into the hike, the trail again levels out in mixed hardwoods. Teaberry and lycopodium abound in the ground cover. Off to the right there is an 8-foot drop to a wet area signaling the appearance of a backwater or **oxbow** along the Songo River. The trail continues closing on this swamp until it parallels the banking. Reeds and open water make the ideal feeding and breeding habitat for muskrats, ducks, and the myriad of smaller creatures making up their food chain.

The banking begins to curve to the right. There are signs of an old dump (yes, humans have been here), and the trail suddenly intersects with an old jeep trail. The blue blaze directs the hiker into a sharp right turn, continuing along the waterway, now 4,600 feet from the trailhead. The walk makes its way out onto a point jutting into the Songo River. A little more than a mile into the hike, the path opens onto the sandy banks of the Songo River proper. The river is about 80 feet wide with a broad sandy beach on the near side. The dark tannin-stained waters hide young fish and the occasional turtle. Take a break at this secluded spot and enjoy the shimmering reflections across the surface of the water.

The ancient Songo Lock is near the entrance to Sebago Lake State Park.

From the beach, the trail cuts left and traces the riverbank. It turns back on itself and meets the old jeep track. From this intersection, the trail turns right and follows an old slough, home to several ducks. As the watercourse drops away on the right, the flat trail moves off into oak and maple forest and at 9,200 feet returns to Thompson Point Road. Directly across the road, the trail moves back into the woods and begins a long easy climb. Just after the trail tops the rise and levels out, there is an abrupt left turn onto a narrow path.

This new turn quickly leads to a drop down a hillside to another jewel on this wilderness trail. Open water marks the back side of Horseshoe Pond rimmed on its southern margin by the Beaver Lodge Trail. The higher elevation of this path and the open water may give a better view of possible beaver activity on the pond. Visiting early in the morning or at dusk will increase your chances of seeing the beavers.

The trail makes a U-turn around the northern end of the pond, coming to an isolated picnic table with one of the nicer views in Sebago Lake State Park. It sits on a knoll and surveys most of Horseshoe Pond, which may have originated as a glacial **kettle hole.** It is a perfect place to sit and snack or just enjoy relaxing from the 2 miles traveled. From here the trail continues alongside the water and makes a radical right turn uphill into the woods. Abruptly, the trail breaks out onto the campground road with a blue diamond on the blacktop. You have walked 2.2 miles from the trailhead and are now a few hundred feet from the park entrance. Unless you left a vehicle at the ranger's booth ahead of time, it is a 1-mile walk along the campground road back to the service area.

The mix of beaches, camping, and trails offered at Sebago Lake State Park meets the needs of many people. Enjoy the trails, leaving them cleaner than you found them, or see if the park's rangers have an area that needs marking or clearing. The present reduction in state funding makes volunteer **support** for the system even more critical than before. You can help make a difference.

Getting There

Route 302/35 is the main thoroughfare past Sebago Lake State Park. About 5.5 miles north of the junction with Route 121 there is a small state park sign. Take a left and after about 1.5 miles down this road, another left turn leads to the picnic and beach area of the park. To get to the campgrounds, continue past this turn across a small bridge. The next left crosses a tiny one-way turntable bridge at the Songo Locks (last one on the old Cumberland and Oxford Canal). Past the bridge, stay right until the next park entrance on your left.

From the north, follow Routes 11/114 in Naples, then the signs for the Songo Locks. The park entrance will come up on the right.

Like all state parks there is an entrance fee for day use and camping. The park is open from early May to mid-October.

For more information call 207-693-6231.

38. Gray Game Farm and Visitors Center

Gray

200 Acres

Woodlands

1 mile

2 hours

Wheelchair accessible: level 1–3 (see p. xiv)

Gray Game Farm and Visitors Center offers two short nature trails, wildlife gardens, interactive educational displays, and a **guaranteed up close look at several species of Maine wildlife.** It also creates **an opportunity to consider and discuss a number of wildlife-related issues,** including game management, wildlife rehabilitation, and human impact on animal habitat.

The farm was purchased in 1931, through a mandate of the Maine legislature. It was charged with raising pheasant that would subsequently be leased to stock hunting areas. In 1982, this program was phased out. In the interim, however, department wardens and biologists had begun bringing injured and orphaned animals to the farm for rehabilitation. It proved well suited for this undertaking. The present game farm and visitors center evolved from these modest beginnings. The

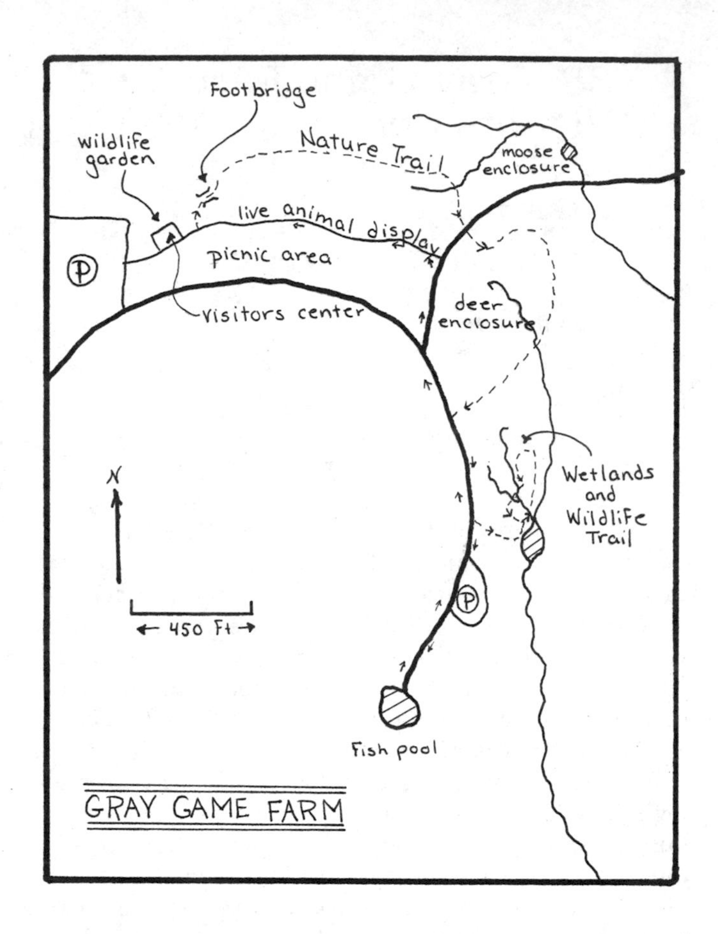

vision for its future expands with its new mission of public awareness, education, and wildlife rehabilitation.

The game farm takes in more than 100 animals each year. Whenever possible, the animals are released back

into the wild. Most of the animals are inju
orphaned, presumed orphaned, or dependent
humans after being raised in captivity. Most disturbi
are the presumed-orphaned and the human-dependen
cases. The largest number of referrals are made in the spring when well-meaning citizens unwittingly separate young from their parents. In the wild, parents must often leave their young temporarily to gather food. If people discover the waiting young, they often conclude that it has been abandoned and remove it from its hiding place, either bringing it to a rehabilitation center or trying to raise it on their own. Meanwhile, the parents return to find their offspring gone and frantically call and search for it to no avail.

In the best of circumstances—a healthy animal in the hands of trained professionals—as few as one in three will survive. The stress of handling and captivity is often enough to cause the death of an animal. Even temporary handling may be fatal: a bird that has been touched by humans will still be accepted by its parents as birds have a poor sense of smell; mammals, on the other hand, have an excellent sense of smell and will often reject young that have been contaminated with the scent of humans. Humans cannot provide the level of care, the proper quantity and quality of nutrition, or the educational lessons that a natural parent does. We cannot teach a bear how to be a bear, how to hunt, track, find a mate, and raise its young, nor can we provide it with the necessary space. A bear's range may be 100 square miles or more.

Many of the animals at the Gray Game Farm can never be released. They have become habituated to peo-

ı deer accustomed to being fed from the hands of ıans will not survive long during hunting season. A nter does not care if the deer thinks she or he is a iend. The same is true for moose, fox, or even coyote. ıf the animal is comfortable with you, it will not last long in the wild.

In addition, an animal removed from the wild is separated from the breeding population and can no longer have young. Populations of endangered or threatened species can be severely affected when this occurs. Wild animals often look cute and cuddly, especially when young, but they are feisty and unmanageable in an enclosed space like your home. As the visitors center brochure clearly states, "If you care, leave them there." A hands-off approach to wildlife is often a humane approach.

The animals at the game farm are all native species except for the ornamental pheasants and the mountain lion, which is now extinct in Maine. While it is an excellent opportunity to see these wild animals, **it may also be distressing to observe them in the confined space of a cage.** This is an opportune time to discuss with children the impact of captivity on the habits of each species. Coyotes naturally roam for miles every day; what happens when it is enclosed by a wall 20 feet across? Captive animals are fed chopped meat and dog food instead of live prey. What would the mountain lion, coyote, and bobcat hunt in the wild?

Begin your walk at the visitors center. Surrounding the building is a wildlife garden. Plaques describe each of the plants and indicate what species of animals are attracted to the fruit, flowers, or vegetation that it provides. As you circle to the left around the back, a large informational display describes how you can create space for wildlife in your back yard at home.

Spend some time investigating the interactive displays inside the visitors center. Topics include tracking, animal rehabilitation, fur-bearing animals, fish, animal size, and habitat. Children and adults get to test their knowledge and have fun.

The Nature Trail begins to the left of the first animal cage (**coyote**). It was designed to demonstrate **white-**

Selected plants attract a variety of wildlife to the visitors center gardens.

tailed deer habitat. The trail swings to the right and drops into a shallow draw crossed by a footbridge. The gentle grade and well-groomed footpath make for easy walking. It is amazing how quickly you can find relative solitude only a few hundred feet from the hustle and bustle of the picnic area. You have entered a northern hardwood forest. Red oak, red maple, and an occasional beech tree surround the trail. The trees provide protection and nourishment for the deer, who may require the tender leaf buds for winter forage. After crossing an intermittent stream and entering a stand of evergreens, the first 0.25 mile of trail emerges between the Canada lynx cage and the moose enclosure.

White-tailed deer often choose hemlock groves for their winter yard. The deer do not fare well in deep snow so they herd up, packing the snow over a large area and gathering together for warmth and protection. Unlike **moose,** their hooves are narrow and give them little aid. When the snow is crusted with ice, they cannot walk on top of it. Their hooves punch through and their legs are torn on the ragged edges of the broken crust, slowing possible escape. Meanwhile, their predators, coyote, bobcat, and domestic dogs, bound across the crust unimpeded. This is when the family pet can often cause great suffering to both individual deer and local herds. Dogs, unlike most wild animals, do not kill their prey before consuming it. Often game wardens will discover deer still alive but partially disemboweled, with dog tracks leading back to the pet owner's home.

Moose are common in the woods of northern Maine. Unlike white-tailed deer, they prefer moist evergreen forests. Their hooves and legs are adapted to winter conditions. They lift their legs up, then stretch them forward over the surface of the snow, instead of plowing through it like deer. In addition, long legs keep their bellies from dragging in the snow. Their massive bodies retain heat better in winter. A large bull moose can weigh close to half a ton, while a white-tailed deer sets records at 300 pounds.

Here in Maine, the ecological boundaries between moose and white-tailed deer meet. The deer are more plentiful in the hardwood forests of southern Maine, while the moose rule the evergreen forests of the north. Deer are much more plentiful in such states as Pennsyl-

Albino porcupines such as this one (protected at the Gray Game Farm) are a rare sight in nature.

ania, where the winters are more forgiving, but in Maine they often grow larger.

As you leave the moose corral, cross the paved road and circle the deer enclosure following the dirt track on the far side. Sharing space with deer are wild turkeys and several species of ducks.

Rejoin the paved road and turn left. In a few hundred yards, turn left again onto a second nature trail. This section is a demonstration project on wetlands. As the information board explains, water is important to all living things. Ponds, streams, lakes, and marshes all attract and support wildlife. Some animals spend only a short amount of time in and about wetlands, drinking then feeding elsewhere, while others are rarely separated from a body of water. These animals—ducks, frogs, turtles, fish, and insect larvae—depend on permanent pools of water for food and shelter.

Return to the paved road. Take a left to reach the fish hatchery and a show pool of the biggest **trout** you are likely to have the pleasure of viewing in this lifetime. Or, turn right and proceed to the visitors center via the wild animal display cages.

As you backtrack along the road, the ornamental **pheasants, owls, hawks, crows, ravens, turkey vultures, bald eagles,** and **turtles** are housed separately in the same compound on your left. Continuing on the paved road take the right fork at the junction, then turn left immediately before the mountain lion enclosure. On your right, you will see **black bear, raccoon, porcupine, pine marten, mink, fisher, coyote,** and more. Each has a plaque beside it describing the animal and its habitat.

Complete the loop back at the visitors center, also on your right.

The Gray Game Farm is hoping to fund and build a new rehabilitation center in the next year. Expansions are planned for many of the enclosures. Much of the work is done with the help of volunteers and donations. The entrance fee goes directly to the farm and is used to fund personnel and maintain and improve the facilities. Your assistance in these endeavors and in following park rules is appreciated.

Getting There

From the intersection of Routes 26, 100, 202, and 4 in Gray, take Route 26 north 3.5 miles. Turn right at the sign for the Gray Game Farm and the Maine State Police.

For more information call 207-657-4977 or TDD #287-4471.

39. Range Ponds State Park

Poland

750 Acres

Woodlands

up to 2 miles

2 hours

Wheelchair accessible: level 1–2 (see p. xiv)

The state of Maine is to be congratulated for the design of this park. It was created with wheelchair access in mind. The result is a highly approachable recreation area for those with physical limitations.

As you drive 3,000 feet down the entrance road, past the tollbooth, the popularity of Range (pronounced rang) Ponds State Park becomes evident from several large parking lots. Reduce the competition for space by visiting on weekdays or evenings during the summer season. Handicapped parking is designated close to the large gray buildings near the pond. From the graveled parking zone, a planked deck leads between the men's and women's rest rooms with their double-wide doors. Step a few feet toward the pond to one of the unique features of Range Ponds State Park: a smooth-surfaced **promenade** parallels the pond for 1,000 feet immediately next to the fine sand beach. Turn right and walk, stroll, or roll past a series of picnic tables (like the parking, some of these are also reserved) that face onto the

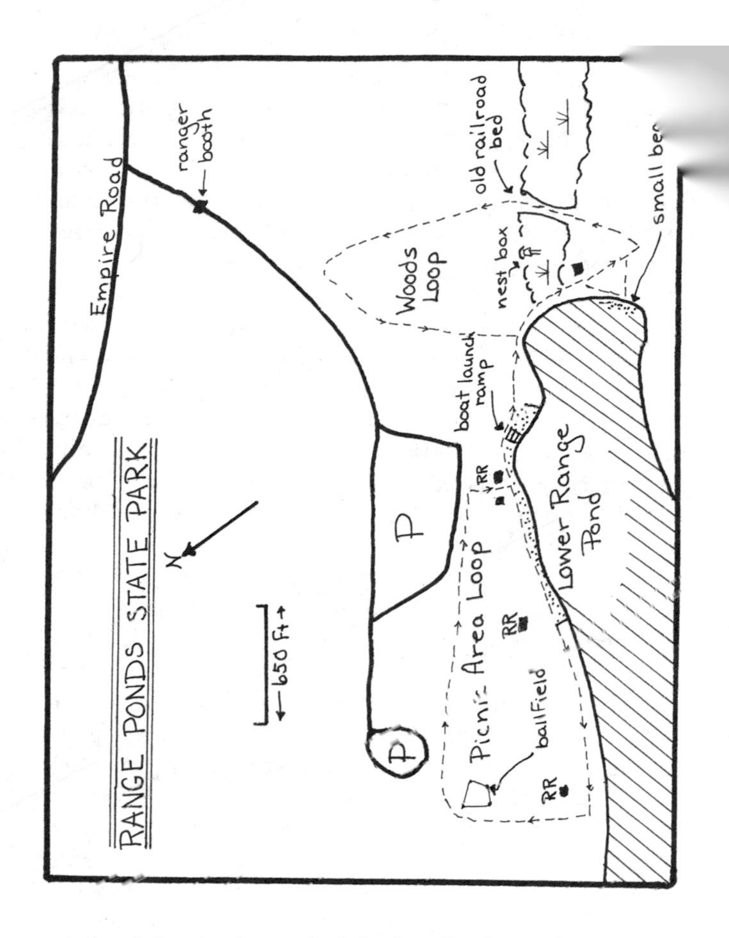

pristine lake. At the end of the beach, the path continues on a surface of leaves and needles straight into the woods and another set of tables strung along the margin of the pond. This **woodland path**, with smaller acing side trails, continues more than 1,000 feet a series of swings, slides, and horseshoe pits. out 1,800 feet from the beach it makes a right angle p into the woods, makes a right turn around a small ball field, and heads back to the parking area. This mile-long loop is accessible and marred by only a few tree roots that should cause no problems for hikers or wheelchairs.

Most of the walking/hiking trails in southern Maine are a corrugated surface of roots and rocks. The compact, moist soils drive tree roots to the surface where they challenge the most ardent hiker. The deep-drained soils of this park allow for a very smooth walking surface. This is particularly evident on the woods loop that heads from the rest rooms east to the boat launch.

Beyond the ramp and open sand there is a series of picnic tables along the water's edge. The trail slips along the arc of the beach onto the remains of the wide trail from the parking lot. It passes through a forest of red (Norway) and white pine and a carpet of ground pine and mosses. The reddish bark and paired six-inch-long needles of the red pine contrast with the dark furrowed bark and three-inch needles (cluster of five) on the white pine. The pine cones are the easiest way to distinguish the two trees. The white pine's cones are up to six inches long and very narrow compared to the two-inch rounded cone of the red pine. Regardless of shape, the **cones** provide nutritious seeds for the squirrel and chipmunk population. Pine cones beneath the trees are cushioned by the ground pine, or lycopodium. This plant, a few inches tall, looks like a miniature pine and carries upright spore cases that look like small pine cones. Lycopodium is a descendant of the plants that dominated the Carboniferous period more than 300 million years ago. The remains of most of these plants is now known as coal.

A few hundred feet farther, another trail intersects at a right angle and dead-ends on the lake to the right. This is the return end of the loop. Four hundred feet past this junction, the path breaks out onto a low gravel stretch skirting the eastern end of Lower Range Pond. On the left is a marsh with **wood duck boxes.** To the right is a view the length of the pond. Beyond the low area, the trail slopes uphill through a planting of young red pine past a rest room on the left and another picnic spot. Farther along, some hikers may wish to follow a narrow trail to the right, up a set of steps leading to a small, quiet beach. The main trail continues straight for another 500 feet, where a small arrow on a gray post points to a left-hand turn. This path, some 10 feet wide and sloping slightly downhill, moves through a mixed forest. The trees and shrubs begin to drop away on each side to reveal an old, smooth **rail bed** elevated about 20 feet above the surrounding landscape. This strange formation in the midst of a marsh is the relic of a train track to the former Poland Spring House. To the left is the bog with the duck boxes. On the right, the marsh continues with leatherleaf, highbush blueberry, and winter holly. The raised portion of the path, canopied by pines, proceeds for about 900 feet. After the trail crosses the bog, the path begins to arc left into the forest on a very smooth jeep trail. Here and there a few black spruce, up to 8 or 10 feet high, grow in the low spots.

Portions of Range Pond allow for solitude and reflection.

This is one of the hardiest evergreens and grows right up to tree line in the Arctic and on mountaintops. Locally its sap was harvested for spruce gum and the young shoots were made into spruce beer. The dense growth and fuzzy coat of needles once made this spruce a popular Christmas tree. Needles on the black spruce are about half an inch long and the twigs and buds are hairy. The rounded half-inch cylindrical cone is much smaller than those of the red or white spruce. The warm green color of the foliage and the dark bark give the tree its name.

The trail heads toward the access road. You can see the ranger toll station to the right through the woods. At this point the path cuts sharply to the left to return to the margin of the pond and parallels the blacktop drive for a short distance. There are a couple of gentle slopes and a smooth spot of ledge as the path makes its return. At the intersection with the lakeside trail, turn right and head back to the boat launch area. The length of this woods loop is just about one mile and is wheelchair accessible the whole way around.

Like the design of Sebago Lake State Park (see p. 281), Range Ponds maintains a centralized busy area combined with trails that allow for escape to the quiet corners of the park. The fact that so much of the park has been made accessible, including trails, is certainly unique and should serve as a model for future outdoor developments.

Getting There

The main artery in this area of Maine is Route 26. Travel north from Gray or south from the Poland and Poland Springs area. Leave Route 26 and pick up 122 north just a few miles north of the Gray Game Farm & Visitors Center, and drive 1.3 miles. Turn left onto Empire Road. The well marked entrance to the park will be 0.7 mile on the left.

40. Thorncrag Bird Sanctuary

Lewiston
230 Acres

Woodlands

2.5 miles

3 hours

Thorncrag Bird Sanctuary is where urban meets country. Within moments of entering the grounds, you forget you are in one of Maine's largest cities. The sanctuary is sizable. In addition, it borders on parcels of undeveloped private land. This allows it to provide truly safe haven for a large and varied animal population. The two resident authorities on Thorncrag wildlife, Jason and Dan, took a break from their frog-catching activities to talk about their experiences with wildlife in the sanctuary. Jason visits almost every day. He's seen white-tailed deer, porcupine, snapping turtles, owls, snakes, and lots of frogs. He was a good teacher. In a few moments' time, he had spied and captured a **garter snake** (which escaped), a **woolly bear caterpillar,** and a **pickerel frog.** All of these he released except the frog, which was going to be a meal for his pet snake. Of course, his mom was going to make him let the snake go before school started. I learned from Jason to delight in little things and to keep my eyes open.

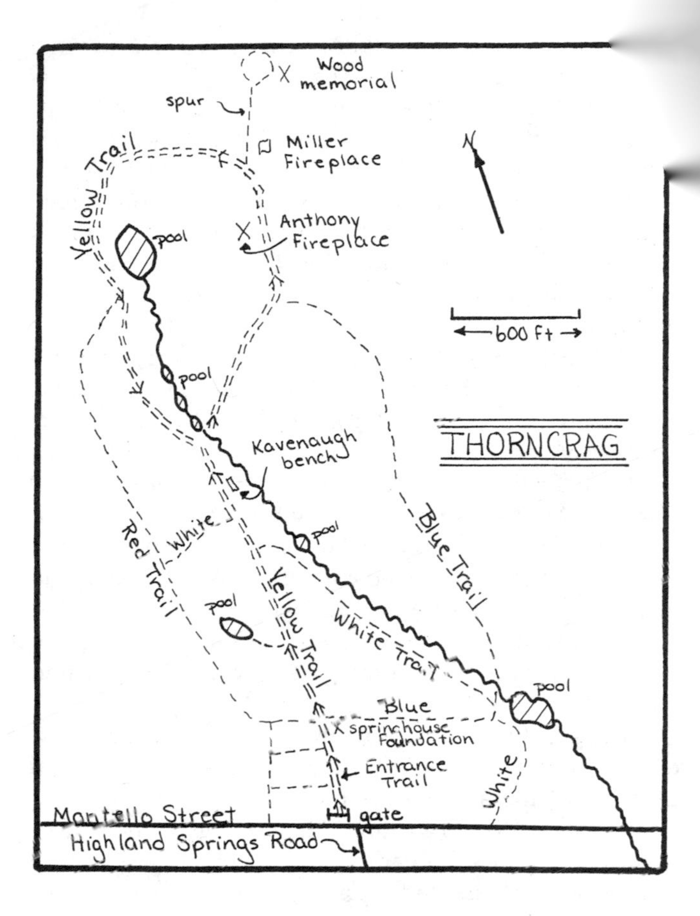

Dr. Alfred Anthony, a professor at Bates College, donated most of the sanctuary's land to the Stanton Bird Club in 1928. The huge stone fireplace and benches at the top of the hill honor his memory. A few hun-

.eet beyond the Anthony fireplace is a bronze ıe set in stone memorializing Mabel Wood's con- ution; she donated the narrow strip of land con- :ting the two larger parcels. Evidence of the founda- ons and fireplaces of earlier residents can be found in .he woods and along the paths. The **old cellar holes and stone walls** are from the early 1900s. The remains of a farmhouse were removed in 1867. It is a place that has been well loved by many and used for farming and lumber.

A brochure outlining the cultural history, natural history, rules of the sanctuary, and information about the Stanton Bird Club is found in the battered mailbox on the right where the drive meets Montello Street. The Entrance Trail is 0.1 mile in length, as is the spur trail from the Anthony fireplace to the Wood memorial. Neither one of these paths is blazed, but each is easy to follow. Other trails are blazed by color. The Blue, Red, and White Trails are each 0.5 mile, and the Yellow Trail is 0.8 mile. All paths frequently intersect, allowing you to see as much or as little of the park as you have time and inclination.

The sanctuary gives the impression that the caretakers are warm people who enjoy sharing this special place with others. There are **numerous benches** provided for the comfort of visitors. They supply a good place to sit while you keep ears open and binoculars poised for spring warblers, fall migrants, and year-round residents like the black-capped chickadee, the red-breasted nuthatch, and the downy woodpecker. The pools excavated in the 1940s and 1950s offer refreshment for

Anthony fireplace is a picnic destination at Thorncrag.

wildlife on an otherwise dry hillside and habitat for reptiles and amphibians.

The Entrance Trail begins in a mixed stand of ash, locust, maple, and oak. The path, an old road, is wide and well groomed. There is a bench immediately on your right. The footway is lined with plantain and thistle. Common plantain was introduced to the New World by Europeans. Tradition has it that the cluster of parallel veined, basal leaves was referred to as whiteman's footprints by Native Americans, who recognized that the plant followed Europeans' westward spread in North America. An abundance of gray squirrels scatter in the trees. At 0.1 mile you enter a large clearing, with the springhouse foundation appearing prominently on your left. The Blue Trail branches right across the open grassy area and enters the pines. The Red Trail leads off ın the northwest corner of the foundation. The .rail continues straight ahead.

you begin the Yellow Trail, notice the golden- Queen Anne's lace, milkweed—whose names are descriptors—and alder on your left. The light green, ee-leafed vine with the egg-shaped leaves is a mem- er of the pea family called hog peanut. It's a rather coarse name for a plant with such delicate pale purple flowers. But it is a practical name. Although the fruit of the visible flowers is inedible, there is a second set of petal-less flowers that produces a pod beneath the ground. This fruit is edible when boiled and served with butter. Hogs discover it when rooting about in the ground and consume it without accoutrements.

Pass through an open understory, overshadowed by pine, birch, and maple. On your left is a wet area graced with a large spread of ferns and a side trail leading a few hundred feet to a pool. Beneath a grand old white pine and edging the pond are two backed benches. Listen for chickadees, red-eyed vireo, wood peewee, and red-breasted nuthatches.

The Yellow Trail soon intersects with the White Trail on the right. They combine for a short distance, then the White Trail departs, leading uphill on the left. One hundred feet beyond is the Kavanaugh bench, the perfect place to rest on a hot sunny day—the stones are refreshingly cool under the shade of overhanging branches. In 200 feet, the Yellow Trail meets itself as it closes the top loop. Continue to the right, the most direct route to the Anthony fireplace.

Although the forest is a rich mixture of hardwood and softwood species, the impression is that of a stand of **pines.** They dominate the senses. The needles remain, cushioning the footpath long after the wind has picked up the oak and maple leaves and carried them to the outstretched arms of some understory thicket. The pines scent the air. Even in winter, the green needles console us with their living presence.

The Blue Trail joins the Yellow on the right 100 feet below the Anthony fireplace and leads downhill to the southeast corner of the sanctuary. From the intersection you can glimpse the clearing surrounding the memorial. The **huge fireplace** is enclosed by a semicircle of large, beautiful **stone masonry benches,** all set beneath the spreading branches of a red oak. The encircling field contains plantain, purple clover, a variety of grasses, and crickets. Look for lightning bugs on early July evenings.

Three hundred feet beyond the memorial, the Yellow Trail makes a sharp left turn and begins a gradual descent. Continuing straight ahead will take you past the Miller fireplace and Wood memorial, both on the right. The northern portion of the sanctuary is accessed along this path, but the trails in this section have not yet been mapped.

Turning left with the Yellow Trail, descend through hemlocks. In 0.1 mile, pass a duck box on the edge of a large pool. From here to the intersection with the Red Trail, the path swings wide around the perimeter of the wooded pond. This area feels more secluded tranquil than the main trail. Many people visit the sanctuary as a destination hike to Anthony fireplace. If you prefer to find a quiet place to yourself, the northwestern sections of the Yellow, Red, and White Trails

Queen Anne's lace blooms in the fields of the bird sanctuary.

make a good loop. You may be accompanied by the constant chatter of black-capped chickadees, the flute-like serenade of **wood thrush and hermit thrush,** and the wake-up call of robins.

Continuing on the Yellow Trail, you will pass two more smaller pools on your left (the last may be dry). Proceed through a bountiful stand of **beech trees** and close the loop just above Kavanaugh bench. The length of the Yellow Trail is 0.8 mile. Returning along this route to your car is a 1.2-mile round-trip. If you choose to descend along the Red Trail instead, you will find yourself paralleling an old stone wall. Chipmunks peek from between rocks, give a warning squeak, then pear. In 0.3 mile the trail takes a sharp left across fr huge white pine. Scan the top for large holes excava in the dead branches, evidence of pileated woodpec ers.

In 300 feet, the Red Trail meets the western terminus of the White Trail. The White Trail cuts diagonally across the preserve from west to southeast intersecting first the Yellow then the Blue Trail before dropping due south to Montello Street. Proceed on the Red Trail. Pass an old chimney, then swing left through white pines. Cross a log bridge to discover yourself once again at the springhouse foundation. Returning to your car via the Entrance Trail, the Yellow and Red Trail loop is 1.5 miles in length.

Getting There

The sanctuary entrance is located at the intersection of Montello Street and Highland Springs Road. There are a multitude of routes leading to the gate. Enter Lewiston on the James B. Longley Memorial Bridge and drive north on Main Street (Routes 202, 11, and 100). In 0.5 mile turn right at the lights onto Sabattus Street (Route 126). Travel 3 miles. Turn left onto Highland Spring Road. A sign for the sanctuary stands on the corner. Highland Spring Road dead-ends onto Montello Street, directly across from the entrance to Thorncrag. Parking is available to the right along Montello Street. Please do not block the gate leading to the sanctuary.

For more information, contact: Stanton Bird Club, PO Box 3177, Lewiston, ME 04243.

Bibliography

Barrows, John Stuart. *Fryeburg Maine.* Fryeburg, Maine: Pequawket Press, 1938.

Caldwell, Bill. *Lighthouses of Maine.* Portland, Maine: Gannet Books, 1986.

Duncan, Roger F. *Coastal Maine.* New York: W. W. Norton, 1992.

Dwelley, Marilyn J. *Trees and Shrubs of New England.* Camden, Maine: Down East Books, 1980.

Epple, Anne Orth. *The Amphibians of New England.* Camden, Maine: Down East Books, 1983.

Ernst, George. *New England in Miniature.* Freeport, Maine: Bond Wheelright, 1961.

Foster, Steven, and James A. Duke. *A Field Guide to Medicinal Plants.* Boston: Houghton Mifflin, 1990.

Gosner, Kenneth L. A *Field Guide to the Atlantic Shore.* Boston: Houghton Mifflin, 1978.

Hansen, Judith. *Seashells in My Pocket: A Child's Nature Guide to Exploring the Atlantic Coast.* Boston: Appalachian Mountain Club Books, 1992.

Harlow, William M., Ph.D. *Fruit and Twig Key to Trees and Shrubs.* New York: Dover Publications, 1946.

Hunter, Malcolm L. Jr., John Albright, and Jane Arbuckle. *The Amphibians and Reptiles of Maine.* Orono, Maine: Maine Agricultural Experiment Station, 1992.

Jacobson, Bruce, with Joel W. Eastman and Anne Bridges. *Tides of Change.* Freeport, Maine: Freeport Historical Society, 1985.

Johnson, Judith B. *The Heritage of Our Maine Wildflowers.* Rockland, Maine: Courier of Maine Books, 1978.

Kendall, David L. *Glaciers & Granite.* Camden, Maine: Down East Books, 1987.

Kennedy, Edward, and Dale Fairar. *A History and Self-guided Tou[r] Steve Powell Wildlife Management Area.* Augusta, Maine: Maine Department of Inland Fisheries and Wildlife, 1977.

Kricher, John C., and Gordon Morrison. *Eastern Forests.* Boston: Houghton Mifflin, 1988.

Lust, John B. *The Herb Book.* New York: Bantam Books, 1974.

Marchand, Peter. *Life in the Cold.* Hanover, N. H. : University Press of New England, 1987.

———. *North Woods: An Inside Look at the Nature of Forests in the Northeast.* Boston: Appalachian Mountain Club Books, 1987.

Morris, Percy A. *Shells of the Atlantic.* Boston: Houghton Mifflin, 1973.

Newcomb, Lawrence. *Wildflower Guide.* Boston: Little, Brown, 1977.

Peterson, Lee Allen. *Edible Wild Plants.* Boston: Houghton Mifflin, 1977.

Robbins, Chandler S., Bertel Bruun, and Herbert S. Zim. *Birds of North America.* New York: Golden Press, 1983.

Roberts, Kenneth. *Boon Island.* Garden City: Doubleday, 1956.

Rowe, William H. *Ancient North Yarmouth and Yarmouth, Maine 1636–1936.* Yarmouth, Maine: Southworth-Anthoensen Press, 1937.

Rowe, William R. *The Maritime History of Maine.* W. W. Norton, 1948.

Simpson, Dorothy. *The Maine Islands.* Nobleboro, Maine: Blackberry Books, 1987.

Smith, Robert L. *Ecology and Field Biology.* 3d ed. New York: Harper and Row, 1980.

Spiller, Virginia S. *Colonial Ramblings.* York, Maine: York Historical Society, (date unknown).

Thompson, Woodrow B. et al. *A Collector's Guide to Maine Mineral Localities.* Maine Geological Survey, Department of Conservation, 1991.

Venning, Frank D. *Wildflowers of North America.* New York: Golden Press, 1984.

Wiggin, Agnes Innes. *Let's Go Back and Reminisce.* West Buxton, Maine: Buxton Press, 1992.

———. *Home.* West Buxton, Maine: Buxton Press, 1988.

About the Authors

JAN M. COLLINS teaches high school biology and chemistry in southern Maine. She received a B.A. from the Rochester Institute of Technology and an M.Ed. in secondary education from the University of Maine. She has spent many summers working as an interpretive specialist for the Appalachian Mountain Club.

JOSEPH E. McCARTHY, Ph.D., teaches biology and marine science in southern Maine. An instructor for more than twenty years at the University of Southern Maine, he has also taught Elderhostel classes in marine topics and medicinal and edible plants at the University of New England. He received a B.A. from St. Francis College (now the University of New England), and an M.S. and Ph.D. from Oregon State University.

About the AMC

The Appalachian Mountain Club pursues an active conservation agenda while encouraging responsible recreation. Founded in 1876, the club has been at the forefront of the environmental protection movement. Our philosophy is that successful long-term conservation depends on firsthand experience of the natural environment. AMC's 67,000 members pursue interests in hiking, canoeing, skiing, walking, rock climbing, bicycling, camping, kayaking, and backpacking, and—at the same time—help safeguard the environment.

The most recent efforts in the AMC Conservation program include river protection, Northern Forest lands policy, Sterling Forest (NY) preservation, and support for the Clean Air Act. The AMC depends upon its active members and grassroots supporters to promote this conservation agenda.

The AMC's Education department offers members and the general public a wide range of workshops, from introductory camping to intensive Mountain Leadership School taught on the trails of the White Mountains. In addition, volunteers in each chapter lead hundreds of outdoor activities and excursions and offer introductory instruction in backcountry sports.

The AMC's Research department focuses on the forces affecting the ecosystem, including ozone levels, acid rain and fog, climate change, rare flora and habitat protection, and air quality and visibility.

.other facet of the AMC is the Trails program, . maintains more than 1,400 miles of trail (including miles of the Appalachian Trail) and more than 50 .lters in the Northeast. Through a coordinated effort of olunteers, seasonal crews, and program staff, the AMC contributes more than 10,000 hours of public service work each summer in the area from Washington, D.C., to Maine.

In addition to supporting our work by becoming an AMC member, hikers can donate time as volunteers. For more information on these public service volunteer opportunities, contact the AMC Trails Program, Pinkham Notch Visitor Center, PO Box 298, Gorham NH 03581; 603-466-2721.

The club operates eight alpine huts in the White Mountains that provide shelter, bunks and blankets, and hearty meals for hikers. Pinkham Notch Visitor Center, at the foot of Mt. Washington, is base camp to the adventurous and the ideal location for individuals and families new to outdoor recreation. Comfortable bunk rooms, mountain hospitality, and home-cooked, family-style meals make Pinkham Notch Visitor Center a fun and affordable choice for lodging. For reservations, call 603-466-2727.

The AMC's offices in Boston and at Pinkham Notch Visitor Center stock the entire line of AMC publications, as well as other trail and river guides, maps, reference materials, and the latest articles on conservation issues. Guidebooks and other AMC gifts can be ordered by calling 800-262-4455 or by writing AMC, PO Box 298, Gorham, NH 03581. Also available from the bookstore or by subscription is *Appalachia*, the country's oldest mountaineering and conservation journal.

Listing of Areas by Ecosystem

Alphabetical Listing of the Areas